Six Ingredients or Less ®

Low-Carb Cooking

Six Ingredients or Less®

Low-Carb Cooking

Carlean Johnson

CJ
Books
Washington

Six Ingredients or Less® Low-Carb Cooking

Copyright© 2004 by Carlean Johnson
Copyright© 2010 new cover design
Printed in the United States of America

Eighth Printing 2010

Notice: The information in this book is true to the best of our knowledge but it is not meant to take the place of skilled professionals and the advice of your doctor. Author and publisher disclaim all liability in connection with the use of this book.

Cover Design by CarrotStick Marketing
Typography and production design by Pattie Graffe

Library of Congress Control Number: 2004095008
ISBN: 978-0-942878-07-3

CJ Books
PO Box 922
Gig Harbor, WA 98335
1-800-423-7184
www.sixingredientsorless.com
email:info@sixingredientsorless.com

Dedication

This book is dedicated to my granddaughter, Paulina. Thank you for your loyal support and your sweet love. I love you, too.

Gramma

Acknowledgements

Putting together a cookbook has many parts before it all starts coming together. This is only made possible with the help of many talented people. I would like to thank my loyal customers, who again have determined what the next book would be. Thank you.

I would like to thank Pattie Graffe, a newcomer I want to introduce to you. Pattie was in charge of the typography and production design. This isn't an easy job, but Pattie came through with flying colors. Thank you for your dedication to the project, your hard work, and at times, very long hours.

Another newcomer is Darlene Lindmark. Darlene spent many long hours proofreading the text and did a wonderful job. Her dedication to her work was unfailing and I thank you for everything you did! And to Corbett Petersen, I appreciate all the typing you did.

My mom is in her eighties but still tells others about my books. Thank you, Mom. Another big thank you to my family and to my daughter, Linda. You are the best. And yes, Ben, Grandma now has time to take you and Patrick to a movie.

Carlean Johnson

# Table of Contents

Ingredient List

Almond Flour - We used Bob's Red Mill. This is a quality almond flour and is found in some supermarkets, but not all. Website is www.bobsredmill.com

Barbecue Sauce - We used low-carb Westbrae, unsweetened un-ketchup at 1 carb per tablespoon.

Bread - We used "I'm Watching My Carbs!" bread distributed by Safeway at 3 net carbs per slice. Just in time for this book, this same company has come out with hamburger and hot dog buns at 9 net carbs each. They taste like buns should taste. The carbs are a little bit on the high side, but by carefully planning your day, you can enjoy those wonderful summer barbeques.

Brianna's Vinaigrette (no-carb) - This is by far the best brand I have found. Del Sol Food Co., Inc., P.O. Box 2243, Breuham, TX 77834. Found in most supermarkets.

Dressings - Because of the lower carb count we usually made our own. See index.

Cheddar Cheese - Bandon, found at the warehouse stores, has the lowest carb count per ounce (0.36) and is very good.

Chocolates - Called *Low Effective Carb* sugarfree. Comes in dark chocolate, milk chocolate and white chocolate. About 1.5g per ounce. Very good and easy to work with. Trader Joe's or call (561) 706-6178.

Deli Meats - Some of the meats do have carbs. Ask to see if they do and how many.

Expert Foods - A line of low-carb products worth checking out. It was too late for me to work with their products, but do check out their website: www.expertfoods.com.

Flour - Only a small amount of all-purpose flour was used in just a few of the recipes.

Fruit Spreads - We used LA Nouba which is 1.6 net carbs per tablespoon. Their nutritional labeling seems to contradict itself, but I was told to use the one where the ingredients are listed. Go to www.lanouba.be or call toll-free 866-697-8477.

Ice Cream - We used Carb Solutions at 3 grams net carbs per 1/2 cup.

Low-Carb Products - Brands vary, but check them out and purchase those of quality, but lowest in carbs.

Oils - We used Extra Light Olive Oil because of its versatility.

Maple Syrup - We used *Joseph's Maple Syrup*, which tastes just like real syrup and has 0 carbs, but it is hard to find. Call 505-546-2839 to see who carries it in your area.

Pasta - Dreamfield's pasta tastes just like what pasta should taste like. At 5 net carbs per 2 ounces, it is the lowest and best I have found on the market. You should be able to find their pastas in most supermarkets. At this time they make spaghetti, linguine, penne and elbow pasta. Go to www.Dreamfields.com or call 800-250-1917.

Peanut Butter Spread - Made by Carb Options and tastes just like real peanut butter. Check your supermarkets.

Salsa's - These are based on 1 net carb per tablespoon.

Soy Sauce - Regular soy sauce has no carbs. Lite soy sauce does have 1 carb.

Spaghetti Sauce - We used Carb Options, found in most supermarkets.

Sugar Free Syrups - These are like the ones popular in coffee drinks. Can usually be found in coffee shops and supermarkets.

Taco Shells - The only low-carb taco shells we found (and they are delicious) is "La Tiara" made by Gladstone Food Products Co. Inc., Gladstone, MO 64118. No phone number or web site was listed. They can be used as taco shells or broken up and used as chips for dips. At 1 net carb per shell, they are worth the trouble it may take to find them.

Tortillas - We used La Tortilla Factory and Mission's White Tortilla.

Unsweetened Shredded Coconut - We used Bob's Red Mill found in most supermarkets. At 2 net carbs per 3 tablespoons, you might be able to find one with fewer carbs. *Atkins' Carb Guide* lists fewer net carbs than we were able to find.

Xylitol - This is an excellent sugar substitute with only 10 calories per teaspoon and no carbs. It is expensive, but is wonderful in recipes where you really need to cut the carbs. It is hard to find, but you can go to www.nowfoods.com. In Gig Harbor, WA it is found at The Whole Foods Market, 253-851-8120.

Introduction

This is not a specific diet plan, but a collection of recipes to be used while on a low-carb diet or as a solution to a lifestyle of low-carb eating long-term.

My loyal customers are always requesting specific types of recipes and although this book is designed for those who are eating low-carb, a lot of the recipes can be used for diabetics as well as those on the Weight Watcher's program.

There is such a wide choice of low-carb diet books available to us that it can be quite confusing. Most of them are a takeoff of the Atkins' diet with some variations and changes. I think it is important to spend some time checking out these books and then choose a plan that best suits your needs. And, of course, always check with your doctor first. With the diet plan chosen and a wide variety of quick and easy recipes available using just Six Ingredients or Less®, you should be well on your way to achieving your goal.

What are NET CARBS? They are total carbs minus fiber.

Enjoy Low-Carb Cooking!

Carlean

About the Author

Carlean Johnson, mother of four, resides in scenic Gig Harbor in the Puget Sound area of Washington state. Her love of cooking inspired her to write a series of Six Ingredients or Less cookbooks. The *New* Low-Carb Cookbook is the sixth book in the series.

Appetizers and Beverages

Pineapple Cheese Spread

MAKES 3-1/4 CUPS

A most requested recipe for over 30 years now.

2   (8-oz) packages cream cheese
1   (8-oz) can crushed pineapple, drained
1   cup finely chopped pecans
¼   cup finely chopped green pepper
2   tablespoons finely chopped onion
1   tablespoon seasoning salt

1. Beat cream cheese until smooth and light. Add remaining ingredients and mix thoroughly. Spoon into a serving bowl, cover and chill at least 2 hours before serving.

Per tablespoon: 49 Cal, 5 Fat, 1g Pro, <1g Sug, 1g Carb, <1g Fib, **NET CARBS: 1**

Sausage Stuffed Mushrooms

MAKES 8 SERVINGS OF 2 EACH

Tiny but tasty little gems.

16   large mushrooms
8   ounces Italian sausage links
¼   cup grated Parmesan cheese

1. Preheat oven to 350°F. Wipe mushrooms with a damp paper towel. Remove stems.
2. Remove casings from sausage. Fill each mushroom with sausage until mounded and rather compact. Place on baking sheet and sprinkle lightly with Parmesan. Bake 25 to 30 minutes or until sausage is cooked through.

Per serving: 71 Cal, 5g Fat, 5g Pro, 1g Sug, 2g Carb, 1g Fib, **NET CARBS: 1**

Vegetable Tray

Use as a vegetable tray for entertaining or keep in the refrigerator for snacks.

Suggestions:

Artichokes
Asparagus
Bell peppers
Broccoli
Cauliflower
Celery sticks
Cherry tomatoes
Cucumber spears
Green onions
Jicama
Mushrooms
Radishes
Snap peas
Zucchini

Quesadillas

MAKES 12 WEDGES

Good served with salsa or guacamole.

4   **(7-inch) low-carb tortillas**
1   **cup (4-oz) Cheddar cheese, shredded**
¼   **cup chopped black olives**
¼   **cup chopped green onion**
¼   **cup diced tomatoes**

1. Preheat oven to 400°F. Place tortillas on a baking sheet and bake 2 minutes.
2. Remove from oven and sprinkle 2 tortillas with cheese, then remaining ingredients. Top with remaining tortillas. Bake until cheese is melted, 3 to 4 minutes. Cut each tortilla into 6 wedges.

Per wedge: 59 Cal, 4g Fat, 4g Pro, <1g Sug, 4g Carb, 3g Fib, **NET CARBS: 1**

Cheese Quesadilla

MAKES 1 SERVING

A lunch time favorite.

1   **(7-inch) low-carb tortilla**
½   **cup (2-oz) shredded cheese blend**

1. Sprinkle cheese over half of tortilla. Fold over to enclose cheese.
2. Heat a lightly sprayed skillet over medium-high heat. Add tortilla and cook until lightly browned on both sides, turning once.

variations: A choice of these additions can be added:

> Cooked, crumbled bacon
> Diced chicken or turkey
> Salsa
> Diced tomatoes
> Chopped green onions
> Diced bell peppers
> Jalapeño peppers
> Cooked sausage

Per serving: 269 Cal, 20g Fat, 18g Pro, 0g Sug, 13g Carb, 8g Fib, **NET CARBS: 5**

Saucy Chicken Wings

MAKES 16 APPETIZERS

Finger food at its best with just 2 ingredients. And--no carbs!

16   **chicken wings**
½   **cup soy sauce**

1. Preheat oven to 400°F. Cut wings into 3 parts, discarding the wing tip.
2. Combine wings with soy sauce, tossing well to coat. Line a 15x10-inch baking sheet with heavy duty foil; spray with cooking spray.
3. Arrange wings on pan, skin-side up. Pour soy sauce over top. Bake 20 minutes. Turn and bake 10 minutes. Turn and bake 8 to 10 minutes or until browned and glazed.

Per 2 pieces: 101 Cal, 7g Fat, 10g Pro, 0g Sug, 0g Carb, 0g Fib, **NET CARBS: 0**

Stuffed Pepper Shells

MAKES 8 SERVINGS

A wonderful addition to a vegetable tray.

4   small red peppers, halved, seeded
1   cup (4-oz) Mozzarella cheese, shredded
2   tablespoons pesto

1. Preheat oven to 375°F. Fill peppers with cheese, mounding slightly. Place on a baking sheet and drizzle with pesto. Bake 10 to 12 minutes to melt the cheese. Serve hot.

Per serving: 72 Cal, 5g Fat, 5g Pro, 2g Sug, 3g Carb, 1g Fib, *NET CARBS: 2*

Baked Camembert

MAKES 4 SERVINGS

Easy! Serve with low-carb vegetables.

1   (8-oz) wooden box Camembert

1. Preheat oven to 350°F. Remove cheese from box and unwrap. Return to box and cover. Remove all labels and place on baking sheet. Bake 25 to 30 minutes or until cheese is soft.
2. Carefully remove the top rind keeping cheese in box.

Per serving: 170 Cal, 14g Fat, 11g Pro, <1g Sug, <1g Carb, 0g Fib, *NET CARBS: <1*

Little Tomatoes with Cheese

PER TOMATO

These are those beautiful little tomatoes that are still attached to the vine.

1   small red tomato, about 1½-inches
1   tablespoon Pepper Jack cheese, shredded
½   teaspoon sliced almonds, coarsely
     crumbled
     Chopped parsley

1. Preheat oven to 350°F. Remove a 1/4-inch slice from stem end of tomatoes. Remove pulp and place upside down on paper towels to drain.
2. Form cheese into a sort of ball and fill tomato. There should be a slight mound above the tomato. Sprinkle with almonds and parsley. Bake 5 minutes to melt cheese. Don't overcook or the tomatoes will be too soft.

Per tomato: 50 Cal, 3g Fat, 3g Pro, 2g Sug, 4g Carb, 1g Fib, *NET CARBS: 3*

Asparagus Tips

Try these when in season.

16 thin asparagus spears
⅓ cup mayonnaise
1½ teaspoons soy sauce

1. Wash asparagus. Snap ends off at breaking point. Place in a steamer rack over hot water. Cover and steam 3 to 5 minutes or until just crisp-tender. Chill until ready to serve.
2. Combine mayonnaise and soy sauce. Chill to blend flavors.   Use as a dip for the asparagus spears.

Per serving: 37 Cal, 4g Fat, <1g Pro, <1g Sug, <1g Carb, <1g Fib, *NET CARBS: <1*

Antipasto

SERVINGS VARY

This makes for a great appetizer platter. If you don't overdo, it should be very few carbs.

Deli ham, halved and rolled
Salami (pork has lowest carbs)
Marinated artichoke hearts
Marinated mushrooms
Provolone cheese, cubed
Kalamata olives, pitted
Red and yellow cherry tomatoes
Pepperoncini peppers

Chicken-Bacon Bites

MAKES 32 APPETIZERS

These can be made ahead and reheated.

2 chicken breast halves, skinned, boned and cut into 32 bite-size pieces
⅓ cup no-carb vinaigrette dressing
16 bacon slices, halved crosswise

1. Marinate chicken in dressing for 30 minutes.
2. Preheat oven to 425°F. Wrap chicken with bacon and secure with wooden toothpicks. Place on a foil-lined 15x10-inch pan and bake 15 to 20 minutes until cooked through.

Per appetizer: 38 Cal, 3g Fat, 3g Pro, 0g Sug, 0g Carb, 0g Fib, *NET CARBS: 0*

Pumpkin Seed Snacks

MAKES 2 CUPS

The kids love to make these.

2 cups fresh pumpkin seeds
1 tablespoon oil
1 tablespoon butter, melted
   Salt

1. Preheat oven to 350°F. Wipe fibers from seeds but do not wash. Place in mixing bowl.
2. Combine oil and butter and pour over seeds. Spread on a large baking sheet. Sprinkle lightly with salt. Bake 30 minutes or until golden and crisp.

Per 1/4 cup serving: 99 Cal, 6g Fat, 3g Pro, 0g Sug, 9g Carb, 6g Fib, *NET CARBS: 3*

Cheese Kabobs

These are also nice as a side-dish serving.

16   broccoli florets
2   cups (8-oz) Pepper Jack cheese, cut into
     ¾-inch cubes (32 cubes)
16   pitted ripe olives
16   small cherry tomatoes

1. Thread 1 broccoli, 2 cheese cubes, 1 olive and one tomato on each small skewer.

Per kabob: 68 Cal, 5g Fat, 4g Pro, <1g Sug, 2g Carb, 1g Fib, *NET CARBS: 1*

Celery Boats

MAKES ABOUT 60, 2-INCH PIECES

Always a favorite on a appetizer tray.

1   small bunch celery
1   (8-oz) package cream cheese
1   (8-oz) can crushed pineapple, drained
     Paprika

1. Trim celery stalks; wash and dry thoroughly.
2. Combine cream cheese and pineapple. Spoon into celery and level with a knife. Sprinkle lightly with paprika. Cover and chill.
3. Cut celery into 2-inch pieces and serve.

Per piece: 16 Cal, 1g Fat, <1g Pro, <1g Sug, 1g Carb, 0g Fib, *NET CARBS: 1*

Teriyaki Kabobs

MAKES 20 KABOBS

These go really fast. Wooden skewers should be soaked in water for 20 minutes.

1   pound beef sirloin
⅓   cup brown Sugar Twin®
⅓   cup soy sauce
2   tablespoons white vinegar
1½   tablespoons Worcestershire sauce
2   thin slices fresh ginger

1. Cut sirloin crosswise into thin strips.
2. Combine remaining ingredients. Add meat; cover and marinate in refrigerator at least 2 hours.
3. Thread about 2 strips of meat on each 4-inch wooden skewer. Place on an oiled, heated grill and cook about 2 minutes. Brush with marinade, turn and cook 1 to 2 minutes or until cooked to desired doneness. For safety reasons do not brush with marinade a second time.

Per kabob: 33 Cal, 1g Fat, 5g Pro, 0g Sug, 0g Carb, 0g Fib, *NET CARBS: 0*

Cook's Tip

Nuts make a nice between meal snack, but watch the carb count.

Tortilla Appetizers

MAKES 40 APPETIZERS

A nice make-ahead appetizer.

2   (8-oz) packages cream cheese
1   (1-oz) package Ranch dressing mix
¼   cup chopped green onions
½   cup finely chopped red peppers
½   cup chopped black olives
4   (10-inch) low-carb tortillas

1. Beat cream cheese until light. Add dressing mix and beat until blended. Add remaining ingredients and spread on the tortillas. Roll up tightly and wrap in wax paper, twisting ends. Chill at least 2 hours. Cut into 1-inch slices.

Per slice: 52 Cal, 4g Fat, 2g Pro, 0g Sug,
3g Carb, 2g Fib, *NET CARBS: 1*

Bacon-Pineapple Appetizers

MAKES 1 SERVING

Pineapple adds very few carbs to a roll-up, but you do have to be aware of how many you eat.

Per Appetizer:

1   slice bacon, halved crosswise
1   whole water chestnut, halved
1   pineapple chunk, drained
    Soy sauce

1. Preheat oven to 400°F. Wrap bacon slice around a pineapple chunk and water chestnut. Secure with a wooden toothpick. Bake on rack in a shallow pan for 15 minutes. Brush with soy sauce and bake 5 to 10 minutes or until bacon is crisp.

Per serving: 58 Cal, 3g Fat, 3g Pro, 2g Sug,
6g Carb, 2g Fib, *NET CARBS: 4*

Dorothy's Coconut Chips

MAKES 1-1/2 CUPS

Place these on your coffee table and watch them disappear.

1   fresh coconut
1½ teaspoons butter, melted
    Salt

1. Preheat oven to 350°F. Pierce eyes in coconut and drain. Place on a baking sheet and bake 30 minutes. Remove. Reduce heat to 250°.

2. Break coconut open with a hammer. Trim off brown skin. Shave coconut with a vegetable peeler. Spread coconut on a large baking sheet. Bake 1 to 1-1/2 hours, or until just lightly browned around the edges. Drizzle with butter. Sprinkle lightly with salt, and toss to coat.

Per 1/4 cup: 204 Cal, 19g Fat, 2g Pro, 3g Sug, 8g Carb, 5g Fib, **NET CARBS: 3**

Teriyaki Chicken Wings

MAKES 20 SERVINGS

Chicken wings are loved by all.

20   chicken wings
 1   cup soy sauce
 1   cup Splenda®
 2   tablespoons lemon juice
 ½   teaspoon ground ginger
 2   garlic cloves, minced

1. Preheat oven to 300°F. Cut wings in half, discarding tips. Place, skin-side down, on a large shallow baking pan.
2. Combine remaining ingredients and pour over chicken. Bake 30 minutes.
3. Turn and bake another 30 minutes. Increase heat to 350° and bake 10 to 15 minutes, basting frequently.

Two pieces: 100 Cal, 7g Fat, 9g Pro, 0g Sug, 0g Carb, 0g Fib, **NET CARBS: 0**

Ham Rolls

MAKES 30 APPETIZERS

Ham must be thinly sliced to allow for easy rolling. Asparagus should not be too soft.

 1   (8-oz) container Herb Cheese Spread, softened
 6   thin slices deli boiled ham
12   cooked asparagus spears

1. Spread cheese evenly over ham. Place 2 asparagus spears on long edge of ham and roll tightly. Wrap each roll in wax paper, twisting ends. Chill at least 2 hours.
2. Cut each roll into 5 slices and place on serving plate.

Per appetizer: 32 Cal, 3g Fat, 2g Pro, <1g Sug, <1g Carb, <1g Fib, **NET CARBS: <1**

Katie's Chicken Wings

MAKES 12 APPETIZERS

Wonderful after school snack, too!

12   chicken wings
1½   tablespoons flour
     Seasoning salt

1. Preheat oven to 400°F. Line a shallow baking pan with foil. Lightly spray the foil.
2. Coat chicken wings with flour, shaking off excess. Place in baking pan. Sprinkle generously with seasoning salt. Bake 30 to 40 minutes or until nicely browned.

Per appetizer: 102 Cal, 7g Fat, 9g Pro, 0g Sug, 1g Carb, 0g Fib, **NET CARBS: 1**

Linda's Guacamole

MAKES 2 CUPS

If not serving right away, cover with a thin layer of mayonnaise, spreading to the edge; cover and refrigerate.

2   ripe avocados
1   garlic clove, minced
1   tablespoon lime juice
    Dash hot pepper sauce
1   small tomato, diced
    Salt and pepper to taste

1. Peel and slice avocados. Combine with garlic, lime juice and pepper sauce, mashing with a fork until blended. Add tomato, salt and pepper. When ready to serve, simply stir in the mayonnaise, if using.

Per tablespoon: 20 Cal, 2g Fat, <1g Pro, <1g Sug, 1g Carb, 1g Fib, **NET CARBS: <1**

Water Chestnut Appetizers

MAKES 36 APPETIZERS

These are good.

1   (8-oz) can whole water chestnuts
¼   cup soy sauce
¼   cup Splenda®
1   pound lean bacon

1. Preheat oven to 400°F. Rinse water chestnuts and cut in half, if too large. Combine soy sauce and sugar; add water chestnuts and marinate 30 minutes.

2. Cut bacon in half crosswise and lengthwise. Wrap each water chestnut with 1 piece bacon; secure with a wooden toothpick. Place on rack in shallow baking pan. Bake 20 to 30 minutes or until bacon is crisp.

Per appetizer: 73 Cal, 5g Fat, 5g Pro, 0g Sug, 1g Carb, <1g Fib, **NET CARBS: 1**

Baked Tortilla Chips

MAKES 24 CHIPS

Use with dips or Taco Salads.

2   (7-inch) low-carb white tortillas
    Salt (optional)

1. Preheat oven to 425°F. Place tortillas on baking sheet and spray both sides with cooking spray. Sprinkle lightly with salt, if using.
2. Cut each tortilla into 12 even wedges. Separate slightly. Bake 5 to 7 minutes or until lightly browned.

Per chip: 4 Cal, <1g Fat, <1g Pro, 0g Sug, <1g Carb, <1g Fib, **NET CARBS: <1**

Apricot Almond Brie

MAKES 10 SERVINGS

Serve with low-carb crackers.

1   (10-oz) wedge Brie cheese
5   tablespoons low-carb apricot spread
1   teaspoon Grand Marnier
1   tablespoon sliced almonds

1. Remove top rind of cheese. Place on serving plate and let soften.
2. In small saucepan, heat apricot spread and Grand Marnier until hot, but not boiling. Spoon over Brie and sprinkle with almonds.

Per 1-oz serving: 120 Cal, 8g Fat, 6g Pro, <1g Sug, 1g Carb, 0g Fib, **NET CARBS: 1**

Curried Almonds

MAKES 2 CUPS

For a more pronounced curry flavor, sprinkle on the curry powder with the salt.

¼   cup butter
2   cups whole almonds
1   tablespoon curry powder
½   teaspoon salt

1. Melt butter in medium skillet. Add almonds. Cook, stirring frequently, until lightly browned, about five minutes. Add curry and cook 2 to 3 minutes, stirring frequently. Drain on paper towels. Sprinkle with salt.

Per 2 tablespoons: 125 Cal, 11g Fat, 4g Pro, <1g Sug, 4g Carb, 2g Fib, **NET CARBS: 2**

Sweet-Sour Wrap-Ups

MAKES 48 APPETIZERS

These go fast. To make ahead, prepare bacon and water chestnuts. Make sauce and refrigerate both until ready to bake.

1   pound lean bacon
2   (8-oz) cans water chestnuts
1½   cups low-carb ketchup
16   packets Splenda®
3   tablespoons lemon juice

1. Preheat oven to 350°F. Cut bacon crosswise into thirds. Cut water chestnuts in half. Wrap 1 piece bacon around each water chestnut. Secure with wooden toothpicks. Place in a sprayed 13x9-inch baking dish and bake for 30 minutes. Drain off fat.
2. Combine remaining ingredients and pour over top. Reduce heat to 325°F. Bake 20 to 30 minutes, basting occasionally, until bacon is crisp. Serve hot.

Per appetizer: 24 Cal, 1g Fat, 1g Pro, <1g Sug, 2g Carb, <1g Fib, **NET CARBS: 2**

MENU

Sausage Stuffed Mushrooms
Saucy Chicken Wings
Baked Camembert
Savory Tomato Brie
Vegetable Tray
Celery Boats
Easy Salsa
0 to 1 net carbs per appetizer.

Salami Stacks

These little wedges add variety to an appetizer tray. Makes a lot, but they go fast.

36 slices salami (watch carbs)
2 (8-oz) packages cream cheese, softened
¼ cup prepared whipped horseradish

1. Pat salami dry with paper towels.
2. Beat cream cheese and horseradish until blended. Spread on salami. Make stacks of 3 layers each. Cover and chill at least 2 hours.
3. Cut each stack into 4 wedges. Place a toothpick in center of each wedge.

Per appetizer: 62 Cal, 6g Fat, 2g Pro, 0g Sug, <1g Carb, 0g Fib, *NET CARBS: <1*

Jicama

JICAMA (HEE-kah-mah) is that wonderful, but funny looking vegetable with a thin brown skin. It should be peeled before serving. The crunchy white flesh is similar to a potato or water chestnut, only sweeter. It can be steamed, baked, boiled or fried and retains its crisp texture when cooked briefly. At only 2.5 net carbs per 1/2 cup, this is a vegetable that should become a staple in your kitchen.

Savory Tomato Brie

MAKES 16 SERVINGS

Serve with a good white wine.

1 (16-oz) Brie cheese
6 oil-packed sun-dried tomatoes, finely chopped
1 tablespoon oil from tomatoes
2 small garlic cloves, minced
1 tablespoon minced fresh basil
2 tablespoons minced parsley

1. Remove top rind from Brie and place on serving plate. Let stand 30 minutes at room temperature
2. Combine remaining ingredients and spread on top of cheese.

Per serving: 105 Cal, 9g Fat, 6g Pro, <1g Sug, <1g Carb, <1g Fib, *NET CARBS: <1*

Heavenly Fruit Dip

MAKES 10 SERVINGS

My favorite dip to serve with fresh fruit.

1   **(1-oz) package sugarfree vanilla
    pudding mix**
1¼ **cups heavy cream**
2   **packets Splenda®**
½   **teaspoon rum extract**
½   **teaspoon vanilla extract**

1. Combine ingredients along with 1-1/4 cups water, on lowest speed of mixer, about 2 minutes. Cover. Chill several hours or overnight.

Per 1/4 cup serving: 114 Cal, 11g Fat, 1g Pro, 0g Sug, 3g Carb, 0g Fib, **NET CARBS: 3**

Artichoke Dip

MAKES 2-1/2 CUPS

*Serve with vegetable sticks or
toasted bread triangles.*

1   **(14-oz) can artichoke hearts, drained,
    coarsely chopped**
1   **(4-oz) can chopped green chilies**
1   **cup mayonnaise**
1   **cup grated Parmesan cheese**

1. Combine ingredients in a medium saucepan and heat through. Serve hot.

variation: add 1 cup cooked cubed chicken.

Per 1/4 cup: 211 Cal, 20g Fat, 4g Pro, 0g Sug, 3g Carb, <1g Fib, **NET CARBS: 3**

Cheese Wafers

MAKES 12 WAFERS

I have also used Cheddar, Monterey Jack, Pepper Jack and Parmesan cheese. Serve with dips, as a snack or crumbled and used on salads.

¾   **cup (3-oz) package Mexican blend cheese**

1. Preheat oven to 400°F. Spoon 1 tablespoon cheese on foil or Silpat-lined baking sheet, about 3 inches apart. Bake 6 to 10 minutes, depending on the type of cheese used.

Per wafer: 28 Cal, 2g Fat, 2g Pro, 0g Sug, <1g Carb, 0g Fib, **NET CARBS: <1**

Dill Dip

MAKES 1-1/3 CUPS

Serve with Jicama sticks and enjoy anytime, especially on those days when you are tempted to go off your diet.

⅔   **cup mayonnaise**
⅔   **cup sour cream**
1   **teaspoon dry minced onion**
1   **teaspoon dill weed**
1   **teaspoon Beau Monde seasoning**

1. Combine ingredients; cover and chill several hours to blend flavors.

Per 1/4 cup: 212 Cal, 23g Fat, <1g Pro, 0g Sug, <1g Carb, 0g Fib, **NET CARBS: <1**

Clam Dip

Can also be gently heated and served hot.

1   (8-oz) package cream cheese
1   (6½-oz) can minced clams, save juice
1   small garlic clove, minced
1   teaspoon lemon juice
¼   teaspoon Worcestershire sauce
    Salt to taste

1. Combine cream cheese and clams. Add enough juice to make a nice consistency for dipping. Add remaining ingredients. Serve or cover and chill.

Per 2 tablespoons: 109 Cal, 10g Fat, 4g Pro, <1g Sug, 2g Carb, 0g Fib, *NET CARBS: 2*

Peppered Cheese Dip

1 OUNCE = 1CARB

So Easy. Serve with low-carb bread or chips.

Shredded Pepper Jack cheese, desired amount

1. Place cheese in a 9-inch pie dish. Microwave until melted or very soft.

Per 1-oz serving: 110 Cal, 9g Fat, 7g Pro, 0g Sug, 1g Carb, 0g Fib, *NET CARBS: 1*

Artichoke and Dill Dip

MAKES 4 SERVINGS

Kids love to dip these little leaves in the sauce.

2   artichokes
⅓   cup mayonnaise
½   teaspoon dried dill weed

1. Wrap each artichoke in a paper towel and microwave until tender. Time varies according to wattage so watch carefully not to overcook. Serve warm or cold.
2. Combine mayonnaise and dill weed. Serve as a dip with the artichokes.

Per serving: 164 Cal, 15g Fat, 2g Pro, 1g Sug, 7g Carb, 3g Fib, *NET CARBS: 4*

Ranch Dip

MAKES 1-3/4 CUP

Serve with your favorite low-carb vegetables.

½   cup Ranch dressing
½   cup mayonnaise
½   cup sour cream
⅓   cup grated Parmesan cheese
½   cup crumbled cooked bacon

1. Combine first 4 ingredients. Cover and chill 1 to 2 hours. Add bacon just before serving.

Per ¼ cup: 267 Cal, 28g Fat, 3g Pro, 1g Sug, 1g Carb, 0g Fib, *NET CARBS: 1*

Hot Crab Dip

MAKES 6 SERVINGS

Serve with toasted bread triangles.

1 (8-oz) package cream cheese, softened
1 cup mayonnaise
½ cup grated Parmesan cheese, reserve 2 tablespoons for top
2 tablespoons finely chopped onion
½ cup chopped artichoke hearts
1 (6-oz) can crab, drained

1. Preheat oven to 350°F. Beat cream cheese until light. Add remaining ingredients, except crab, and beat until blended. Stir in crab.

2. Spoon into sprayed shallow dish. You want the mixture about 1-inch thick. Smooth top. Sprinkle with reserved Parmesan. Bake 15 to 20 minutes or until heated through.

variation: Top with 1 tablespoon sliced almonds.

Per serving: 476 Cal, 45g Fat, 14g Pro, <1g Sug, 3g Carb, 0g Fib, **NET CARBS: 3**

Vegetable Dip

MAKES 2 CUPS

Vegetable dippers could be snap peas, zucchini spears, red peppers and jicama.

2 (3-oz) packages cream cheese
1 cup sour cream
1 tablespoon chopped green onion
⅓ cup finely chopped cucumber
1 small garlic clove, minced
    Dash Salt

1. Beat cream cheese until light; beat in sour cream. Add remaining ingredients. Cover and chill.

Per 1/4 cup: 137 Cal, 13g Fat, 3g Pro, <1g Sug, 2g Carb, 0g Fib, **NET CARBS: 2**

Cook's Tip Pork Rinds are good when you want something crispy to use with dips and salsa.

Pineapple Salsa

Serve on salmon fillets or grilled chicken.

1   cup coarsely chopped fresh pineapple
½   cup chopped Plum tomatoes
¼   cup chopped cilantro
1   teaspoon minced fresh jalapeños
¼   teaspoon salt

1. Combine ingredients and mix well.

Per tablespoon: 4 Cal, 0g Fat, 0g Pro, 1g Sug, 1g Carb, <1 Fib, **NET CARBS: 1**

Tomato Salsa

MAKES 2 CUPS

Serve over grilled chicken or fish.

1   cup chopped red tomato
1   cup chopped yellow tomato
1   tablespoon red wine vinegar
½   teaspoon dried basil

1. Combine ingredients; cover and chill several hours to blend flavors.

Per tablespoon: 2 Cal, 0g Fat, <1g Pro, <1g Sug, <1g Carb, 0g Fib, **NET CARBS: <1**

Mayonnaise-Salsa

MAKES 2/3 CUP

At about 1 carb per tablespoon of salsa, we have to use discretion. Serve with low-carb taco shells or jicama sticks.

½   cup mayonnaise
2   tablespoons drained salsa

1. Combine ingredients and chill until ready to serve.

Per tablespoon: 81 Cal, 9g Fat, 0g Pro, 0g Sug, 0g Carb, 0g Fib, **NET CARBS: 0**

Easy Salsa

MAKES 3-1/2 CUPS

Serve as a dip or as a topping for meats, salads and hamburgers.

3   cups chopped Plum tomatoes
¼   cup chopped onion
1   (4-oz) can chopped green chilies
1   tablespoon oil
1   tablespoon apple cider vinegar
¾   teaspoon salt

1. Combine ingredients; cover and chill several hours to blend flavors.

Per tablespoon: 5 Cal, <1g Fat, <1g Pro, <1g Sug, <1g Carb, <1g Fib, **NET CARBS: <1**

Almond Iced Tea

*Lemon and almond makes a
refreshing combination.*

6   tea bags
1   tub Crystal Light® lemonade mix
24 packets Splenda®
½   teaspoon almond extract

1. Heat 2 cups water to boiling. Add tea bags
and let steep 5 minutes.
2. Remove tea bags and add remaining
ingredients. In large container, combine mixture
with 9 cups water. You may wish to adjust
sweetener to taste. Serve over ice.

Per cup: 13 Cal, 0g Fat, 0g Pro, 0g Sug,
2g Carb, 0g Fib, *NET CARBS: 2*

Fruit Champagne

Place 3 strawberries, raspberries,
blueberries, or peach slices in each
champagne flute or wine glass. Fill
with four ounces champagne.

Sun Tea

MAKES 1 GALLON

*This is very easy to make,
especially for a crowd.*

1   gallon cold water
7   tea bags

1. Fill a gallon glass jar with water. Add tea
bags; put lid on. Place outside in sun and leave
several hours or until desired strength is
achieved.

Per serving: 0 Cal, 0g Fat, 0g Pro, 0g Sug,
0g Carb, 0g Fib, *NET CARBS: 0*

Paulina's Italian Cream Soda

MAKES 1 SERVING

*If desired, garnish with a dollop of whipped
cream and a strawberry slice.*

2   tablespoons sugar-free strawberry syrup,
    or to taste
1   cup chilled club soda
1   tablespoon heavy cream

1. Pour syrup into a glass filled with ice cubes.
Add club soda. Stir in the cream.

Per serving: 51 Cal, 5g Fat, 0g Pro, 0g Sug,
<1g Carb, 0g Fib, *NET CARBS: <1*

Strawberry Lemonade

MAKES 18 CUPS

A little bit rich, but oh so good.

6   cups sliced strawberries
1½ cups Xylitol
1   tub Crystal Light® lemonade mix
9   cups diet lemon-lime soda, chilled

1. Purée strawberries in blender or food processor. Combine purée with Xylitol, lemonade mix and 6 cups water. Cover and chill.
2. When ready to serve, mix equal parts strawberry mixture with soda, or to taste.

Per cup: 60 Cal, <1g Fat,< 1g Pro, 3g Sug, 4g Carb, 1g Fib, *NET CARBS: 3*

Lime Spritzer

MAKES 1 SERVING

Good wine choices are: Chardonnay, Chablis, Reisling, etc.

½   cup dry white wine
1   lime (1 tablespoon juice and 1 slice)
½   cup diet lemon-lime soda, or to taste

1. Combine wine, lime juice and soda. Pour over ice. Garnish with a lime slice.

Per serving: 84 Cal, 0g Fat,<1g Pro, <1g Sug, 2g Carb, 0g Fib, *NET CARBS: 2*

7-Up® Punch

MAKES 36 PUNCH CUP SERVINGS

This makes a nice holiday punch.

2   quarts low-carb vanilla ice cream
3   quarts diet 7-Up, chilled

1. Spoon ice cream into a large punch bowl. Stir in 7-Up, leaving small bits of ice cream.

Per serving: 62 Cal, 4g Fat, 2g Pro, 1g Sug, 3g Carb, 2g Fib, *NET CARBS: 1*

Raspberry Cooler

MAKES 3 CUPS

You may substitute strawberries.

1   cup raspberries
¼   cup Xylitol
¼   cup heavy cream
½   teaspoon vanilla extract
6   ice cubes

1. Combine first 4 ingredients and 1-3/4 cups water in blender. Blend until smooth.
2. Add ice cubes, one at a time, and blend until thoroughly crushed. The ice may not crush quite as thoroughly in a food processor.

Per cup: 132 Cal, 8g Fat, 1g Pro, 2g Sug, 6g Carb, 3g Fib, *NET CARBS: 3*

Peach Fizz

MAKES 1 SERVING

*Just the thing to make when you get a
craving for something sweet.*

1   (12-oz) can diet golden peach soda
1   tablespoon heavy cream

1. Pour soda into a tall glass. Add cream and
stir.

Per serving: 51 Cal, 5g Fat, <1g Pro, 0g Sug,
<1g Carb, 0g Fib, *NET CARBS: <1*

Vanilla-Raspberry Treat

MAKES 1 SERVING

*This makes that little-bitty 1/2-cup serving
of ice cream go a little farther.*

½   cup low-carb vanilla ice cream
½   cup diet raspberry soda, chilled

1. Place ice cream in a 12-ounce glass and pour
raspberry soda over top.

Per cup: 140 Cal, 10g Fat, 4g Pro, 2g Sug,
7g Carb, 4g Fib, *NET CARBS: 3*

Raspberry Drink

MAKES 2 CUPS

You may also use any choice of flavors.

1   cup low-carb vanilla ice cream
2   tablespoons sugar-free raspberry syrup
1   cup diet lemon-lime soda

1. Place ingredients in blender and blend until
smooth.

Per cup: 140 Cal, 10g Fat, 4g Pro, 2g Sug,
7g Carb, 4g Fib, *NET CARBS: 3*

Root Beer Float

MAKES 1 SERVING

Let the kids make these.

½   cup low-carb vanilla ice cream
1   (12-oz) can diet root beer, chilled

1. Place ice cream in a tall glass and slowly add
root beer.

variation: Vanilla ice cream and diet orange
soda.

Per serving: 140 Cal, 10g Fat, 4g Pro, 2g Sug,
7g Carb, 4g Fib, *NET CARBS: 3*

Easy Eggnog

MAKES 8 SERVINGS

People at risk may wish to avoid the use of uncooked eggs. This isn't as thick as regular eggnog, but it is rich.

1	**(1-oz) package sugar-free instant vanilla pudding**
2	**large eggs, lightly beaten**
⅓	**cup Xylitol**
1	**teaspoon vanilla extract**
1½	**cups heavy cream**
	Nutmeg

1. Using mixer on low speed, combine first 4 ingredients.
2. Combine cream with 4-1/2 cups water. Gradually add to egg mixture, mixing thoroughly. Chill until ready to serve.

Per serving: 206 Cal, 18g Fat, 3g Pro, <1g Sug, 4g Carb, 0g Fib, **NET CARBS: 4**

Orange-Almond Hot Chocolate

MAKES 4 CUPS

The orange is a perfect match with the chocolate.

2	**ounces low-carb dark chocolate**
6	**packets Splenda®**
¾	**cup heavy cream**
2	**teaspoons grated orange zest**
¼	**teaspoon almond extract**
4	**cinnamon sticks (optional)**

1. Melt chocolate in 1 cup water in heavy medium saucepan. Add sugar and bring to a boil. Cook, stirring frequently, 5 minutes.
2. Add cream, zest, extract and 2-1/4 cups water and heat until hot. Beat with rotary beater or on low speed of mixer, until frothy. Serve with cinnamon stick in each cup.

Per cup: 220Cal, 21g Fat, 2g Pro, 0g Sug, 4g Carb, 2g Fib, **NET CARBS: 2**

Cocoa Mix

MAKES 2 CUPS

Convenient to have on hand for a quick hot drink for the kids.

1	**cup cocoa**
1	**cup Xylitol**
¼	**teaspoon salt**
¼	**teaspoon cinnamon (opt.)**

1. Combine ingredients. Cover and store in pantry.
2. For each drink, add 1 tablespoon cocoa mix to 1 cup boiling water and 3 tablespoons heavy cream. If a sweeter cocoa is desired add 1 to 2 teaspoons Xylitol.

Per tablespoon of mix: 21 Cal, <1g Fat, <1g Pro, 0gSug, 1g Carb, <1g Fib, **NET CARBS: <1**

White Hot Chocolate

Can you believe our passion for flavored coffees. Using low-carb ingredients, we can now enjoy this delicious hot coffee drink without guilt.

4   ounces low-carb white chocolate
⅔   cup hot decaf coffee
1   teaspoon vanilla extract
⅔   cup heavy cream

1. Coarsely chop white chocolate. Melt in a large heavy saucepan over very low heat.

2. Gradually add remaining ingredients, mixing until smooth. Add 2-1/3 cups water and heat through. Simmer, but do not boil.

3. Carefully pour mixture into a blender and blend until frothy, making sure the lid is on tight. (This step is optional.)

Per cup: 267 Cal, 15g Fat, 2g Pro, <1g Sug, 3g Carb, 0g Fib, *NET CARBS: 3*

Cook's Tip

If a recipe calls for milk, combine 2 tablespoons heavy cream with water to measure 1 cup. This combination is 0.8g carbs compared to 11 carbs for 1 cup whole milk.

Dessert Coffee

MAKES 1 SERVING

Sugarfree syrup makes this a wonderful low-carb drink.

1   cup hot decaf coffee
2   tablespoons heavy cream
2   teaspoons sugar free white chocolate syrup
1   packet Splenda®

1. Combine all ingredients in a mug and enjoy.

Per serving: 110 Cal, 11g Fat, 1g Pro, 0g Sug, 3g Carb, 0g Fib, *NET CARBS: 3*

Frappacino

MAKES 4 SERVINGS

For a more flavorful drink, you need to use strong brewed coffee.

4   cups strong decaf coffee
1   cup whipping cream
6   packets Splenda®, or to taste

1. Combine ingredients and chill. Serve over ice.

Per serving: 211 Cal, 22g Fat, 1g Pro, 0g Sug, 3g Carb, 0g Fib, *NET CARBS: 3*

Mochalicious

MAKES 4 SERVINGS

Delicious! The taste testers loved this one.

½   cup whipping cream
2   packets Splenda®
1   teaspoon vanilla
½   ounce low-carb dark chocolate, grated
2   cups hot decaf coffee

1. Combine whipping cream, Splenda and vanilla and beat until soft peaks form. Fold in chocolate.
2. Pour coffee into 4 small coffee cups. Top with whipped cream.

Per serving: 125 Cal, 12g Fat, 1g Pro, <1g Sug, 2g Carb, <1g Fib, *NET CARBS: 2*

Caramel Coffee Delight

MAKES 1 SERVING

Variations can be easily made by using Irish cream, hazelnut or other assorted sugar-free syrups.

1   tablespoon sugar-free caramel syrup (or to taste)
1   cup hot decaf coffee
2   tablespoons whipped cream

1. Pour syrup into a 10-ounce mug. Add coffee and top with whipped cream. If desired, garnish with cocoa powder or grated chocolate.

Per serving: 61 Cal, 7g Fat, 1g Pro, 0g Sug, <1g Carb, 0g Fib, *NET CARBS: <1*

Maple Coffee Drink

MAKES 2 SERVINGS

Can't always make it to Starbucks. You can make this delicious coffee drink at home.

½   cup heavy cream
1   to 2 tablespoons no-carb maple syrup
1   cup hot decaf coffee

1. Combine ingredients with 1/2 cup water. Heat in microwave and serve.

Per serving: 212 Cal, 22g Fat, 1g Pro, 0g Sug, 2g Carb, 0g Fib, *NET CARBS: 2*

Breads

⚘ Breakfast
⚘ Breads
⚘ Muffins

Oven Pancake

This doesn't puff up as much as the traditional pancake, but it is still very good and also very rich. Offset the richness by serving with fresh berries and sausage links.

2   **tablespoons butter**
2   **large eggs, lightly beaten**
2   **tablespoons heavy cream**
⅓   **cup almond flour**

1. Preheat oven to 425°F. Place butter in 9-inch pie dish and melt in oven.
2. Meanwhile, combine remaining ingredients with 6 tablespoons water. Pour into pie dish and bake 12 to 15 minutes or until golden. Serve immediately.

Per serving: 187 Cal, 17g Fat, 7g Pro, <1g Sug, 3g Carb, 1g Fib, *NET CARBS: 2*

Maple   Butter

MAKES 2/3 CUP

Use as a topping for French toast, pancakes or waffles.

½   **cup butter, softened**
¼   **cup no-carb maple syrup**

1. In a mixer bowl, beat butter until fluffy.
2. Gradually add maple syrup, beating until well-mixed and light.

NET CARBS: 0

Nutty Pancakes

MAKES 10 PANCAKES

If you really don't want to give up your pancakes, these make a fairly good substitute.

1½   **cups almond flour**
2   **large eggs, lightly beaten**
½   **cup club soda**
2   **tablespoons heavy cream**

1. Combine ingredients until blended. Spoon about 2 tablespoons into an oiled hot skillet or griddle. Spread to make a 3-inch circle. Cook as for regular pancakes, turning gently to prevent breaking.

Per serving: 121 Cal, 10g Fat, 5g Pro, 0g Sug, 4g Carb, 2g Fib, *NET CARBS: 2*

Atkins' Low-Carb Rolls

MAKES 10 SERVINGS

It's a stretch to call these light, airy puffs rolls, but they aren't too bad.

3   large eggs, separated
¼   teaspoon cream of tartar
3   tablespoons small curd cottage cheese
2   packets Splenda®

1. Preheat oven to 300°F. Beat egg whites and cream of tartar until stiff peaks form (do not overbeat).
2. Combine egg yolks with cottage cheese and Splenda and mix well. Carefully fold into egg whites until just mixed. You don't want to deflate the whites. Working quickly, spoon onto a sprayed baking sheet, making rounds about 2-inches high. Bake 30 to 35 minutes or until a deep golden brown.

Per serving: 26 Cal, 2g Fat, 2g Pro, <1g Sug, 1g Carb, 0g Fib, **NET CARBS: 1**

French Toast

MAKES 8 SERVINGS

What a treat! The milk mixture will make enough for about 12 slices, depending on the size of the bread. Extra slices can be frozen and used as needed.

¼   cup butter, divided
2   large eggs
½   cup whipping cream
12   slices low-carb white bread

1. Heat half of the butter in large skillet or brush on a heated griddle.
2. Combine eggs, cream, and 1/2-cup water. Dip bread in mixture, coating both sides. Cook in butter, until golden, turning once. Add a little extra butter as needed.

Per serving: 210 Cal, 14g Fat, 12g Pro, <1g Sug, 9g Carb, 4g Fib, **NET CARBS: 5**

Bread Crumbs How-To

Dry Bread Crumbs

Place low-carb white bread on a baking sheet and bake at 350°F 10 to 12 minutes or until bread is quite dry. Break into smaller pieces and process in blender or food processor to make dry crumbs.

FOUR SLICES WILL MAKE 1 CUP

Soft Bread Crumbs

Soft bread crumbs are made from fresh low-carb white bread. Process in a blender or food processor until soft crumbs form.

TWO SLICES WILL MAKE 1 CUP

Almond-Cranberry Muffins

MAKES 12 MUFFINS

These freeze well.

½ cup butter, softened
6 packets Splenda®
5 large eggs, room temperature
1 teaspoon baking powder
2 cups almond flour
36 Dried cranberries

1. Preheat oven to 350°F. In a mixer bowl, beat butter and Splenda until smooth.

2. Add eggs, one at a time, and beat until somewhat blended. It doesn't mix very well and may look curdled, but that is okay.

3. Add baking powder and almond flour and beat until well mixed. Spoon into sprayed muffin tin. Press 3 cranberries into top of each muffin. Bake 18 to 25 minutes or until tester inserted in center comes out clean. Remove and place on rack.

variation: Sprinkle each muffin with a little brown Sugar Twin® and chopped nuts.

Per serving: 214 Cal, 19g Fat, 7g Pro, 2g Sug, 7g Carb, 2g Fib, *NET CARBS: 5*

Almond Bread

MAKES 12 SERVINGS

Serve with eggs, salads, chili or as a bread with dinner. Even better, spread with a little low-carb fruit spread.

½ cup butter, softened
3 packets Splenda®
5 large eggs, room temperature
1 teaspoon baking powder
2 cups almond flour

1. Preheat oven to 350°F. In a mixer bowl, beat butter and Splenda. Add eggs one at a time and mix, stirring often. This doesn't mix very well and may look curdled, but that is okay.

2. Add baking powder and almond flour and beat until well mixed. Pour into sprayed 9-inch springform pan. Bake 25 to 30 minutes or until tester inserted in center is dry. The bread will brown somewhat, but not much.

Per serving: 205 Cal, 19g Fat, 7g Pro, <1g Sug, 4g Carb, 2g Fib, *NET CARBS: 2*

Tomato Herb Toast

These are excellent for an appetizer tray or with salads.

4	slices low-carb white bread
1	tablespoon olive oil
2	small Plum tomatoes, chopped
½	teaspoon dried basil
	Salt and pepper to taste
½	cup (2-oz) Cheddar cheese, shredded

1. Preheat oven to 375°F. Brush top side of bread with oil. Place on baking sheet and bake 6 to 8 minutes or until toasted.
2. Combine tomato and basil. Add salt and pepper to taste. Spoon onto bread slices. Sprinkle with cheese. Bake 3 to 4 minutes to melt cheese. Cut into triangles.

Per serving: 152 Cal, 9g Fat, 11g Pro, 1g Sug, 7g Carb, 3g Fib, **NET CARBS: 4**

Parmesan Sticks

Serve with soups or salads.

4	slices low-carb white bread
¼	cup butter, melted
2	tablespoons grated Parmesan cheese

1. Preheat oven to 325°F. Remove crusts from bread. Cut each slice into three 1-inch slices.
2. Combine butter and cheese. Brush on both sides of bread. Bake 10 to 12 minutes or until lightly toasted.

Per serving: 57 Cal, 4g Fat, 3g Pro, 0g Sug, 2g Carb, 1g Fib, **NET CARBS: 1**

Croutons

MAKES 2 CUPS

4	slices low-carb white bread
1½	tablespoons oil
3	tablespoons grated Parmesan cheese

1. Preheat oven to 400°F. Cut bread into small cubes and place in mixing bowl.
2. Toss with oil and Parmesan. Spread in a single layer in shallow baking pan and bake 5 to 8 minutes or until golden.

Per 1/4 cup: 61 Cal, 4g Fat, 4g Pro, 0g Sug, 3g Carb, 1g Fib, **NET CARBS: 2**

Eggs & Cheese

♟ Omelets
♟ Casseroles
♟ Quiches

Basic Omelet

MAKES 2 SERVINGS

Once you learn the basics you can make a variety of your favorite omelets.

1   **tablespoon butter**
3   **large eggs, lightly beaten**
     Salt and pepper

1. Heat butter in a 9-inch nonstick skillet over medium heat.
2. Combine eggs, salt, pepper and 1 tablespoon water, mixing until lightly blended. Add to skillet. As eggs begin to set, lift edges to allow uncooked portions to flow underneath. When eggs are lightly set, fold, then cut in half to serve.
note: For 1 serving, use 2 teaspoons butter and 2 eggs.

Per serving: 161 Cal, 13g Fat, 9g Pro, 1g Sug, 1g Carb, 0g Fib, *NET CARBS: 1*

Baked Bacon Omelet

MAKES 6 SERVINGS

Have cooked bacon on hand in the freezer for this tasty omelet.

6   **large eggs, lightly beaten**
⅓   **cup Half & Half**
3   **slices bacon, cooked, crumbled**
¼   **teaspoon pepper**
1   **cups (4-oz) Cheddar cheese, shredded**
¼   **cup chopped green onion**

Cook's Tip   Omelets are easier to make if cooked in a slope-sided non-stick skillet.

1. Preheat oven to 400°F. Combine eggs, Half & Half and 1/3 cup water. Add bacon, pepper, cheese and onion. Pour into a sprayed 8x8-inch baking dish. Bake 18 to 20 minutes or until center is set.

Per serving: 185 Cal, 14g Fat, 12g Pro, 1g Sug, 2g Carb, <1g Fib, *NET CARBS: 2*

Ham & Cheese Omelet

MAKES 1 SERVING

I added a little apple here, not much, just 1 tablespoon, but a treat!

1   **tablespoon butter**
1   **tablespoon diced apple**
2   **large eggs**
⅓   **cup diced ham**
¼   **cup (1-oz) Swiss cheese, shredded**

1. Melt butter in a 9-inch nonstick skillet. Add apple and cook until just tender. Remove apple and set aside.
2. Combine eggs with 1 tablespoon water. Add to skillet and cook until eggs begin to set. Then gently lift edges to allow egg to flow underneath. When eggs are lightly set, spoon apple, ham, and cheese over one side. Let cook about 1 minute. Fold in half and serve.

Per serving: 431 Cal, 31g Fat, 32g Pro, 2g Sug, 3g Carb, <1g Fib, *NET CARBS: 3*

Omelet For Two

MAKES 2 SERVINGS

*Quick and easy. Just what
you need in the morning.*

2   teaspoons oil
¼   cup finely chopped onion
4   eggs, lightly beaten
    Salt and pepper

1. Heat oil in a 9-inch nonstick skillet Add
onion and cook until soft.
2. Combine eggs with salt, pepper and 2
tablespoons water. Add to skillet and cook over
medium heat, lifting gently to allow uncooked
portion to flow underneath. When eggs are
lightly set, fold, then cut in half to serve.

Per serving: 195 Cal, 15g Fat, 13g Pro, 2g Sug,
3g Carb, <1g Fib, **NET CARBS: 3**

Omelet Crepes

MAKES 1 SERVING

*There's a restaurant in Missouri that makes
their omelets this way, filling them with all sorts
of delicious fillings and toppings. If you have
trouble making omelets, try this easy method.*

2   large eggs
    oil

1. Thoroughly combine eggs with 2 tablespoons water, whisking until smooth.
2. Heat a 9-inch nonstick skillet over medium

heat. When hot, brush lightly with oil. Add eggs
and cook until top is only slightly moist. Turn
and cook 2 to 3 seconds. Remove. Fill omelets,
non-browned side out, with desired filling and/or
toppings. Roll up and serve.

Per serving: 147 Cal, 10g Fat, 13g Pro, 1g Sug,
1g Carb, 0g Fib, **NET CARBS: 1**

Baked Eggs & Cheese

MAKES 1 SERVING

Especially easy for just 1 or 2 servings.

2   large eggs
2   tablespoons whipping cream
¼   cup (1-oz) Pepper Jack cheese, shredded
    Chopped parsley

1. Preheat oven to 350°F. Place eggs in a
sprayed 10-ounce ramekin. Pour cream over
eggs and sprinkle with cheese. Sprinkle with
parsley.
2. Bake 18 to 20 minutes or until egg yolks are
almost set. Let stand 5 minutes before serving.

Per serving: 360 Cal, 30g Fat, 20g Pro, 1g Sug,
3g Carb, 0g Fib, **NET CARBS: 3**

Sausage Burritos

Variety is what helps us stay on our diet. To save time, keep cooked sausage on hand and you can make these in just a few minutes.

8   ounces sausage
4   large eggs, lightly beaten
    Salt and pepper
4   (7-inch) low-carb tortillas
¾   cup (3-oz) Cheddar cheese, shredded
½   cup salsa

1. Cook sausage and drain off fat.
2. Scramble eggs in same skillet, adding salt and pepper to taste.
3. Warm tortillas in microwave, if desired. Spoon eggs just off center of each tortilla. Top with cheese and salsa. Roll tortilla to enclose.

variation: Omit sausage and add cooked onions and peppers.

Per serving: 330 Cal, 24g Fat, 21g Pro, 1g Sug, 14g Carb, 8g Fib, **NET CARBS: 6**

Chicken Frittata

Just a small amount of chicken is all you need for this recipe.

2   tablespoons butter
1   cup cubed cooked chicken
1   tablespoon heavy cream
6   large eggs
¼   teaspoon salt
½   cup salsa

1. Heat butter in an oven-proof 10-inch skillet. Spoon chicken over bottom. Combine cream, eggs, salt and 3 tablespoons water and pour over chicken. Spoon salsa over top.
2. Cook over low heat 6 to 8 minutes or until almost set.
3. Broil about 6 inches from heat, 2 to 3 minutes, or until set.

Per serving: 214 Cal, 15g Fat, 16g Pro, 1g Sug, 2g Carb, <1g Fib, **NET CARBS: 2**

Frittata

A frittata is easier to make than several omelets.

6   large eggs
¼   cup heavy whipping cream
1   tablespoon butter, melted
¼   teaspoon salt
¼   teaspoon pepper
1   cup (4-oz) Cheddar cheese, shredded

1. Preheat oven to 400°F. By hand, beat first 5 ingredients and 3/4 cup water until blended. Pour into sprayed deep 10-inch pie dish. Sprinkle with cheese and bake 20 minutes or until golden.

variations: Sprinkle top with ham, bacon, sausage, vegetables, etc.

Per serving: 301 Cal, 25g Fat, 17g Pro, 1g Sug, 1g Carb, 0g Fib, **NET CARBS: 1**

Sausage Egg Scramble

MAKES 4 SERVINGS

Mixture can be served in a low-carb tortilla. Just add 3 carbs per serving.

4 ounces sausage
¼ cup chopped onion
2 tablespoons chopped green pepper
6 large eggs
½ cup (2-oz) Pepper Jack cheese, shredded

1. Cook sausage, onion and green pepper in a medium skillet; drain.
2. Combine eggs with 1/4-cup water. Add to sausage and cook over medium heat, stirring occasionally.   Sprinkle with cheese and serve.

Per serving: 225 Cal, 17g Fat, 15g Pro, 1g Sug, 2g Carb, <1g Fib, *NET CARBS: 2*

Quick Crab & Eggs

MAKES 4 SERVINGS

A good pantry-type recipe.

¼ cup butter
8 large eggs
1 (6.5-oz) can crab, drained
1 teaspoon prepared mustard

1. Melt butter in a medium skillet. Combine eggs, crab and mustard and add to skillet. Scramble mixture until cooked through, but still moist.

Per serving: 279 Cal, 21g Fat, 19g Pro, 1g Sug, 1g Carb, 0g Fib, *NET CARBS: 1*

Ham and Egg Scramble

MAKES 2 SERVINGS

An easy way to use up that last little bit of ham.

1 tablespoon butter
2 tablespoons chopped onion
¼ cup chopped mushrooms
½ cup diced ham
4 large eggs, lightly beaten
  Salt and pepper, to taste

1. Melt butter in a medium skillet. Add onion and cook until almost soft. Add mushrooms and cook through. Stir in the ham.
2. Add eggs, salt and pepper. Cook, stirring frequently, until almost set.

Per serving: 256 Cal, 17g Fat, 22g Pro, 1g Sug, 2g Carb, < 1g Fib, *NET CARBS: 2*

Baked Cheddar Egg Dish

A great brunch dish.

2 cups (8-oz) Cheddar cheese, shredded
½ cup heavy cream
½ teaspoon salt
¼ teaspoon pepper
2 teaspoons prepared mustard
12 large eggs, lightly beaten

1. Preheat oven to 325°F. Sprinkle cheese in a sprayed 13x9-inch baking dish.
2. Combine cream, 1/2 cup water, salt, pepper, and mustard. Pour half the mixture over cheese. Add eggs; then, remaining milk mixture. Bake 30 to 35 minutes or until set.

Per serving: 274 Cal, 22g Fat, 17g Pro, 1g Sug, 1g Carb, 0g Fib, *NET CARBS: 1*

Company Swiss Eggs

Surprise your family and make this a special meal for them---and YOU! Serve with sausage links and sliced strawberries.

2 cups (8-oz) Swiss cheese, shredded
¼ cup butter
1 cup whipping cream
½ teaspon salt
⅛ teaspoon pepper
12 large eggs, lightly beaten

1. Preheat oven to 325°F. Sprinkle cheese in a sprayed 13x9-inch baking dish. Dot with butter.
2. Combine cream, salt and pepper, and pour half over cheese. Pour eggs over top and then remaining cream. Bake 30 to 35 minutes or until set.

Per serving: 292 Cal, 25g Fat, 14g Pro, 1g Sug, 2g Carb, 0g Fib, *NET CARBS: 2*

MENU

Baked Cheddar Cheese Egg Dish
3 Sausage Links
Almond Bread
3 net carbs per meal.

Egg Nests

MAKES 1 SERVING

Not just for kids.

1   slice low-carb white bread
1   large egg
    Salt and pepper

1. Make a hole in center of bread and place both pieces in a sprayed skillet. Drop egg into hole and sprinkle with salt and pepper. Cook over medium heat until toasted on bottom. Turn both pieces and cook as desired.

Per serving: 133 Cal, 6g Fat, 13g Pro, <1g Sug, 6g Carb, 3g Fib, **NET CARBS: 3**

Sausage & Egg Casserole

MAKES 8 SERVINGS

For mushroom lovers. Spicy with a chewy cheese topping.

6   large eggs
¼   cup sour cream
12 ounces sausage
4   ounces fresh mushrooms, sliced
1   (4-oz) can diced green chilies
4   cups (16-oz) Mozzarella cheese, shredded

1. Preheat oven to 400°F. Combine eggs and sour cream. Pour into a sprayed 13x9-inch baking dish. Bake 10 to 12 minutes or until set, but not firm.

2. Meanwhile, cook sausage; drain. Add mushrooms and chilies and cook 2 to 3 minutes. Spoon over eggs. Sprinkle with cheese. Bake 10 to 15 minutes or until golden.

Per serving: 332 Cal, 25g Fat, 23g Pro, 1g Sug, 4g Carb, 0g Fib, **NET CARBS: 4**

Chile Relleno Loaf

MAKES 4 SERVINGS

A taste tester's favorite.

1   (7-oz) can whole green chiles
2   cups (8-oz) Pepper Jack cheese, shredded
2   large eggs, lightly beaten
¼   cup heavy cream
    Salt and pepper

1. Preheat oven to 375°F. Split chilies lengthwise and remove seeds. Fill with 3/4 of the cheese. Roll up starting at narrow end. Place, seam-side down, in a sprayed 9x5-inch loaf pan.

2. Combine eggs, cream, salt and pepper with 3/4-cup water. Pour over chilies and sprinkle top with remaining cheese. Bake 50 to 60 minutes or until golden and custard is set. When cutting, pour off any excess liquid in bottom of pan.

Per serving: 312 Cal, 26g Fat, 16g Pro, <1g Sug, 4g Carb, 0g Fib, **NET CARBS: 4**

Scotch Eggs

MAKES 4 SERVINGS

Worth the extra effort this recipe produces.

16   ounces pork sausage
 4   hard-boiled eggs
 1   egg, lightly beaten
 ½   cup low-carb dry white bread crumbs
     oil

1. Divide sausage into 4 equal parts. Form sausage around hard-boiled eggs.

2. Roll in lightly beaten egg, then in bread crumbs. Deep fry in hot oil until browned and cooked through. Cut in half crosswise.

Per serving: 401 Cal, 34g Fat, 17g Pro, 1g Sug, 4g Carb, 1g Fib, **NET CARBS: 3**

Asparagus-Egg Dish

MAKES 1 SERVING

Vegetable, meat and dairy, all in one recipe.

4   cooked asparagus spears
1   poached or fried egg
2   slices bacon, cooked

1. Place asparagus on a serving dish. Top with egg and bacon.

Per serving: 155 Cal, 10g Fat, 12g Pro, 1g Sug, 3g Carb, 1g Fib, **NET CARBS: 2**

Tortilla Egg Casserole

MAKES 6 SERVINGS

This is a little on the hot side.

8   large eggs
½   medium green pepper, chopped
2   cups (8-oz) Pepper Jack cheese, shredded
6   (7-inch) low-carb white tortillas

1. Preheat oven to 350°F. Lightly beat eggs with 1/4 cup water. Cook along with peppers in a medium skillet until scrambled, but still moist.

2. Spoon 1/6 of the mixture down center of each tortilla. Sprinkle with half the cheese. Roll tightly and place, seam-side down, in a sprayed 8x8-inch baking dish. Sprinkle with remaining cheese. Bake 15 to 20 minutes or until heated through.

Per serving: 295 Cal, 21g Fat, 22g Pro, 1g Sug, 13g Carb, 8g Fib, **NET CARBS: 5**

Ham & Cheese Egg Roll

I hadn't make this for years, but it fits nicely into a low-carb diet. A great company recipe.

12 large eggs
¼ teaspoon pepper
1 tablespoon prepared mustard
8 ounces thinly sliced deli ham
2 cups (8-oz) Swiss Cheese, shredded
1 tablespoon chopped green onions

1. Preheat oven to 350°F. Lightly spray a 15x10-inch jelly roll pan. Line with waxed paper and lightly spray.

2. Whisk eggs with pepper. Pour into pan and bake 12 to 15 minutes or until eggs are set. Invert onto foil and carefully remove waxed paper.

3. Spread with mustard. Layer with ham, overlapping slices. Sprinkle with cheese. Carefully roll up like a jelly roll starting on long side. Wrap tightly in foil. Place on a baking sheet and bake 12 to 15 minutes or until heated through. Slice and sprinkle cut side with onion.

Per slice: 165 Cal, 11g Fat, 15g Pro, 1g Sug, 2g Carb, 0g Fib, **NET CARBS: 2**

Breakfast Casserole

Plan ahead and assemble a day ahead.

1½ pounds bulk pork sausage
1 cup chopped onion
6 slices low-carb white bread
6 large eggs, lightly beaten
1 cup heavy cream
1 cup (4-oz) Cheddar Cheese, shredded

1. Cook sausage and onion until cooked through; drain.

2. Cube bread and place in a sprayed 13x9-inch baking dish. Spoon sausage over top.

3. Combine eggs and cream with 1 cup water. Pour over sausage and sprinkle with cheese. Cover and chill overnight.

4. Preheat oven to 350°F. Uncover and bake 35 to 40 minutes or until golden and center is set.

Per serving: 291 Cal, 24g Fat, 13g Pro, 1g Sug, 5g Carb, 2g Fib, **NET CARBS: 3**

Deviled Eggs

*This may seem like a lot,
but they make great snacks.*

8   hard-boiled eggs
3   tablespoons mayonnaise
2   teaspoons dill pickle relish
¼   cup finely chopped ham
    Salt and pepper to taste

1. Slice eggs in half lengthwise.
2. Remove yolks and combine with remaining ingredients. Fill whites. Cover. Chill.

note: Fill deviled eggs by spooning egg mixture in a small resealable plastic bag. Cut off one corner of the bag and squeeze to fill.

Per half: 57Cal, 5g Fat, 3g Pro, <1g Sug, <1g Carb, 0g Fib, **NET CARBS: <1**

Hard-Boiled Eggs

This is the way I like to hard-boil eggs. I place the eggs in a single layer in a saucepan. Add water to cover eggs by 1 inch. Bring water to a boil then immediately remove from the heat. Let stand 20 minutes. Drain and rinse with cold water until eggs are cool.

note:
Overcooking the eggs will cause those unattractive green rings around the yolks.

Ham & Egg Casserole

An easy brunch or supper dish.

1   cup diced ham
¼   cup sliced green onions
1   cup (4-oz) Monterey Jack cheese, shredded
12   large eggs, lightly beaten
1   cup heavy cream
⅛   teaspoon pepper

1. Preheat oven to 350°F. Sprinkle ham in a sprayed 11x7-inch baking dish. Add onion and top with cheese.
2. Combine eggs with cream, 1 cup water and pepper. Pour over cheese. Bake 40 to 45 minutes or until set.

Per serving: 294 Cal, 24g Fat, 18g Pro, 1g Sug, 2g Carb, <1g Fib, **NET CARBS: 2**

Sunny-Side Up Eggs

MAKES 1 SERVING

If you have problems getting your eggs just right, try this method.

1 **large egg**
   Salt and pepper

1. Cook egg in a heavily sprayed small skillet until white is set.
2. Add 1 tablespoon water. Cover and let cook briefly until yolk is cooked to desired firmness.

Per serving: 73 Cal, 5g Fat, 6g Pro, <1g Sug, <1g Carb, 0g Fib, *NET CARBS: <1*

Eggs Creole

MAKES 4 SERVINGS

Tomatoes add a nice touch to egg dishes.

⅓ **cup sliced mushrooms**
2 **tablespoons chopped onion**
2 **tablespoons butter**
¾ **cup chopped Plum tomatoes**
6 **large eggs, lightly beaten**

1. Sauté mushrooms and onion in butter until tender. Add tomatoes and heat through.
2. Add eggs and cook until scrambled, but not firm, stirring gently. Serve immediately.

Per serving: 166 Cal, 13g Fat, 10g Pro, 1g Sug, 2g Carb, <1g Fib, *NET CARBS: 2*

Hamburger Quiche

MAKES 6 SERVINGS

When you don't know what to cook for breakfast, lunch or dinner--make a quiche.

½   **pound lean ground beef**
1½ **cups (6-oz) Swiss cheese, shredded**
3   **tablespoons heavy cream**
1   **tablespoon cornstarch**
3   **large eggs, lightly beaten**

1. Preheat oven to 350°F. Brown ground beef; drain thoroughly.
2. Meanwhile, sprinkle cheese in a sprayed 9-inch pie dish. Top with ground beef.
3. Combine cream and cornstarch with enough water to make 2/3 cup. Add eggs and mix well. Pour over ground beef. Bake 30 to 40 minutes or until custard is set.

note: Not as good reheated.

Per serving: 241 Cal, 18g Fat, 17g Pro, 1g Sug, 3g Carb, 0g Fib, *NET CARBS: 3*

Chicken-Broccoli Quiche

MAKES 6 SERVINGS

A nice creamy quiche

2   cups small broccoli florets
1   cup (4-oz) Swiss cheese, shredded
1   cup cubed cooked chicken
2   large eggs, lightly beaten
1   cup whipping cream

1. Preheat oven to 350°F. Place broccoli in a sprayed 9-inch pie dish; add cheese and chicken.
2. Combine eggs and cream until well mixed. Pour over chicken mixture, pressing down to cover ingredients as much as possible. Bake 30 to 40 minutes or until custard is set. Let stand 5 to 10 minutes before serving.

Per serving: 278 Cal, 22g Fat, 16g Pro, <1g Sug, 3g Carb, 1g Fib, **NET CARBS: 2**

Broccoli-Ham Quiche

MAKES 6 SERVINGS

If you need just a small amount of ham, buy a 1/4-inch slice of deli ham.

3   large eggs, lightly beaten
1   cup heavy cream
1   cup small broccoli florets
½   cup cubed ham
½   cup (2-oz) Gruyére cheese, shredded

1. Preheat oven to 375°F. Combine eggs and cream. Add remaining ingredients and pour into a sprayed 9-inch pie dish. Bake 20 to 25 minutes or until center is set.

Per serving: 234 Cal, 21g Fat, 10g Pro, <1g Sug, 2g Carb, <1g Fib, **NET CARBS: 2**

Bacon-Onion Quiche

MAKES 6 SERVINGS

This popular dish is served with a nice tossed salad and fresh berries.

1   pound bacon, cooked, crumbled
2   cups (8-oz) Swiss cheese, shredded
¼   cup finely chopped onion
5   large eggs, lightly beaten
½   cup heavy cream

1. Preheat oven to 350°F. Place half the bacon in a sprayed 9-inch pie dish. Sprinkle with half the cheese. Repeat layers. Sprinkle with onion.

2. Combine eggs, cream and 1/2 cup water. Pour over cheese. Bake 40 to 45 minutes or until center is set.

Per serving: 404 Cal, 32g Fat, 25g Pro, 1g Sug, 4g Carb, <1g Fib, *NET CARBS: 4*

Quiche Lorraine

MAKES 6 SERVINGS

Swiss cheese may be used for this dish, but Gruyére has more flavor.

6   slices bacon, cooked, crumbled
1   small onion, thinly sliced
1   cup (4-oz) Gruyére cheese, shredded
¼   cup grated Parmesan cheese
4   large eggs, lightly beaten
2   cups heavy cream

1. Preheat oven to 450°F. Cook onion in 1 tablespoon of the bacon drippings until tender.

2. Sprinkle bacon, onion, then cheese in sprayed 9-inch pie dish.

3. Combine eggs and cream and pour over cheese. Bake 20 to 25 minutes or until center is set.

Per serving: 454 Cal, 42g Fat, 15g Pro, 1g Sug, 4g Carb, <1g Fib, *NET CARBS: 4*

Sausage Quiche

MAKES 6 SERVINGS

Serve with Almond Cranberry Muffins, page 39.

8   small sausage links, cooked
2   cups (8-oz) Swiss cheese, shredded
5   large eggs, lightly beaten
½   cup heavy cream

1. Preheat oven to 350°F. Cut sausage into 1/4-inch slices. Place half in a sprayed 9-inch pie dish. Sprinkle with half the cheese. Repeat layers.

2. Combine eggs, cream and 1/2 cup water. Pour over cheese. Bake 35 to 40 minutes or until center is set. Let stand 5 minutes before serving.

Per serving: 342 Cal, 28g Fat, 18g Pro, 1g Sug, 3g Carb, 0g Fib, *NET CARBS: 3*

Meats & Seafoods

⌂ Ground Beef
⌂ Beef
⌂ Pork
⌂ Lamb
⌂ Salmon
⌂ White Fish
⌂ Shellfish

Selecting the Best Roasts

When selecting meat, freshness is of the utmost importance. There should be no offensive odors, yellow or brown discoloration on fat or sticky surfaces. The color should be bright and without dark spots.

Beef

Unlike some cuts of meat, a beef roast should have some marbling of fat. Restaurants usually get the Prime cuts of meat, so most of our choices will be Choice or Select, with Choice being the better of the two. Many supermarkets carry only Select cuts. These are okay but if cooked beyond medium-rare stage, may tend to be dry and less tender.

Pork

Pork tends to be lean with very little marbling. The meat should be firm and slightly moist. The color should be a pale reddish-pink. To prevent dryness, most pork should be cooked to no more that 140°. The temperature will rise as it stands. Pork is a great choice for brining, see page 213, but make sure the pork doesn't have additives. This may be labeled on the package as tender or flavor enhanced.

Lamb

I sometimes have a hard time finding good lamb, but look for meat that is light red in color. The fat should be smooth and white. As with pork, lamb should not be overcooked.

When cooking meats, I highly recommend you invest in an accurate thermometer. The one I like best has an external display that you can place on your counter with a cord attached to a probe that you insert into the meat. You simply set the desired temperature and the thermometer will beep to alert you when it has reached that degree. Do not rely on thermometers that have preset temperatures for Rare, Medium Rare, etc., we usually find these settings to be too high. Probably the most important thing to remember when cooking roasts, turkey or a whole chicken is to allow time for the meat to stand after roasting. Your meat will be juicier and easier to carve.

Beef Roasting Chart

Beef Cut	Oven Temp	Lbs	Approx. Total Cooking Hours	Remove when Temp Reaches
Eye Round Roast	325°F	2-3	Med. Rare: 1½ to 1¾	135° F
Rib Eye Roast (small end)	350° F	4-6	Med. Rare: 1¾ -2 / Med: 2-2½	135° F / 140° F
		6-8	Med. Rare: 2¼ / Med: 2½-2¾	135° F / 140° F
Rib Eye Roast (large end)	350° F	4-6	Med. Rare: 2-2½ / Med: 2½-3	135° F / 140° F
		6-8	Med. Rare: 2¼-2½ / Med: 2½-3	135° F / 140° F
Rib Roast (prime rib)	350° F	6-8	Med. Rare: 2¼-2½ / Med: 2¾-3	135° F / 140° F
		8-10	Med. Rare: 2½-3 / Med: 3-3½	135° F / 140° F
Round Tip Roast	325° F	4-6	Med. Rare: 2-2½ / Med: 2½-3	140° F / 150° F
		6-8	Med. Rare: 2½-3 / Med: 3-3½	140° F / 150° F
Tenderloin Roast	425° F	2-3	Med. Rare: 35-40 min. / Med. 45-50 min	135° F / 140° F
		4-5	Med. Rare: 50-60 min. / Med. 60-70 min	135° F / 140° F
Tri-Tip Roast	425° F	1½-2	Med. Rare: 30-40 min. / Med. 40-45 min	135° F / 140° F
Ground Beef				160°F

Olive Oils

Extra Virgin Olive Oil	Fragrant and strong flavor. Drizzle on pasta, meats and vegetables. Not for high temperature cooking.
Virgin Olive Oil	Lighter and less fruity. Can use the same as extra virgin oil but doesn't have the same flavor.
Refined Olive Oil	Made from lower-quality oils. Use in frying, cooking and salad dressings.
Pure Olive Oil	Has a mild flavor. Cheaper than above oils. Use as an all-purpose oil, and in dressings, salads and marinades.
Extra Light* Olive Oil	Composed of refined olive oils and virgin olive oils. A mild taste and light color. Can withstand higher temperatures. *This is the one I used for this book.*
Pomace	Made from previous pressings. Bland flavor, but good for dressings, cooking and deep-frying.

Menu Ideas

Organization is the key to stress-free cooking. In the long run, it will save you time as well as money.

Make it simple and plan a 4-week cycle of menus. Once this is done, the hardest part is over and you are on your way to preparing more nutritious meals for your family.

As long as you know what the main course is, filling in the rest is fairly easy. At least once a week, prepare a ham, roast, chicken or turkey and plan for the use of leftovers.

A sample weekly menu might be:

> Sun - Ham
> Mon - Pizza
> Tue - Noodles & Ham Casserole
> Wed - Roasted Chicken
> Thur - Fish
> Fri - Ham Fettuccine
> Sat - A Chicken Casserole

Stuffed Burgers

MAKES 4 SERVINGS

If desired, serve on lettuce leaf with dill pickles.

1½   pounds lean ground beef
1   cup (4-oz) Cheddar cheese, shredded
4   tablespoons Barbecue Sauce, page 209

1. Divide meat into 8 equal portions and shape into thin patties.
2. Sprinkle cheese in center of half the patties. Press remaining patties over cheese and press to seal. Place on grill and cook over direct heat to 160°, turning once. Brush with barbecue sauce toward end of cooking time.

Per serving: 420 Cal, 30g Fat, 33g Pro, 1g Sug, 2g Carb, 0g Fib, **NET CARBS: 2**

Tortilla Hamburgers

MAKES 4 SERVINGS

A different twist on how to serve a hamburger.

1   pound lean ground beef
⅓   cup finely chopped onion
1   teaspoon salt
4   (7-inch) low-carb tortillas
2   cups shredded lettuce
¼   cup salsa

1. Combine first 3 ingredients and shape into 4 patties. Broil or grill patties until cooked (160°).
2. Warm tortillas if desired, and place on serving plates. Top with lettuce, burger patty and salsa.

Per serving: 260 Cal, 16g Fat, 23g Pro, 1g Sug, 13g Carb, 8g Fib, **NET CARBS: 5**

Burger Towers

MAKES 6 SERVINGS

Nice for even your carb friends.

2   pounds lean ground beef
1   teaspoon seasoning salt
4   ounces mushrooms, sliced
2   tablespoons butter
2   medium tomatoes

1. Lightly mix ground beef with salt. Shape into 6 patties about 1-inch thick. Pan-fry, grill or broil until cooked (160°), turning once.
2. Meanwhile, cook mushrooms in butter until tender; drain.
3. Place meat patties on serving plates. Slice tomatoes and place on patties. Top with mushrooms.

Per serving: 314 Cal, 22g Fat, 24g Pro, 2g Sug, 3g Carb, 1g Fib, **NET CARBS: 2**

Ground Beef

Safety reasons show that all ground beef must be cooked to 160°F. The correct temperature is extremely important and well worth the investment in an accurate thermometer with the sensor in the tip, thus reducing any margin for error.

Taco Burgers

*I have used 8-ounce burgers here for those
days when you are really hungry.*

1   **pound lean ground beef**
½   **cup salsa**
2   **slices Cheddar cheese**
1   **cup shredded lettuce**
2   **Plum tomatoes, chopped**

1. Combine ground beef and salsa. Form
ground beef into 2 oval patties, about 3/4-inch
thick. Broil or grill until cooked to 160°.
2. Top each with cheese, lettuce and tomato.

Per serving: 538 Cal, 37g Fat, 43g Pro, 3g Sug,
6g Carb, 2g Fib, *NET CARBS: 4*

Southwestern Cheeseburgers

MAKES 4 SERVINGS

*Any cheese can be substituted for
the Pepper Jack.*

1½   **pounds lean ground beef**
¼   **cup finely chopped onion**
4   **slices Pepper Jack cheese**
4   **tomato slices**

1. Combine ground beef and onion. Divide and
shape into 8 thin slices. Top 4 patties with
cheese, cutting cheese to fit. Cover with remaining patties and seal. Broil or grill until cooked to
160°. Top with tomato slice and serve.

Per serving: 413 Cal, 30g Fat, 32g Pro, 1g Sug,
2g Carb, <1g Fib, *NET CARBS: 2*

Bleu Cheese Burgers

MAKES 4 SERVINGS

*If you don't care for Bleu cheese,
just omit that ingredient.*

1   **pound lean ground beef**
⅓   **cup Bleu cheese, crumbled**
½   **teaspoon garlic salt**
⅛   **teaspoon cayenne**
4   **(½-inch) slices onion**
1   **tablespoon olive oil**

1. Combine first 4 ingredients and shape into 4
patties. Cook on heated grill over direct heat 12
to 15 minutes or until cooked to 160°, turning
once.
2. Last 5 minutes of cooking time, brush onion
slices with oil and grill until tender, turning once.
Serve on patties.

Per serving: 296 Cal, 21g Fat, 20g Pro, 3g Sug,
7g Carb, 1g Fib, *NET CARBS: 6*

MENU

Bleu Cheese Burgers
Asparagus & Bacon
Tossed Salad with Mushrooms
Coconut Custard
8 net carbs per meal.

Swiss with Dill Burgers

*Serve hamburgers with your choice of
condiments and fresh vegetables.*

1   **pound lean ground beef**
2   **tablespoons sour cream**
¼   **teaspoon dried dill weed**
4   **slices Swiss cheese**

1. Combine first 3 ingredients, mixing lightly.
Shape into 4 patties and grill over direct heat
until cooked through (160°). Top with cheese and
cook until melted.

Per serving: 321 Cal, 23g Fat, 25g Pro, <1g Sug,
2g Carb, 0g Fib, *NET CARBS: 2*

Swiss Burgers

*If desired, meat can be divided
into smaller burgers.*

1   **pound lean ground beef**
    Salt and pepper
2   **slices Swiss cheese**
4   **slices bacon, cooked**

1. Form ground beef into 2 patties. Broil or
grill until cooked through (160°). Sprinkle with
salt and pepper and top with cheese last couple
minutes of cooking time.
2. Top with bacon and serve.

Per serving: 473 Cal, 41g Fat, 47g Pro, <1g Sug,
2g Carb, 0g Fib, *NET CARBS: 2*

Bacon Cheeseburgers

Just like fast food minus the bun.

1   **pound lean ground beef**
1   **medium onion**
    Salt and pepper
4   **slices Cheddar cheese**
4   **slices bacon, cooked**

1. Form ground beef into 4 patties and slice
onion into 4 slices. Place on oiled, heated grill.
Cook over direct heat, turning once. Meat should
register 160° and onion should be tender.
Sprinkle lightly with salt and pepper.
2. Top meat with cheese and cook until melted.
Top each pattie with an onion slice and 2 bacon
halves.

Per serving: 358 Cal, 26g Fat, 27g Pro, 1g Sug,
3g Carb, <1g Fib, *NET CARBS: 3*

Reuben Burgers

A delicious way to serve a beef patty.

1½ **pounds lean ground beef**
1   **cup sauerkraut, drained**
4   **slices Swiss cheese**

1. Shape ground beef into 4 oval patties and
grill or cook as desired, to 160°.
2. Top each patty with sauerkraut, then cheese.
Place under broiler to melt the cheese.

Per serving: 412 Cal, 29g Fat, 34g Pro, 1g Sug,
3g Carb, 1g Fib, *NET CARBS: 2*

Ground Beef Fajitas

MAKES 8 SERVINGS

A slight twist to the popular beef fajitas.

1   pound lean ground beef
1   medium green pepper, cut into narrow strips
1   small onion, thinly sliced
8   (7-inch) low-carb tortillas
¾   cup well-drained salsa
½   cup sour cream

1. Brown ground beef, green pepper and onion in a large skillet. Cook until beef is lightly browned and cooked through. Drain off fat.
2. Divide mixture evenly and spoon onto tortillas. Top each with 2 tablespoons salsa and 1 tablespoon sour cream. Roll up and serve.

Per serving: 190 Cal, 12g Fat, 14g Pro, 1g Sug, 14g Carb, 9g Fib, **NET CARBS: 5**

Tacos

MAKES 10 SERVINGS

Low-carb taco shells give us a wider variety of recipes that we can now use.
Only 1 net carb per shell!

1   pound lean ground beef
1   (1.25-oz) package taco seasoning mix
10 low carb taco shells (approximately)
½   cup (2-oz) Cheddar cheese, shredded
½   cup shredded lettuce
½   cup chopped tomatoes

1. Brown ground beef and drain. Add seasoning mix and 3/4-cup water. Bring to a boil, reduce heat, and simmer 10 to 15 minutes or until liquid is absorbed.
2. Carefully spoon into taco shells. Sprinkle with cheese, lettuce and tomato.

Per serving: 191 Cal, 14g Fat, 10g Pro, 2g Sug, 6g Carb, 3g Fib, **NET CARBS: 3**

Taco Meat

MAKES 6 SERVINGS

Use mixture for tacos, taco burgers, pizzas, etc.

1¼ pounds lean ground beef
1   cup chopped onion
1½ teaspoons garlic salt
2   teaspoons chili powder
¼   teaspoon cumin
¼   teaspoon crushed red pepper flakes

1. In a medium skillet, brown ground beef and onion; drain. Add 1 cup water along with remaining ingredients. Bring to a boil, reduce heat and simmer 18 to 20 minutes or until liquid is absorbed.

Per serving: 209 Cal, 14g Fat, 18g Pro, 1g Sug, 2g Carb, <1g Fib, **NET CARBS: 2**

Linda's Spaghetti Sauce with Red Peppers

MAKES 6 SERVINGS

Everyone enjoys Linda's spaghetti. The mild flavor of the red pepper blends well with the spaghetti sauce giving it a slightly sweet taste. Serve over spaghetti squash or low carb pasta.

1   **pound lean ground beef**
4   **ounces fresh mushrooms, sliced**
1   **small red pepper, coarsely chopped**
3   **cups low-carb spaghetti sauce**
    Salt and pepper to taste

1. Brown the ground beef. Add mushrooms toward end of cooking time; drain.
2. Add remaining ingredients and bring to a boil. Reduce heat and simmer 15 to 20 minutes or to desired thickness.

Per serving: 220 Cal, 14g Fat, 14g Pro, 5g Sug, 8g Carb, 2g Fib, **NET CARBS: 6**

Layered Hamburger Bake

MAKES 6 SERVINGS

If a smaller or larger recipe is desired, you may need to decrease or increase ingredients and pan size accordingly.

2   **pounds lean ground beef**
     Salt and pepper
1   **tablespoon prepared mustard**
1   **small onion, thinly sliced**
2   **small tomatoes, sliced**
½   **green pepper, sliced**

1. Preheat oven to 350°F. Pat half of the ground beef into a deep 8 or 9-inch round cake pan. Sprinkle with salt and pepper. Spread with mustard. Cover with onion, 1 tomato and green pepper.
2. Pat remaining ground beef evenly over top. Arrange remaining tomato slices on top. Bake 25 to 30 minutes or until meat reaches 160°.

Per serving: 280 Cal, 19g Fat, 23g Pro, 1g Sug, 3g Carb, 1g Fib, **NET CARBS: 2**

Italian Meatballs

MAKES 16 MEATBALLS

If you can afford the carbs, serve meat balls with low-carb spaghetti sauce and low-carb pasta. Otherwise, enjoy just the meatballs.

1   **pound lean ground beef**
½   **cup low-carb soft white bread crumbs**
1   **teaspoon Italian seasoning**
1   **large egg, lightly beaten**
¼   **cup low-carb spaghetti sauce**
½   **cup (2-oz) Mozzarella cheese**

1. Preheat oven to 400°F. Combine first 5 ingredients. Mix lightly.
2. Cut cheese into 16 cubes. Divide meat mixture into 16 parts and shape around cheese cubes. Place in a shallow baking pan and bake 18 to 20 minutes or until cooked to 160°.

variation: Make larger meatballs by dividing meat mixture and cheese into 8 portions.

Per meatball: 72 Cal, 5g Fat, 6g Pro, 0g Sug, <1g Carb, <1g Fib, **NET CARBS: <1**

Swedish Meatballs

MAKES 40 MEATBALLS

If desired, meatballs can be served in a gravy. Make gravy, add meatballs and heat through.

2   pounds, lean ground beef
1½ cups low-carb white soft bread crumbs, crust removed
⅓   cup very finely chopped onion
1   teaspoon salt
½   teaspoon nutmeg
1   (14.5-oz) can beef broth

1. Preheat oven to 425°F. Combine first 5 ingredients. Form into walnut-size meatballs. Place in a shallow baking pan and bake 10 minutes.
2. Add broth to pan. Cover tightly with foil and bake 8 minutes or until cooked to 160°.

Per meatball: 45 Cal, 3g Fat, 4g Pro, 0g Sug, <1g Carb, <1g Fib, **NET CARBS: <1**

Basic Meatballs

MAKES 6 DOZEN MEATBALLS

Use for stroganoff, spaghetti or as a snack between meals. The meatballs may be frozen before or after baking. Keep a bag in the freezer for last minute meals.

3   pounds lean ground beef
3   large eggs, lightly beaten
2   tablespoons whipping cream
4   slices low-carb white bread, torn
½   cup chopped onion
    Salt and pepper

1. Preheat oven to 425°F. In a large bowl, combine the ingredients with 1/3 cup water. Chill mixture if too soft to form into balls. Shape into meatballs and place on a 15x10-inch baking pan. Bake 15 to 20 minutes or until cooked to 160°.

Per meatball: 41 Cal, 3g Fat, 4g Pro, 0g Sug, <1g Carb, <1g Fib, **NET CARBS: <1**

Salsa Meatloaf

MAKES 6 SERVINGS

A good meatloaf recipe.

1½ pounds lean ground beef
½   cup finely chopped green pepper
½   cup finely chopped onion
1   teaspoon salt
1   tablespoon prepared mustard
⅓   cup salsa

1. Preheat oven to 350°F. Gently combine ingredients until well mixed.
2. Place in a sprayed 11x7-inch baking dish and shape into a loaf. Bake 50 to 60 minutes or until cooked to 160°. Let stand 5 to 10 minutes before slicing.

Per serving: 208 Cal, 14g Fat, 17g Pro, <1g Sug, 1g Carb, <1g Fib, **NET CARBS: <1**

MENU

Salsa Meatloaf
Mock Mashed Potatoes
Steamed Green Beans
Spinach-Orange Salad
8 net carbs per meal.

Southwestern Meatloaf

MAKES 6 SERVINGS

What do you do with that last bit of salsa!
You make this recipe.

1½   **pounds lean ground beef**
¾   **cup thick and chunky salsa**
1   **large egg, beaten**
½   **cup low-carb soft white bread crumbs**
¾   **cup (3-oz) Cheddar cheese, shredded**

1. Preheat oven to 350°F. Combine ingredients and place in a sprayed 9x5-inch loaf pan. Bake 60 to 70 minutes or until meat reaches 160°. Carefully pour off fat and let stand 5 to 10 minutes before slicing.

Per serving: 293 Cal, 19g Fat, 23g Pro, 2g Sug, 3g Carb, <1g Fib, *NET CARBS: 3*

Stuffed Green Peppers

MAKES 8 SERVINGS

Only 6 carbs for these stuffed peppers.

1½   **pounds lean ground beef**
¾   **cup chopped onion**
4   **Plum tomatoes, chopped**
   Salt and pepper to taste
4   **medium green peppers**
1   **(8-oz) can tomato sauce**

1. In a large skillet, brown ground beef and onion; drain. Add tomatoes, salt and pepper.
2. Preheat oven to 325°F. Meanwhile, cut peppers in half lengthwise; remove seeds. Place, cut-side up, in a sprayed 13x9-inch baking dish.

Fill with meat mixture. Spoon remaining mixture around peppers. Pour tomato sauce over top. Add 1/4 cup water to dish. Bake 50 to 60 minutes or until peppers are tender.

Per serving: 178 Cal, 11g Fat, 14g Pro, 4g Sug, 7g Carb, 1g Fib, *NET CARBS: 6*

Patty Melts

MAKES 4 SERVINGS

Cooked onions and ground beef make
a very tasty combination.

1   **pound lean ground beef**
   Salt and pepper
4   **slices Monterey Jack cheese**
2   **small onions, sliced**

1. Form ground beef into 4 patties.
2. Cook in a large skillet until cooked to 160°, turning once. Sprinkle with salt and pepper. Top with cheese. Remove and keep warm.
3. In drippings in skillet, cook onion, stirring frequently until tender. Season with salt and pepper. Serve over patties.

Per serving: 318 Cal, 22g Fat, 25g Pro, 2g Sug, 3g Carb, <1g Fib, *NET CARBS: 3*

Grilled Steaks

Use steaks such as New York strip, porterhouse, T-bone or sirloin.

1   (4-oz) beef tenderloin
   Minced garlic
   Freshly ground black pepper
   Salt

1. Trim steak of excess fat. Firmly rub steak with garlic (both sides). Sprinkle with pepper. Set aside while preparing coals. Sprinkle 1 side of steak with salt. Place salt-side down, on grill. Sprinkle with salt. Cook 4 to 6 minutes. Turn and cook to desired doneness.

Per serving: 276 Cal, 14g Fat, 35g Pro, 0g Sug, 0g Carb, 0g Fib, **NET CARBS: 0**

Teriyaki Tri-Tip Steaks

MAKES 4 SERVINGS

Allow time for meat to marinate.

1   (1½-pound) tri-tip beef steak
½   cup soy sauce
2   tablespoons brown Sugar Twin®
½   teaspoon ground ginger

1. Place meat in a large resealable bag. Combine remaining ingredients with 1/4 cup water. Pour over meat. Seal. Marinate in refrigerator for 6 to 8 hours.
2. Grill over hot coals until cooked to desired doneness, turning once.

note: Tri-tip steaks are sometimes cut into 4 to 6-ounce boneless steaks and sometimes cut into long narrow strips. They can also be used for beef kabobs.

Per 4 oz serving: 208 Cal, 9g Fat, 31g Pro, <1g Sug, <1g Carb, 0g Fib, **NET CARBS: <1**

Teriyaki Strips

MAKES 4 SERVINGS

Remember to pre-soak wooden skewers.

1   (1-lb) flank steak
¼   cup oil
¼   cup soy sauce
¼   cup dry sherry
1½   teaspoons freshly grated ginger
1   small garlic clove, minced

1. Cut beef crosswise into thin strips.
2. Combine remaining ingredients in a shallow dish. Add beef and marinate 1 hour.
3. Place beef, accordian style, on 4 skewers. Grill or broil until cooked through, turning at least once.

Per 4 oz serving: 227 Cal, 11g Fat, 32g Pro, 0g Sug, <1g Carb, 0g Fib, **NET CARBS: <1**

MENU

Teriyaki Tri-Tip Steaks
Family Favorite Asparagus
Brie Salad
5 net carbs per meal.

Beef & Vegetable Kabobs

If using sirloin, or other less tender cuts of meat, marinate at least 8 hours before cooking. See marinades, page 214.

Place ingredients on skewers as listed:
- Cherry tomato
- Beef
- Green pepper square
- Beef
- Small whole mushroom
- Beef
- Onion wedge
- Cherry tomato
- Beef
- Onion wedge
- Green pepper square

note: Use 3-ounces of beef total on each skewer.

Per kabob: 211 Cal, 8g Fat, 27g Pro, 3g Sug, 6g Carb, 1g Fib, **NET CARBS: 5**

Beef Kabobs

If using wooden skewers, don't forget to soak in water for about 20 minutes.

1	(1½-lb) top sirloin
1	cup dry white wine
⅔	cup olive oil
⅓	cup soy sauce
2	large garlic cloves, minced
1	medium onion (8 wedges)

1. Cut meat into 16 (1-1/2 inch) cubes. Combine next 4 ingredients. Reserve 1/4-cup for basting. Add meat; cover and marinate in refrigerator at least 2 hours.

2. Thread the meat with onion on 4 skewers. Place on grill or under broiler and cook to desired doneness or about 3 minutes per side, basting frequently with the 1/4 cup sauce.

Per kabob: 312 Cal, 16g Fat, 34g Pro, 1g Sug, 3g Carb, <1g Fib, **NET CARBS: 3**

Stuffed Flank Steak

MAKES 6 SERVINGS

*For a 2 ingredient recipe, this one has
a lot of flavor. And leftover steak makes
delicious sandwiches.*

1   **(1 to 1½-lb) flank steak**
12 **ounces bulk Italian sausage**

1. Preheat oven to 350°F. Pound steak,
rounded side down, to flatten and make even.
2. Crumble sausage over meat to within one
inch of edge. Starting at the short end, roll
tightly. Tie with kitchen string in 5 or 6 places,
making sure ends are tied to enclose filling.
String should be tight, making a compact loaf.
3. Place, seam-side down, on a rack in a
roasting pan. Bake 75 to 85 minutes or until both
meats are cooked through. Slice into 1/4-inch
slices.

Per 4-oz serving: 242 Cal, 14g Fat, 26g Pro, <1g Sug,
1g Carb, <1g Fib, **NET CARBS: <1**

Kid's Favorite Flank Steak

MAKES 4 SERVINGS

Simple and delicious

1   **(1¼-lb) flank steak**
¼   **cup soy sauce**

1. Put steak in a large resealable bag. Add soy
sauce and seal bag. Marinate in refrigerator 60
minutes, turning bag frequently.
2. Grill or broil steak to 140°, turning once. Do
not overcook. Slice crosswise to serve.

Per serving: 214 Cal, 10g Fat, 29g Pro, 0g Sug,
0g Carb, 0g Fib, **NET CARBS: 0**

Grilled Rib-Eye Steaks

MAKES 4 SERVINGS

*If desired, rub steaks with a dry
rub mix, see page 81.*

4   **(1-inch) rib-eye steaks**
    Salt and pepper
4   **(½-inch) onion slices**
2   **teaspoons olive oil**

1. Preheat grill to medium heat. Sprinkle steaks
rather generously with salt and pepper. Brush
onion slices with oil and place steaks and onions
on grill. Grill, uncovered, about 10 to 15 minutes,
turning once. Cooking time will vary according
to desired degree of doneness.

Per 4 oz serving: 328 Cal, 19g Fat, 32g Pro, 3g Sug,
7g Carb, 1g Fib, **NET CARBS: 6**

Basic Pot Roast

We all need a good basic pot roast recipe.

1   (3 to 4-lb) rump roast
¼   cup oil
1   medium onion, sliced
    Salt and pepper to taste
1½ teaspoons mixed herbs

1. Preheat oven to 350°F. Brown meat in heated oil in a heavy pot or Dutch oven. Add remaining ingredients along with 1 cup water. Cover and bake 2 to 2-1/2 hours or until meat is tender, adding more water if necessary.

Per 4 oz serving: 265 Cal, 14g Fat, 33g Pro, 1g Sug, 1g Carb, <1g Fib, **NET CARBS: 1**

Pepper Roast

MAKES 4 SERVINGS

A sirloin roast is best when thinly sliced.

1   (2-lb) sirloin tip roast
2½ teaspoons seasoned salt
3   teaspoons coarsely ground black pepper

1. Preheat oven to 350°. Rub meat with salt and pepper. Place on a rack in a small roasting pan. Bake about 60 minutes or until temperature reaches 140° for medium rare. Cover with foil and let stand 10 to 15 minutes for easier carving.

Per 4 oz serving: 238 Cal, 13g Fat, 30g Pro, 0g Sug, <1g Carb, <1g Fib, **NET CARBS: <1**

Rib-Eye Roast

MAKES 10-12 SERVINGS

A rib-eye roast takes the stress out of what to serve for a special company dinner, but do use an accurate meat thermometer.

1   (5 to 5½-lb) rib-eye roast, small end
½   teaspoon lemon pepper

1. Preheat oven to 350°F. Place roast, fat-side up, on rack in a shallow roasting pan. Sprinkle with lemon pepper. Bake to 140° for medium-rare or desired degree of doneness. Cover lightly with foil and let stand 15 to 20 minutes before slicing.

Per 4 oz serving: 280 Cal, 17g Fat, 31g Pro, 0g Sug, 0g Carb, 0g Fib, **NET CARBS: 0**

What is a Rib-Eye Roast?

A rib-eye roast is one of the most expensive roasts you can buy. The rib bones are removed as well as any other bones and all the fat and cap meat has been removed, leaving only the tender eye meat. Some argue that you don't get the flavor you normally would get from the attached bones, but I doubt if most of us would notice the difference. A rib-eye roast is perfect for that special holiday or company meal. And slicing is a breeze.

Grilled Prime Rib

If you can get beyond the price of what one of these roasts cost, this popular cut, when grilled, takes on a wonderful smokey flavor. As you know, I prefer charcoal, but a gas grill works as well.

1   **(9 to 11-lb) prime rib roast**
    Salt and pepper
    Dry rub, page 81 (optional)
3   **cups hickory chips, soaked for 1 hour, drained**

1. Trim roast of excess fat. Sprinkle with salt and pepper or dry rub.

2. Prepare your grill for indirect heat (coals on each side with drip pan in the middle). Heat should be medium, 325°F to 350°F. Sprinkle half the wood chips on the coals. (Use remaining chips as needed.)

3. Place roast, fat-side up, on center of rack over drip pan. Cover grill. Grill about 2 hours for rare 130°, or about 2-1/2 hours for medium-rare 140°. Grill time can vary with charcoal, depending on how even the heat is. Be prepared to add additional hot charcoal about half way through cooking time. (I like to use a charcoal chimney for this.) When desired doneness is achieved cover meat loosely with foil and let stand 20 minutes before carving.

Per 6 oz serving: 602 Cal, 53g Fat, 42g Pro, 0g Sug, 0g Carb, 0g Fib, **NET CARBS: 0**

Standing Rib Roast

Always an elegant meal.

1   **standing prime rib roast (4 ribs)**
    Seasoning, if desired

1. Preheat oven to 350°F. Place roast, rib-side down, on rack in a shallow roasting pan. Sprinkle with seasoning, if using. Bake to 140° for medium-rare, or to desired degree of doneness. Cover lightly with foil and let stand 15 to 20 minutes before slicing.

Per 6 oz serving: 602 Cal, 53g Fat, 42g Pro, 0g Sug, 0g Carb, 0g Fib, **NET CARBS: 0**

"What to Buy"

A prime rib is made up of ribs 6 through 12. You want to purchase, if possible, the loin end which is ribs 9 through 12. It is mostly one muscle, so there's very little intermuscular fat and it is the most tender cut of a prime rib.

2 Rib Roast = 4 to 5 pounds and should serve 4 to 6 people.

4 Rib Roast = 7 to 9 pounds and should serve 8 to 10 people.

Tri-Tip Roast

A tri-tip roast is a delicious and economical roast that has become quite popular in recent years. Meat should be cooked at a high temperature.

1 **(1½ to 2½-lb) beef tri-tip roast**
  Salt and pepper

1. Generously sprinkle meat all over with salt and pepper. Rub into meat and let stand at room termperature for 1 hour.
2. Preheat oven to 450°F. Place meat, fat-side up, on a rack in a shallow roasting pan. Place in oven and begin checking temperature after 20 minutes. For rare, remove at 120°. For medium-rare, remove at 140°. Temperature will rise as meat stands. Let stand 10 minutes. Carve into thin slices across the grain.

Per 4 oz serving: 206 Cal, 9g Fat, 30g Pro, 0g Sug, 0g Carb, 0g Fib, **NET CARBS: 0**

Rump Roast

A rump roast is often called something else, depending on where you live.

1 **(4-lb) boneless rump roast**
  Salt and pepper

1. Preheat oven to 325°F. Place roast, fat-side up, on rack in a shallow roasting pan. Sprinkle with salt and pepper. Bake 2 to 2-1/2 hours or until temperature reaches 140° for medium rare or 150° for medium. Let stand 10 minutes before slicing.

tip: To make Au Jus, skim off excess fat from meat juices. Add a little water to pan. Bring to a simmer and cook 3 to 4 minutes, stirring in the crusty pieces. Strain.

Per 4 oz serving: 214 Cal, 13g Fat, 22g Pro, 0g Sug, 0g Carb, 0g Fib, **NET CARBS: 0**

Steak with Mushroom Sauce

MAKES 2 SERVINGS

You don't have to buy a whole bottle of brandy. Purchase one of those airline size bottles at the liquor store.

2	(6-oz) New York steaks
¼	cup butter
½	cup chopped onion
8	mushrooms, sliced
2	teaspoons Worcestershire sauce
2	tablespoons brandy

1. Melt butter in a medium skillet. Brown steaks quickly on one side. Reduce heat and add onion and mushrooms. Cook 2 minutes. Turn steaks and cook about 6 minutes or to desired degree of doneness. Add Worcestershire sauce and brandy. Cook about 2 minutes.

Per serving: 667 Cal, 49g Fat, 38g Pro, 4g Sug, 7g Carb, 1g Fib, *NET CARBS: 6*

Swiss Steak

MAKES 6 SERVINGS

Let bake in the oven while you are busy doing other things.

1	(2-lb) round steak, 1-inch thick
	Salt and pepper
3	tablespoons oil
½	cup chopped onion
1	(16-oz) can diced tomatoes, with juice

1. Preheat oven to 350°F. Sprinkle meat with salt and pepper.

2. Heat oil in a Dutch oven or large skillet; add meat and brown both sides. Top with onion and tomatoes. Cover and bake 1-1/2 to 2 hours or until tender, adding water if necessary.

Per 4-oz serving: 261 Cal, 15g Fat, 26g Pro, 3g Sug, 5g Carb, 1g Fib, *NET CARBS: 4*

Beef Tenderloins

MAKES 4 SERVINGS

A delightful recipe that takes only about 15 minutes and you are ready to eat.

2	(8-oz) beef tenderloins, 1-inch thick
1	tablespoon oil
	Salt and pepper
1	medium onion
⅓	cup Sauterne

1. Cut each tenderloin into two 1/2-inch slices, making 4 tenderloins. Trim off excess fat.

2. Heat a 9-inch nonstick skillet with oil. Add tenderloins and cook, over medium heat, about 3 to 4 minutes on each side, turning once until medium rare or as desired. Sprinkle with salt and pepper. Remove and keep warm.

3. Add onions and Sauterne to skillet. Cook covered, until onion is just crisp tender, stirring occasionally. Add salt and pepper to taste. Serve over tenderloins.

Per serving: 239 Cal, 13g Fat, 24g Pro, 1g Sug, 5g Carb, <1g Fib, *NET CARBS: 5*

Beef Tenderloin with Mustard Caper Sauce

MAKES 6 SERVINGS

The sauce makes this wonderful beef cut even more special. It can also be served with roast pork or pork chops.

1   (3-lb) beef tenderloin, butt end
2   tablespoons butter, divided
3   green onions, divided
2   cups heavy cream
3   tablespoons Dijon mustard
1½ tablespoons capers, rinsed

1. Preheat oven to 425°F. Trim tenderloin of any fat and silver skin; pat dry.

2. Melt 1 tablespoon of the butter and brush over meat. Place on rack in a small roasting pan and bake 35 to 45 minutes or until temperature reaches 140° for medium rare or 150° for medium. Lightly cover with foil. Let stand 10 to 15 minutes before slicing.

3. Meanwhile, melt remaining butter in a heavy medium sauce pan. Chop 1 tablespoon from white part of onion and cook in butter until soft. (Thinly slice some of the green part for garnish and set aside).

4. Add cream and bring to a boil. Reduce heat and simmer 10 to 15 minutes or until mixture thickens, stirring occasionally. Remove from heat; add mustard and capers.

4. Spoon some of the sauce on each dinner plate and top with tenderloin. Sprinkle with green onion.

note: The Mustard Caper Sauce can be made up to 2 hours ahead and kept warm in a small thermos. Gently reheat, if necessary.

Per 6 oz serving: 688 Cal, 53g Fat, 49g Pro, <1g Sug, 4g Carb, <1g Fib, *NET CARBS: 4*

Beef Tenderloins with Mushrooms

MAKES 4 SERVINGS

Save this recipe for a special dinner.

4   (6-oz) beef tenderloins
     Salt and pepper
2   tablespoons butter
4   bacon slices, ½-inch pieces
¼   cup chopped onion
12 ounces mushrooms, sliced

1. Sprinkle tenderloins with salt and pepper.

2. Heat butter in a medium skillet and cook fillets over medium-high heat, turning once, until browned and cooked to medium rare (140°) or medium (150°). Place on serving platter and keep warm.

3. Meanwhile, cook bacon and onion in skillet until bacon is cooked through. Add mushrooms, a little salt and pepper, and cook until mushrooms are tender. Spoon over fillets.

note: If butter starts to burn, add a little oil to the skillet.

Per serving: 382 Cal, 23g Fat, 40g Pro, 2g Sug, 4g Carb, 1g Fib, *NET CARBS: 3*

Mushroom Round Steak

MAKES 4 SERVINGS

An easy economical meal.

1   **(1-lb) top round steak**
4   **ounces fresh mushrooms, sliced**
1   **medium onion, sliced**
1   **(14.5-oz) can beef broth**
    Salt and pepper to taste
2   **tablespoons cornstarch**

1. Preheat oven to 325°F. Cut meat into 4 serving size pieces. Place in a Dutch oven. Add mushrooms, onion, broth, and salt and pepper. Cover. Bake 2-1/2 to 3 hours or until tender.
2. Remove meat and keep warm. Combine cornstarch with about 1/2 cup water. Stir into broth mixture. Place on a burner and cook over medium heat until thickened. Taste for seasoning.

Per serving: 227 Cal, 9g Fat, 28g Pro, 2g Sug, 7g Carb, 1g Fib, **NET CARBS: 6**

Pepper Steak

MAKES 4 SERVINGS

A quick top of the stove meal.

1   **(1-lb) top round steak**
1   **teaspoon cornstarch**
2   **tablespoons soy sauce**
1   **tablespoon Splenda®**
2   **medium green peppers, cut into narrow strips**
2   **medium tomatoes**

1. Cut steak crosswise into 1/8-inch strips.

2. Combine cornstarch, soy sauce and Splenda. Pour over steak; marinate in refrigerator 2 to 3 hours or overnight.
3. When ready to serve, quickly brown steak in a sprayed nonstick skillet. (Do not overcook or meat will be tough).
4. Remove meat from pan. Add green peppers, cook until just crisp-tender. If peppers stick to pan, add a little oil. Add tomatoes and beef and cook until heated through.

Per serving: 226 Cal, 9g Fat, 28g Pro, 4g Sug, 8g Carb, 2g Fib, **NET CARBS: 6**

Steak Au Poivre

MAKES 2 SERVINGS

This is very good, but you must be a pepper fan.

2   **(6-oz) New York steaks**
2   **tablespoons black peppercorns**
1   **teaspoon salt**
3   **tablespoons butter**
3   **tablespoons oil**
⅓   **cup cognac**

1. Coarsely grind peppercorns. Sprinkle each side of steaks with about 1-1/2 teaspoons pepper. Press into meat. Let stand 15 minutes. Sprinkle one side with salt.
2. Heat butter and oil in a medium skillet over medium-high heat. Place steaks, salted-side down, in skillet and cook 3 minutes. Salt steaks, turn and cook 3 minutes.
3. Reduce heat and cook about 3 minutes per side or until cooked to desired doneness. Remove and keep warm.
4. Remove pan from heat; add cognac and carefully ignite. Pour over steaks.

Per serving: 807 Cal, 55g Fat, 48g Pro, 0g Sug, 3g Carb, 2g Fib, **NET CARBS: 1**

Marinated Beef Fajitas

MAKES 6 MEAT SERVINGS OF 2 FAJITAS EACH

Low-carb tortillas allow us to have Fajitas again.

1   (1-lb) flank steak
1   tablespoon oil
2   tablespoons fresh lime juice
½   teaspoon ground cumin
1   teaspoon chili powder
¼   teaspoon garlic powder

1. Trim any fat from meat and place in a shallow dish. Combine remaining ingredients; pour over meat, turning to coat. Cover and refrigerate 2 to 3 hours.

2. When ready to cook, remove meat from marinade. Slice, across the grain, into 1/8-inch slices.

3. Cook about 1/4 of the meat at a time in a nonstick skillet, adding more oil if needed. Heat should be fairly hot to cook meat quickly.

note: Serve with warm low-carb tortillas, sautéed peppers and onions, salsa and sour cream.

Per serving: 137 Cal, 8g Fat, 16g Pro, <1g Sug, <1g Carb, <1g Fib, ***NET CARBS: <1***

Veal Scallopini

MAKES 4 SERVINGS

Veal must be thinly sliced.

1   (1-lb) thinly sliced veal scallopini
    Lemon pepper
    Paprika
1   tablespoon oil
2   tablespoons fresh lemon juice
    Parsley

1. Sprinkle veal lightly with lemon pepper and paprika. Heat oil in a medium skillet and quickly cook veal, 1 to 2 minutes per side, or until lightly browned and tender, being careful not to over-cook. Remove and keep warm.

2. Add lemon juice and 1/4 cup water to skillet. Heat through, stirring in any brown bits in the pan. Spoon over veal; sprinkle with parsley.

Per serving: 313 Cal, 23g Fat, 21g Pro, <1g Sug, 1g Carb, 0g Fib, ***NET CARBS: 1***

Roasted Pork Shoulder

MAKES ABOUT 8 SERVINGS

This cut of pork is a picnic shoulder, very tasty and moist. If you are tired of the traditional ham, this is a nice change.

1　**(7-lb) picnic shoulder**
　Salt and pepper

1. Preheat oven to 325°F. Trim pork of excess fat. Sprinkle with salt and pepper. Place on a rack in a roasting pan.
2. Bake about 4 hours or to 185°, brushing occasionally with drippings. Cover loosely with foil; let stand 20 minutes before slicing.

Per 4 oz serving: 281 Cal, 14g Fat, 37g Pro, 0g Sug, 0g Carb, 0g Fib, **NET CARBS: 0**

Roasted Fresh Ham

MAKES 15 TO 20 SERVINGS

The whole pork leg is known as a fresh un-cured ham. When cooked. it doesn't look like ham, but is very tender and moist and ideal for large holiday dinners. For more accurate cooking time and doneness, use a reliable meat thermometer.

1　**(15-20-lb) bone-in pork leg (fresh ham)**
2　**tablespoons oil**
　Salt and pepper
2　**teaspoons dried oregano or rosemary**
2　**cups dry white wine**

1. Preheat oven to 425°F. Remove skin from pork; score fat. Combine seasonings and rub into roast. Place in a large roasting pan.
2. Bake 30 minutes, then reduce temperature to 325°. Bake 60 minutes; pour wine over meat. Cook 2-1/2 to 3-1/2 hours or until meat reaches 185°. Cover loosely with foil and let stand 30 to 60 minutes before slicing.

Per 4 oz serving: 160 Cal, 7g Fat, 23g Pro, 0g Sug, 0g Carb, 0g Fib, **NET CARBS: 0**

Pork Roasts

In case you were wondering, picnic shoulder roasts and pork leg (fresh ham) roasts are not cooked the same way as pork loin roasts. They are cooked at a lower oven temperature of 325° and to a higher internal temperature of 185°. Because of their size and cooking variables, the exact cooking time is hard to pin down. The nice thing is that while the meat is standing before carving, you can put the final touches to the rest of your meal.

Pork Gravy

Skim off the fat from drippings in pan. Add 1 cup chicken broth (can use part dry white wine). Bring to a boil, stirring to loosen brown pieces in bottom of pan. Cook over medium-high heat 2 to 3 minutes. Pour over meat slices on platter and serve. Less than one carb per serving (per 8 servings).

Maple Ham

MAKES ABOUT 10 SERVINGS

For the holidays, you may want to purchase a 12 pound ham, otherwise, a 7 or 8 pound ham is an ideal size.

1   (7-lb) fully cooked bone-in ham
1   teaspoon dry mustard
2   teaspoons cider vinegar
½   cup no-carb maple syrup

1. Preheat oven to 350°F. Trim ham of excess fat. Score top of ham. Place, fat-side up, on a rack in a shallow roasting pan.

2. Bake 15 to20 minutes per pound or until temperature reaches 140°, about 1-1/2 hours.

3. Meanwhile, combine remaining ingredients and spoon over ham last 30 minutes of cooking time. I usually add this after ham has baked about an hour. Then I baste a couple of times. Let stand 10 minutes before slicing.

Per 4 oz serving: 218 Cal, 14g Fat, 21g Pro, 0g Sug, <1g Carb, 0g Fib, *NET CARBS: <1*

Ham Loaf

MAKES 8 SERVINGS

A good ham loaf recipe is hard to find.

1   (1-lb) cooked ham, ground
1   pound lean ground beef
2   egg whites
¼   cup finely chopped onion
¾   cup low-carb soft white bread crumbs
2   tablespoons heavy cream

1. Preheat oven to 350°F. Place first 5 ingredients in a mixing bowl. Add enough water to the cream to equal 2/3 cup. Combine with ingredients in bowl, mixing lightly to blend.

2. Spoon mixture into a sprayed 8x8-inch baking dish. Form into a loaf, about 6x7-inches in size. Bake 45 to 60 minutes or to 160°.

Per serving: 218 Cal, 11g Fat, 25g Pro, <1g Sug, 2g Carb, 1g Fib, *NET CARBS: 1*

Pork

Grilled Pork Loin Roast

Grilling is one of my favorite ways to cook pork. I like to use a charcoal grill which imparts a wonderful smoky flavor, but other grills will work. If desired, you can choose to use a dry rub, page 81.

1   **(3-lb) boneless pork loin**
    Salt and pepper

1. Sprinkle pork with salt and pepper. The heat in the grill should be low, around 200°F to 250°F. Place pork, fat-side up, over indirect heat. Cover grill and cook about 1-1/2 to 2 hours or until meat registers 140°.
2. Wrap in foil and let stand 10 to 15 minutes before slicing.

Per serving: 270 Cal, 12g Fat, 37g Pro, 0g Sug, 0g Carb, 0g Fib, **NET CARBS: 0**

Pork Medallions with Dijon Sauce

MAKES 6 SERVINGS

Serve with Steamed Green Beans, page 242.

2   **pork tenderloins, about ¾-lb each**
6   **tablespoons butter, divided**
2   **tablespoons finely chopped onioin**
½   **cup white wine**
1   **cup heavy cream**
2   **tablespoons Dijon mustard**

nderloins into 2-inch slices.
1/4-inch thickness.

2. Heat 2 tablespoons butter in a large nonstick skillet. Add medallions and cook 1-1/2 to 2 minutes on each side to cook through (do not overcook.) Remove and keep warm.
3. Add onion to skillet and cook until soft. Add the wine. Cook, over medium heat, until liquid is reduced by half, 3 to 4 minutes.
4. Add the cream and cook until thickened. Remove from heat and quickly stir in the remaining 4 tablespoons butter and the mustard.
5. Place medallions on individual serving plates and top with sauce.

Per serving: 388 Cal, 30g Fat, 24g Pro, <1g Sug, 2g Carb, <1g Fib, **NET CARBS: 2**

Pork Roast Dijon

MAKES 6 SERVINGS

An easy family or company roast.

1   **(2½-lb) boneless pork loin**
2   **teaspoons Dijon mustard**
½   **teaspoon dried rosemary**
    Salt and pepper

1. Preheat oven to 350°F. Place roast on a rack in a roasting pan; spread with mustard and sprinkle with rosemary, salt and pepper.
2. Bake 40 to 50 minutes or until meat reaches 140°. Cover with foil and let stand 15 minutes before slicing.

Per serving: 278 Cal, 13g Fat, 38g Pro, 0g Sug, <1g Carb, 0g Fib, **NET CARBS: <1**

Pork Loin Roast

MAKES 8 SERVINGS

Brining the meat (see page 213) in a salt solution improves the flavor and tenderness of the pork. This cut of meat is sometimes called Rack of Pork.

1   (8-rib) pork loin roast (about 6 pounds)
⅔   cup kosher salt
½   cup no-carb maple syrup
1   teaspoon dried rosemary, crushed
1   teaspoon ground black pepper

1. Wash and trim roast.
2. In a large stockpot, dissolve salt in 4 quarts water. Add maple syrup.
3. Place pork in brine. If pork isn't covered, make additional solution. Cover. Refrigerate 24 hours.
4. Preheat oven to 350°F. Remove pork from brine and pat dry. Place, rib-side down, in a shallow roasting pan. Combine rosemary and pepper and sprinkle over roast. Bake 80 to 90 minutes or until temperature reaches 140°. Cover loosely with foil and let stand 15 minutes before serving.

Per serving: 385 Cal, 18g Fat, 53g Pro, 0g Sug, <1g Carb, 0g Fib, **NET CARBS: <1**

Pan-Fried Pork Chops

MAKES 4 SERVINGS

Today's pork is very lean, but can be tough and dry if overcooked. Brining will help increase the pork's moisture content and tenderness.

¼   cup kosher salt
4   (1-inch) center-cut pork chops
    Salt and pepper
1   tablespoon olive oil

1. Combine kosher salt with 4½ cups water, stirring until melted. Put in a large resealable bag. Add pork chops and seal bag. Let stand in refrigerator at least 8 hours.
2. Remove pork chops and pat dry. Sprinkle with salt and pepper.
3. Heat oil in large skillet and cook pork chops over medium-high heat, to 140°F, turning once.

Per serving: 227 Cal, 14g Fat, 24g Pro, 0g Sug, 0g Carb, 0g Fib, **NET CARBS: 0**

Dry Rub Recipe

MAKES 1/2 CUP

2   tablespoons salt
2   tablespoons Splenda®
2   teaspoons pepper
2   teaspoons paprika
2   teaspoons fresh lemon peel

Combine ingredients and mix well. Amounts can be increased as needed. I use about 1 recipe per rack of baby back ribs. Can also be used on chicken.

Per recipe: 37 Cal, 1g Fat, 1g Pro, 1g Sug, 9g Carb, 3g Fib, **NET CARBS: 6**

Lemon Pepper Pork Chops

Watch carefully and do not overcook.

4   (1-inch) loin-cut pork chops
1½   tablespoons oil
     Lemon pepper
1   cup chicken broth

1. Brown pork chops quickly in heated oil over medium-high heat, about 2 minutes per side. Sprinkle with lemon pepper. Add broth and cook over low heat until cooked through and temperature reaches 140°, about 5 to 6 minutes.

Per serving: 555 Cal, 33g Fat, 61g Pro, 0g Sug, 0g Carb, 0g Fib, **NET CARBS: 0**

Pork Chops & Gravy

MAKES 4 SERVINGS

Fortunately we don't have to give up all gravy.

4   (½-inch) loin-cut pork chops,
     Salt and pepper
     Mixed herbs
¾   cup heavy cream

1. Trim fat from pork chops. Quickly brown on both sides in a large nonstick skillet sprayed with cooking spray. Sprinkle with salt, pepper and mixed herbs.
2. Add 1/2 cup water; cover and simmer 20-30 minutes or until pork chops are tender. Remove and keep warm.

3. Add cream to drippings in skillet. Cook until thickened, stirring frequently. If mixture becomes too thick, add a little water to thin. Taste for seasoning.

Per serving: 409 Cal, 30g Fat, 31g Pro, 0g Sug, 1g Carb, 0g Fib, **NET CARBS: 1**

Company Pork Chops

MAKES 4 SERVINGS

If you have time, brining helps add back moisture to today's drier pork chops, see page 213.

4   (1-inch) loin-cut pork chops
2   tablespoons oil
4   (¼-inch) onion slices
1   chicken bouillon cube, crushed
2   teaspoons prepared mustard
     Salt and pepper

1. Preheat oven to 350°F. Heat oil in a large skillet and quickly brown pork chops.
2. Place onion slices in a sprayed 11x7-inch baking dish. Top with pork chops.
3. Combine bouillon cube and mustard with 1/4 cup hot water, stirring to dissolve bouillon. Pour over pork chops and sprinkle with salt and pepper. Bake 45 minutes or until meat reaches 140°.

Per serving: 579 Cal, 35g Fat, 61g Pro, 1g Sug, 1g Carb, <1g Fib, **NET CARBS: 1**

Grilled Pork Chops Dijon

MAKES 4 SERVINGS

Due to their lower fat content, pork chops should not be overcooked.

4 (½-inch) loin-cut pork chops,
3 tablespoons Dijon mustard
¼ teaspoon dried tarragon
¼ teaspoon garlic powder
   Cracked pepper

1. Trim pork chops of all fat. Place on a heated grill that was sprayed with cooking spray. Cook 4 minutes; turn.

2. Combine mustard, tarragon and garlic powder. Brush on top of each pork chop. Cook 2 to 3 minutes or until cooked through or 140°. Temperature will rise after cooking. Sprinkle lightly with pepper.

Per serving: 270 Cal, 15g Fat, 31g Pro, 0g Sug, 2g Carb, <1g Fib, **NET CARBS: 2**

Sweet & Sour Pork Chops

MAKES 4 SERVINGS

You must try this recipe. It's a winner.

4 (1-inch) pork chops
2 tablespoons oil
2 teaspoons soy sauce
¼ cup cider vinegar
4 packets Splenda®
1 medium onion, sliced

1. Brown pork chops, in heated oil in a large skillet over medium-high heat, turning once.

2. Combine soy sauce, vinegar and Splenda and pour over meat.

3. Separate onion into rings and add to skillet.

4. Cover skillet and cook on low heat about 40 to 45 minutes or until tender. Check occasionally making sure heat isn't too high. You want some of those tasty juices to remain in the pan.

variation: Substitute 4 ounces sliced fresh mushrooms for the onions.

Per serving: 589 Cal, 35g Fat, 62g Pro, 2g Sug, 5g Carb, <1g Fib, **NET CARBS: 5**

Cook's Tip
Cooking spray should be sprayed on grill before heating.

Chicken Fried Pork

Have you ever wondered what to do with those last 2 boneless pork chops you buy in a family pack? Well, you can cut them in half horizontally and make 4 servings instead of two. This recipe is like Chicken Fried Steak only I have used pork.

2   **thick-cut boneless pork chops
    (1 to 1½-inch)
    Salt and pepper**
¼   **cup flour**
⅓   **cup oil**

1. Cut meat into 2 thin pork chops. Place between plastic wrap and pound to 1/4-inch thickness.

2. Sprinkle with salt and pepper. Coat with flour, shaking off excess.

3. Heat oil in a large heavy skillet. Add pork and cook until nicely browned, about 3 to 4 minutes on each side.

variation: If gravy is desired, pour off all but 2 tablespoons of the fat. Add 1/4 cup heavy cream and 3/4 cup water. Heat to boiling, scraping up all the browned bits. Cook until thickened.

note: Amount of oil and flour is marginal for calculating net carbs as the meat only absorbs 1 tablespoon or less.

Per serving: 329 Cal, 21g Fat, 31g Pro, 0g Sug, 3g Carb, <1g Fib, **NET CARBS: 3**

Delicious Baby Back Ribs

You won't believe the flavor you get from using just salt and pepper, but if you really want the barbecue sauce, brush with Barbecue Sauce, page 209, the last 15 minutes of cooking time.

1   **small rack of baby back ribs
    Salt and pepper**

1. Preheat oven to 400°F. Trim ribs and pat dry. Sprinkle both sides rather generously with the salt and pepper.

2. Place in a shallow roasting pan, meaty-side down, in a single layer. Bake 30 minutes. Turn ribs and bake 30 to 40 minutes or until very tender. The cooking time may vary according to the number of ribs in the pan and how hot your oven cooks. For easier slicing, wrap in foil and let stand 15 to 20 minutes.

Per 8 oz serving: 397 Cal, 33g Fat, 23g Pro, 0g Sug, 0g Carb, 0g Fib, **NET CARBS: 0**

Roast Pork Tenderloin

MAKES 4 SERVINGS

Pork tenderloins are the most tender cuts of pork.

2 (¾-lb) pork tenderloins
1 tablespoon coarse grain mustard
½ teaspoon salt
½ teaspoon pepper
3 tablespoons oil
¼ cup dry white wine

1. Trim pork and remove silver skin. Place in a resealable bag.
2. Combine remaining ingredients and pour over pork. Release air from bag and seal. Marinate 2 hours in refrigerator. Drain.
3. Preheat oven to 400°F. Place tenderloins in an 11x7-inch sprayed baking dish. Bake 25 to 30 minutes or until temperature reaches 140°. Remove and let stand 10 minutes before slicing.

Per serving: 297 Cal, 16g Fat, 34g Pro, 0g Sug, <1g Carb, 0g Fib, **NET CARBS: <1**

Pork-Mushroom Kabobs

MAKES 4 SERVINGS

To prevent ingredients from falling off the skewers, top off with a large garlic clove.

1 (1-lb) pork tenderloin
8 ounces fresh mushrooms
1 medium onion, cut into 8 wedges
⅓ cup no-carb vinaigrette dressing

1. Trim fat and silver skin from pork. Cut into 1-1/2 inch cubes.
2. Thread meat and vegetables on four 12-inch skewers, leaving some space between each.
3. Grill kabobs on a sprayed rack over direct heat. Cook 12 to 14 minutes, turning occasionally, and brushing with dressing until cooked through. Do not overcook or pork will be dry.

Per serving: 254 Cal, 15g Fat, 25g Pro, 2g Sug, 5g Carb, 1g Fib, **NET CARBS: 4**

Hot Dogs & Sauerkraut

MAKES 4 SERVINGS.

The caraway seeds and Swiss cheese softens the tartness of the sauerkraut.

1 (32-oz) jar sauerkraut, drained
2 teaspoons caraway seeds
8 hot dog franks
1½ cups (6-oz) Swiss cheese, shredded

1. Preheat oven to 350°F. Place sauerkraut in a sprayed 11x7-inch baking dish. Sprinkle with caraway seeds and mix with a fork. Arrange hot dogs over top and sprinkle with cheese. Bake 25 to 35 minutes or until heated through.

Per serving: 605 Cal, 48g Fat, 33g Pro, 4g Sug, 10g Carb, 5g Fib, **NET CARBS: 5**

Italian Sausage Dinner

MAKES 4 SERVINGS

Hearty and flavorful.

4   Italian sausages
1   tablespoon oil
1   small onion, sliced
1   small green pepper, sliced
3   Plum tomatoes, sliced
    Salt and pepper

1. Brown sausages in hot oil in a medium skillet. Add onion and green pepper and cook until vegetables are just crisp tender. Add tomatoes, salt and pepper and heat through.

Per serving: 279 Cal, 22g Fat, 14g Pro, 3g Sug, 7g Carb, 1g Fib, **NET CARBS: 6**

❧ Baked Bacon ❧

A very easy way to cook bacon.

1   pound bacon (more or less)

1. Preheat oven to 350°F. Arrange bacon slices on a roasting pan rack. Bake 20 to 25 minutes or until cooked through. Drain on paper towels.

Per slice: 34 Cal, 3g Fat, 2g Pro, 0g Sug, 0g Carb, 0g Fib, **NET CARBS: 0**

Sausage-Cheese Meatballs

MAKES 8 LARGE MEATBALLS

These are so easy to make I like to keep some in the refrigerator or freezer at all times. Serve with eggs, omelets, spaghetti, etc.

1   pound bulk sausage
3   ounces Mozzarella cheese

1. Preheat oven to 425°F. Divide sausage into 8 sections. Cut cheese into 8 cubes.
2. Form sausage evenly around a cheese cube, sealing completely. Place in a shallow baking pan. Bake 20 to 25 minutes or until browned and cooked through.

Per meatball: 147 Cal, 13g Fat, 7g Pro, 0g Sug, 1g Carb, 0g Fib, **NET CARBS: 1**

Company Maple Sausages

MAKES 4 SERVINGS

A nice change. Serve with Almond Bread, page 39, and scrambled eggs.

16   pork sausage links
¼   cup brown Sugar Twin®
½   cup no-carb maple syrup

1. Place sausages in a 12-inch nonstick skillet and cook, turning occasionally, until browned and cooked through, but not overcooked.
2. Combine sugar and syrup and pour over sausages. Bring to a boil, reduce heat and simmer until nicely glazed, 10 to 15 minutes.

Per serving: 228 Cal, 19g Fat, 7g Pro, 1g Sug, 3g Carb, 0g Fib, **NET CARBS: 3**

Lamb Chops

Very tender if not over-cooked. Medium is good.

8   (1-inch) lamb chops
    Salt and pepper
1   tablespoon oil
1   tablespoon butter

1. Sprinkle lamb chops with salt and pepper.
2. Heat oil and butter in a large heavy skillet over medium-high heat. Add lamb chops and cook 4 to 5 minutes on each side for medium-rare or 5 to 6 minutes on each side for medium.

Per serving: 459 Cal, 36g Fat, 32g Pro, 0g Sug, 0g Carb, 0g Fib, **NET CARBS: 0**

Leg of Lamb

MAKES 6 SERVINGS

I hate to tell you to cheat, but lamb isn't really lamb unless served with a little mint sauce.

1   (5-lb) leg of lamb
    Salt and pepper

1. Preheat oven to 350°F. Sprinkle lamb with salt and pepper. Place on a rack in roasting pan and bake about 1-1/2 hours or until meat registers 145° for medium-rare or 155°. for medium. Cover lightly with foil and let stand 10 minutes before carving.

Per 4 oz serving: 484 Cal, 17g Fat, 78g Pro, 0g Sug, 0g Carb, 0g Fib, **NET CARBS: 0**

Lamb Chops with Mustard Cream

MAKES 4 SERVINGS

If desired, substitute pork chops for the lamb chops

4   (6-oz) loin-cut lamb chops
1   tablespoon oil
    Salt and pepper
½   cup heavy cream
2   tablespoons dry sherry
2   tablespoons Dijon mustard

1. Brush lamb chops with oil. Sprinkle with salt and pepper.
2. Broil or grill, about 4 minutes on each side or until cooked to desired doneness.
3. Meanwhile, in a small saucepan, cook cream until slightly reduced. Stir in sherry and mustard and heat through. Spoon over lamb chops.

Per serving: 457 Cal, 38g Fat, 26g Pro, 0g Sug, 2g Carb, 0g Fib, **NET CARBS: 2**

Grilled Butterflied Lamb

This is much easier to slice without the bone.

1   (3-lb) butterflied boneless lamb leg
¼   cup fresh oregano, chopped
¼   cup fresh mint, chopped
1   large garlic clove, minced
3   tablespoons lemon juice
3   tablespoons oil

1. Trim lamb of any fat. Place in a 13x9-inch baking dish.
2. Combine remaining ingredients and pour over lamb; turn to coat. Cover. Marinate at least 6 hours or overnight.
3. Place lamb on a sprayed, then heated grill. Cook over medium heat, turning occasionally, 15 to 20 minutes for medium-rare, or to desired doneness. Let stand 10 minutes before slicing.

Per 4-oz serving: 258 Cal, 16g Fat, 27g Pro, <1g Sug, 1g Carb, 0g Fib, **NET CARBS: 1**

Rack of Lamb

A very expensive cut of lamb. Save for special occasions or perhaps a Valentine's dinner for two (in that case, reduce the recipe.)

2   racks of lamb (about 2½-lbs total)
    Salt and pepper
2   tablespoons oil
2   rosemary sprigs, chopped
2   thyme sprigs, chopped

1. Preheat oven to 475°F. Salt and pepper lamb all over.
2. Heat oil in large ovenproof heavy skillet over high heat. Add racks and quickly sear all sides. Remove and let stand about 5 minutes. If skillet isn't ovenproof, use a small roasting pan. Sprinkle herbs over meat. Place, bone-side down, in pan or skillet. Bake 15 to 20 minutes or to 125° for medium rare or 135° for medium.
3. Cover loosely with foil and let stand 5 minutes before carving. Temperature will rise 5° to 10°.

note: To prevent bone ends from burning, cover with pieces of foil.

Per serving: 577 Cal, 45g Fat, 41g Pro, 0g Sug, 0g Carb, 0g Fib, **NET CARBS: 0**

Cooking Time for Fish

Measure fish at its thickest point.
Estimate 10 minutes total cooking time per inch.

Total cooking time applies to whatever cooking method is being used—baking, broiling, frying, etc. If baking a salmon or other fish and the fish measures 3 inches at its thickest point, bake 30 minutes at 450°. If broiling a steak 1½ inches thick, divide the total time and broil 7½ minutes on each side. Cooking times may vary somewhat according to the thickness and size of the fish, the temperature of the fish at cooking time and how hot your oven bakes. Watch carefully though, and remember that the fish will continue to cook somewhat after removing from heat. The internal temperature of fish should be 137 degrees. Salmon cooked in foil or stuffed may take a little longer.

Baked Whole Salmon

A great Pacific Northwest treat.

Whole salmon, cleaned, wiped dry
Salt & pepper
1 large lemon, sliced
1 medium onion, sliced
6 slices bacon

1. Preheat oven to 450°F. Sprinkle salmon with salt and pepper, inside and out. Place on a large sheet of heavy duty foil in a large shallow baking pan.
2. Place 3 bacon slices lengthwise inside salmon. Stuff with lemon and onion slices. Place remaining bacon on top. Wrap foil to seal.
3. Bake 10 minutes per inch measuring salmon at its thickest part (a large salmon may take a little longer). Test for doneness with a toothpick or knife tip. When opaque all the way through, it should be done. Discard bacon, lemon and onion.

tip: Salmon cooked in foil or stuffed may take a little longer to cook.

Per 4 oz serving: 158 Cal, 5g Fat, 27g Pro, 0g Sug, 3g Carb, 0g Fib, *NET CARBS: 3*

Baked Salmon Steaks

MAKES 4 SERVINGS

Salmon is one of the "good" high fat fish.

4 (6-oz) salmon steaks
2 tablespoons butter, melted
½ teaspoon Worcestershire sauce
1 teaspoon fresh lemon juice

1. Place salmon in a sprayed shallow baking pan.
2. Combine remaining ingredients and brush salmon with some of the sauce. Bake at 450°F for 10 minutes, basting occasionally with the sauce. Test for doneness after 8 minutes.

Per serving: 252 Cal, 12g Fat, 34g Pro, <1g Sug, <1g Carb, 0g Fib, *NET CARBS: <1*

Company Baked Salmon

SERVING SIZE IS 4 OUNCES

My mother-in-law cooked her salmon this way.

Small whole salmon
Salt and pepper
Bacon slices

1. Preheat oven to 450°F. Sprinkle inside of salmon with salt. Salt and pepper outside. Place bacon slices inside and crosswise over top tucking ends under bottom of fish.
2. Wrap fish in heavy-duty foil; seal and place on a baking pan. Bake 10 minutes per inch measuring salmon at its thickest point. Test for doneness and cook a little longer, if necessary. Discard bacon before serving.

Per 4 oz serving: 158 Cal, 5g Fat, 27g Pro, 0g Sug, 0g Carb, 0g Fib, *NET CARBS: 0*

Salmon Steaks

MAKES 4 SERVINGS

A quick, easy dinner.

4   (6-oz) salmon steaks
2   tablespoons oil
2   tablespoons lemon juice
1   garlic clove, minced
2   tablespoons minced fresh basil

1. Pat salmon dry and place on a broiler pan.
2. Combine remaining ingredients; brush some of the mixture over salmon. Broil 8 to 10 minutes, or until cooked through, basting once or twice with the sauce. You do not need to turn the salmon.

Per 4-oz serving: 264 Cal, 13g Fat, 34g Pro, <1g Sug, 1g Carb, <1g Fib, *NET CARBS: 1*

Teriyaki Salmon Steaks

MAKES 4 SERVINGS

Serve with vegetable kabobs.

4   (6-oz) salmon steaks
¼   cup oil
2   tablespoons fresh lemon juice
2   tablespoons soy sauce
½   teaspoon dry mustard
½   teaspoon ground ginger

1. Place salmon in a sprayed 11x7-inch baking dish. Combine remaining ingredients; pour over top. Marinate 1 hour in refrigerator, turning occasionally.
2. Drain off marinade. Place salmon on rack in broiling pan. Broil 5 minutes, turn and broil 5 minutes more or until cooked through. Brush lightly with additional oil if salmon appears dry.

Per serving: 214 Cal, 8g Fat, 34g Pro, <1g Sug, <1g Carb, <1g Fib, *NET CARBS: <1*

Tarragon Salmon Fillet

MAKES 4 SERVINGS

Tarragon teams well with salmon.

1   (1¼-lb) salmon fillet
½   teaspoon oil
¼   teaspoon dried tarragon
1   tablespoon Dijon mustard
¼   cup white wine
1   tablespoon butter

1. Preheat oven to 450°F. Place fillet, skin-side down, on a sprayed shallow baking pan.
2. Combine remaining ingredients in a small saucepan. Bring to a boil; reduce heat and simmer about 2 minutes. Pour over salmon. Bake 10 to 12 minutes or until fish tests done. Cut crosswise into 4 pieces.

Per serving: 202 Cal, 9g Fat, 27g Pro, 0g Sug, 1g Carb, 0g Fib, *NET CARBS: 1*

Baked Salmon with Sour Cream

SERVING SIZE IS 4 OUNCES

The sour cream keeps the salmon moist.

1 (2½-lb) salmon fillet
  Salt and pepper
2 tablespoons fresh lemon juice
1 cup sour cream
2 teaspoons finely chopped onion

1. Preheat oven to 450°F. Place salmon in a sprayed 13x9-inch baking dish. Season with salt and pepper; sprinkle with lemon juice.
2. Spread sour cream over top, then the onion. Bake 10 minutes per inch, measuring at its thickest point.

Per 4 oz serving: 220 Cal, 11g Fat, 28g Pro, <1g Sug, 2g Carb, 0g Fib, **NET CARBS: 2**

Pan-Roasted Salmon

MAKES 4 SERVINGS

Simple but delicious. If desired, serve on a bed of Sautéed Kale, page 248.

4 (6-oz) salmon fillets, skin on
  Kosher salt
  Ground black pepper
2 tablespoons oil

1. Preheat oven to 350°F. Sprinkle fillets with salt and pepper.
2. Heat oil in a medium nonstick ovenproof skillet. Add salmon, skin-side up, and cook over medium-high heat until nicely browned, 3 to 4 minutes. Turn skin-side up.
3. Place in oven and bake, 3 to 4 minutes or until cooked through.

Per serving: 261 Cal, 13g Fat, 34g Pro, 0g Sug, 0g Carb, 0g Fib, **NET CARBS: 0**

Pesto Salmon

MAKES 2 SERVINGS

Husband's night to cook.

4 tablespoons pesto
2 (6-oz) salmon fillets, skinned

1. Preheat oven to 450°F. Spread 3 tablespoons pesto in a sprayed 8x8-inch baking dish. Add salmon and spread with remaining pesto. Bake 10 to 12 minutes or until cooked through.

Per serving: 356 Cal, 20g Fat, 40g Pro, 0g Sug, 2g Carb, 1g Fib, **NET CARBS: 1**

Red Snapper & Peppers

MAKES 4 SERVINGS

Lots of color in this recipe

1   **(1-lb) red snapper fillet**
4   **teaspoons soy sauce**
¼   **teaspoon ground ginger**
1   **tablespoon olive oil**
2   **small peppers (1 red, 1 green), julienned**
4   **ounces fresh mushrooms, sliced**

1. Preheat broiler. Place fillet in a sprayed shallow baking pan.
2. Combine soy sauce and ginger; brush over fish. Place under broiler and broil about 8 to 10 minutes or until fish tests done.
3. Meanwhile, heat oil in a large nonstick skillet. Cook peppers and mushrooms until just crisp-tender. Serve with or over the snapper.

Per serving: 157 Cal, 5g Fat, 24g Pro, 2g Sug, 3g Carb, 1g Fib, **NET CARBS: 2**

Red Snapper Fillets

MAKES 4 SERVINGS

Easy and good.

4   **red snapper fillets**
1½ **teaspoons oil**
    Salt and pepper
2   **tablespoons lime juice**
2   **tablespoons butter, melted**

1. Preheat grill to medium-hot. Brush fillets with oil and sprinkle generously with salt and pepper. Grill until cooked through, turning once. Approximately 8 to 10 minutes total cooking time.

2. Brush with lime juice and spoon butter over top.

Per serving: 175 Cal, 9g Fat, 22g Pro, <1g Sug, 1g Carb, 0g Fib, **NET CARBS: 1**

Linda's Favorite Halibut

MAKES 4 SERVINGS

This recipe is good with most white fish.

1   **(1-lb) halibut, 1 inch thick**
½   **teaspoon garlic salt**
3   **tablespoons sour cream**
1   **green onion, chopped**
2   **tablespoons grated Parmesan cheese**

1. Preheat oven to 450°F. Place halibut in a sprayed shallow baking dish. Sprinkle with garlic salt.
2. Combine sour cream and onion; spread over fish. Sprinkle with Parmesan. Bake 10 minutes or until cooked through.

Per serving: 165 Cal, 6g Fat, 26g Pro, 0g Sug, 1g Carb, <1g Fib, **NET CARBS: 1**

Cook's Tip

It's always a good idea to check your oven temperature before each use. You will be surprised at the fluctuation in temperature in various ovens.

Halibut & Tomato

MAKES 4 SERVINGS

Halibut is low in carbs, fat and calories.

1   (1-lb) halibut, 1 inch thick
¼   cup fresh lemon juice
2   Plum tomatoes, chopped
2   green onions, sliced diagonally
¼   teaspoon dried basil
¼   teaspoon salt

1. Preheat oven to 450°F. Place halibut in a sprayed shallow baking dish. Pour lemon juice over fish. Sprinkle remaining ingredients over top.
2. Bake 10 minutes or until fish tests done.

Per serving: 142 Cal, 3g Fat, 25g Pro, 1g Sug, 3g Carb, 1g Fib, **NET CARBS: 2**

Easy Grilled Halibut

MAKES 4 SERVINGS

Simple is often the best.

4   (6-oz) halibut fillets, skin on
    Salt and pepper
2   tablespoons olive oil

1. Sprinkle halibut with salt and pepper. Brush with olive oil and place, flesh side down, on a sprayed heated grill. Grill about 5 minutes.
2. Brush skin with oil and turn. Cook 4 to 5 minutes or until the center turns white.

Per serving: 255 Cal, 11g Fat, 37g Pro, 0g Sug, 0g Carb, 0g Fib, **NET CARBS: 0**

Baked Halibut

MAKES 4 SERVINGS

The lemon juice and onion adds a lot of flavor.

4   (6-oz) halibut steaks
3   tablespoons fresh lemon juice
1   teaspoon salt
½   teaspoon paprika
½   cup chopped onion
2   tablespoons butter

1. Combine lemon juice, salt and paprika in a shallow dish. Add halibut, turning to coat. Chill 1 hour to marinate, turning once or twice.
2. Preheat oven to 450°F. Sauté onion in heated butter until soft. Place halibut in a sprayed 11x7-inch baking dish; top with onions. Bake 10 minutes or until cooked through.

Per serving: 251 Cal, 10g Fat, 37g Pro, 1g Sug, 2g Carb, <1g Fib, **NET CARBS: 2**

Halibut-Shrimp Bake

MAKES 4 SERVINGS

Colorful and tasty.

4   small halibut steaks or fillets
½   cup butter, melted
½   cup fresh lemon juice
½   cup sour cream
½   cup (2-oz) Cheddar cheese, shredded
⅓   cup small cooked shrimp

1. Preheat oven to 350°F. Place halibut in a 13x9-inch baking dish. Combine butter and lemon juice; pour over halibut. Bake 10 to 12 minutes or until fish tests done.

2. Top each fillet with a dollop of sour cream. Sprinkle with cheese. Place under broiler to melt cheese. Garnish top with shrimp.

Per serving: 394 Cal, 25g Fat, 37g Pro, <1g Sug, 3g Carb, 0g Fib, **NET CARBS: 3**

Halibut-Cheese Bake

MAKES 4 SERVINGS

Take advantage of fresh halibut when in season.

4	(6-oz) halibut steaks
½	cup butter, melted
¼	cup white wine
2	tablespoons fresh lemon juice
12	ounces shrimp, cooked
1	cup (4-oz) Cheddar cheese, shredded

1. Preheat oven to 350°F. Place halibut in a sprayed shallow baking dish. Combine butter, wine and lemon juice and pour over fish. Cover with foil and bake 15 to 20 minutes or until cooked through.

2. Top each halibut with 1/4 of the shrimp and cheese. Bake until cheese melts.

variation: If desired (and because we can have it) serve halibut with a dollop of sour cream and a sprinkle of chopped green onions.

Per serving: 497 Cal, 26g Fat, 63g Pro, 0g Sug, 1g Carb, 0g Fib, **NET CARBS: 1**

Broiled Fish Fillets

SERVING SIZE IS 4 OUNCES

Use your choice of white fish fillets.

Fillets (any white fish)
Melted butter
Fresh lemon juice

1. Place fillets on roasting pan rack. Combine melted butter and lemon juice and brush over fillets. Broil about 5 minutes each side or until cooked through.

note: Use about 1 tablespoon lemon juice to 1/4 cup butter.

Per serving (approx): 125 Cal, 6g Fat, 17g Pro, 1g Sug, 1g Carb, 0g Fib, **NET CARBS: 1**

Lemon Pepper Spice

MAKES ABOUT 1/2 CUP

Especially good on meats, seafood and poultry.

5	tablespoons lemon pepper
1	tablespoon seasoning salt
2½	teaspoons garlic powder

Combine ingredients and store tightly covered.

Ling Cod Fillets

MAKES 4 SERVINGS

Can be made in about 15 minutes.

1 (1-lb) ling cod fillet
2 tablespoons butter, melted
1½ teaspoons dry mustard
¼ teaspoon lemon pepper

1. Preheat broiler. Cut fish into 4 serving pieces. Place in a sprayed shallow baking pan.
2. Combine remaining ingredients; brush some of the sauce on the fillets. Place under broiler and cook 5 to 10 minutes, or until fish tests done, brushing occasionally with remaining sauce.

Per serving: 154 Cal, 7g Fat, 21g Pro, 0g Sug, <1g Carb, <1g Fib, **NET CARBS: <1**

Baked Ling Cod

MAKES 4 SERVINGS

Another low carb, low-fat and low calorie fish.

4 ling cod fillets
   Salt and pepper
1 (14.5-oz) can diced Italian-style toma-toes, drained
¼ cup chopped ripe olives

1. Preheat oven to 450°F. Place fillets in a sprayed 13x9-inch baking dish. Sprinkle with salt and pepper. Spoon tomatoes and olives over top. Bake 10 to 12 minutes or until cooked through.

Per serving: 170 Cal, 2g Fat, 27g Pro, 5 Sug, 8g Carb, 2g Fib, **NET CARBS: 6**

Baked Catfish Parmesan

MAKES 4 SERVINGS

The Parmesan coating isn't exactly a Southern or Mid-western way to cook catfish, but do give it a try. It is delicious. (I still haven't convinced my Mother that there are other ways to cook catfish, other than just cornmeal and/or flour).

1 (1-lb) catfish fillet
3 tablespoons sour cream
⅓ cup grated Parmesan cheese
2 tablespoons flour
⅛ teaspoon pepper
¼ teaspoon paprika

1. Preheat oven to 450°F. Cut fish into 4 equal portions. Brush lightly with sour cream.
2. Combine remaining ingredients. Dip fish in mixture, turning to coat both sides. Place on a sprayed shallow baking pan. Bake 8 to 12 minutes, or until fish tests done.

Per serving: 208 Cal, 12g Fat, 21g Pro, 0g Sug, 4g Carb, <1g Fib, **NET CARBS: 4**

Jamaican Jerk Mahi-Mahi

MAKES 4 SERVINGS

Jerk seasoning isn't for everyone, but it takes beautifully to grilled fish, pork, and chicken. Team with a fruity salsa. In case you are wondering, jerk seasoning is not the same as Cajun seasoning.

4   (1-inch) mahi-mahi fillets or steaks
1   tablespoon oil
2   tablespoons Jamaican jerk seasoning

1. Lightly spray the grill rack. Place over medium-hot heat.
2. Brush mahi-mahi with oil. Sprinkle with seasoning and rub in. Grill fish, turning once until opaque in the center, about 3 to 4 minutes per side.

note: Any firm white fish may be substituted for the mahi-mahi.

Per 4-oz serving: 154 Cal, 5g Fat, 27g Pro, 0g Sug, 0g Carb, 0g Fib, **NET CARBS: 0**

Baked Trout Fillets

MAKES 4 SERVINGS

Baked trout lends itself to these ingredients.

4   trout fillets
2   tablespoons heavy cream
2   tablespoons oil
½   cup chopped onion
    Salt and pepper
½   cup dry white wine

1. Preheat oven to 450°F. Place fillets in a resealable plastic bag. Combine cream, oil, onion, salt and pepper and pour over fish. Close bag and chill for 1 hour to marinate.
2. Place fillets and marinade in a sprayed 11x7-inch baking dish. Spoon wine over top. Cover with foil and bake 10 to 12 minutes or until fish tests done.

Per 4-oz serving: 274 Cal, 14g Fat, 30g Pro, 1g Sug, 2g Carb, <1g Fib, **NET CARBS: 2**

Rainbow Trout

MAKES 4 SERVINGS

Allow time for marinating.

1   (1-lb) Rainbow trout
2   tablespoons olive oil
2   tablespoons fresh lemon juice
¼   teaspoon dried oregano
¼   teaspoon salt
⅛   teaspoon pepper

1. Preheat oven to 450°F. Cut trout into 4 serving pieces. Place in a shallow baking dish.
2. Combine remaining ingredients and pour over fish. Cover and marinate in refrigerator about an hour, turning occasionally. Remove fish and place in a sprayed shallow baking dish. Bake 8 to 10 minutes or until fish tests done.

Per serving: 193 Cal, 12g Fat, 20g Pro, <1g Sug, <1g Carb, 0g Fib, **NET CARBS: <1**

Easy Skillet Fish Dish

MAKES 4 SERVINGS

This makes a colorful dish, but only if you remember to remove from heat when the peppers are still a bright color.

1 **pound orange roughy**
1 **tablespoon oil**
2 **small peppers (1 red, 1 green), julienned**
½ **cup coarsely chopped onion**
½ **teaspoon dried basil**
   Salt and pepper to taste

1. Cut fish into 4 serving pieces.
2. Heat oil in a large nonstick skillet. Add peppers and onion. Arrange fish on top. Sprinkle with seasonings. Cover; cook over low heat 8 to 10 minutes. Uncover; continue cooking until fish tests done and vegetables are crisp tender.

Per serving: 128 Cal, 4g Fat, 18g Pro, 2g Sug, 4g Carb, 1g Fib, **NET CARBS: 3**

Mushroom Fillet Bake

MAKES 6 SERVINGS

Delicious!

2 **pounds white fish fillets**
1 **medium onion, finely chopped**
8 **ounces fresh mushrooms sliced**
1 **cup (4-oz) Swiss cheese, shredded**
   Salt and pepper
1 **cup whipping cream**

1. Preheat oven to 400°F. Pat fish dry. Sprinkle onion evenly in a sprayed 11x7-inch baking dish. Add three-fourths of the mushrooms. Sprinkle with half the cheese.
2. Place fillets over the top; sprinkle with salt and pepper. Add remaining mushrooms, then the cheese. Pour cream over top. Bake 20 minutes or until cooked through.

Per serving: 433 Cal, 29g Fat, 37g Pro, 2g Sug, 5g Carb, 1g Fib, **NET CARBS: 4**

Fillet of Sole with Dill

MAKES 4 SERVINGS

Use fresh dill if you just happen to have some.

4 **sole fillets**
2 **tablespoons fresh lime juice**
1 **small garlic clove, minced**
¼ **teaspoon dried dill weed**
   Salt and pepper

1. Preheat broiler. Place fillets in a sprayed shallow baking pan.
2. Combine lime juice, garlic and dill weed. Brush some of the sauce on fillets. Sprinkle lightly with salt and pepper. Place under broiler; cook 5 to 10 minutes, depending on thickness, brushing occasionally with remaining sauce.

Per 4-oz serving: 136 Cal, 2g Fat, 27g Pro, <1g Sug, 1g Carb, 0g Fib, **NET CARBS: 1**

Lemon-Dill Sole

MAKES 4 SERVINGS

*This has to marinate, but then
takes only minutes to cook.*

4   sole fillets
2   green onions, sliced
1   lemon
2   tablespoons Dijon mustard
¼   cup olive oil
½   teaspoon dried dill weed

1. Place fillets in a sprayed 11x7-inch baking
dish. Sprinkle green onion over fish.
2. Squeeze juice from lemon and combine with
remaining ingredients. Spoon over fish. Cover
and marinate in refrigerator for 60 minutes.
3. Preheat oven to 450°F. Bake 8 to 10 minutes
or until cooked through.

Per 4-oz serving: 267 Cal, 16g Fat, 28g Pro, <1g Sug,
2g Carb, <1g Fib, *NET CARBS: 2*

Easy Bake Parmesan Sole

MAKES 4 SERVINGS

*You could also use halibut
or orange roughy in this recipe.*

4   sole fillets
2   tablespoons butter, melted
⅓   cup low-carb dry white bread crumbs
2   tablespoons grated Parmesan cheese
1   teaspoon paprika

1. Preheat oven to 450°F. Brush fillets with
butter. Combine bread crumbs, Parmesan and
paprika. Dip sole in bread crumbs and place in a
sprayed shallow baking pan.
2. Bake 8 to 10 minutes or until cooked
through. If coating appears dry, brush with a little
melted butter.

Per 4-oz serving: 205 Cal, 8g Fat, 29g Pro, 0g Sug,
2g Carb, 1g Fib, *NET CARBS: 1*

Crab Divan

MAKES 4 SERVINGS

Another oldie but goodie.

1	(6.5-oz) can crab
2	cups broccoli florets, cooked
½	cup mayonnaise
1	teaspoon prepared mustard
1	tablespoon chopped onion
½	cup (2-oz) Cheddar cheese, shredded

1. Preheat oven to 350°F. Drain the crab. Arrange broccoli in a sprayed 1-quart casserole. Spoon crab over top.

2. Combine mayonnaise, mustard and onion. Spread over crab. Sprinkle with cheese. Bake 20 to 30 minutes or until heated through.

Per serving: 301 Cal, 27g Fat, 11g Pro, <1g Sug, 2g Carb, 1g Fib, **NET CARBS: 1**

Sautéed Scallops

MAKES 6 SERVINGS

Remember, scallops take very little time to cook.

1½	pounds scallops
¼	cup butter
3	slices fresh ginger
	Salt and pepper
1	tablespoon chopped parsley

1. Rinse scallops and pat dry. Melt butter in a large skillet. Add ginger, then scallops, and cook until just heated through and lightly browned.

Remove ginger. Sprinkle with salt, pepper and parsley.

Per serving: 172 Cal, 9g Fat, 19g Pro, 0g Sug, 3g Carb, 0g Fib, **NET CARBS: 3**

Scallop Piccata

MAKES 2 SERVINGS

To make this a true piccata dish, you probably should add capers, but if you don't have a jar in your cupboard, you may not want to add them. They are quite expensive.

1	teaspoon minced shallots
2	tablespoons butter, divided
4	ounces sea scallops (10 to 15)
2	tablespoons white wine
1	teaspoon lemon juice

1. In a medium skillet, sauté the shallots in 1 tablespoon butter. Add scallops and brown. Remove and keep warm.

2. Deglaze by adding the wine to the hot skillet and stirring quickly. Add lemon juice, then add the remaining butter and cook until slightly thickened. Return scallops and quickly heat through, if needed.

Per serving: 173 Cal, 13g Fat, 9g Pro, <1g Sug, 2g Carb, 0g Fib, **NET CARBS: 2**

"Fresh" Canned Shrimp

This simple method really does improve the taste.

Canned shrimp
1   **teaspoon salt**

1. Drain shrimp and rinse several times. Place in a quart-size jar; add salt and cover with ice water. Refrigerate overnight.
2. Drain shrimp and pat dry.

Per serving: 35 Cal, 1g Fat, 7g Pro, 0g Sug, <1g Carb, 0g Fib, **NET CARBS: <1**

Shrimp Scampi

MAKES 6 SERVINGS

This is similar to Easy Baked Shrimp, but we put it in a skillet and call it Scampi.

2   **pounds shrimp**
⅓   **cup oil**
2   **small garlic cloves, minced**
1   **teaspoon salt**
½   **teaspoon pepper**
¼   **cup fresh lemon juice**

1. Peel and devein shrimp. Heat oil in a large skillet. Stir in remaining ingredients. Add shrimp and cook until almost pink. Reduce heat and cook until liquid is absorbed and shrimp is opaque and pink.

Per serving: 198 Cal, 10g Fat, 24g Pro, <1g Sug, 1g Carb, <1g Fib, **NET CARBS: 1**

Grilled Shrimp Kabobs

MAKES 4 SERVINGS

Remember to soak wooden skewers in water for 20 minutes before using.

16   **large shrimp**
16   **Chinese pea pods, cooked crisp tender**
2   **tablespoons butter, melted**
2   **teaspoons fresh lemon juice**
¼   **teaspoon dried dill weed**
     Dash pepper

1. Spray grill with cooking spray and preheat. Wrap a pea pod around each shrimp and secure with a wooden toothpick. Place 4 on each skewer.
2. Combine remaining ingredients and brush shrimp with some of the sauce. Place on hot grill. Cooking time can vary according to the size of the shrimp and temperature of the grill. Cook on one side, turn and baste with sauce. Cook until cooked through.

Per serving: 78 Cal, 6g Fat, 5g Pro, 1g Sug, 1g Carb, <1g Fib, **NET CARBS: 1**

Spicy Garlic Shrimp

MAKES 4 SERVINGS

The red pepper is just what this recipe needs.

3   tablespoons olive oil
1½ pounds large shrimp
    Salt and pepper
3   small garlic cloves, chopped
¼ teaspoon crushed red pepper
1   tablespoon lemon juice

1. Heat oil in a large skillet over medium-high heat. Add shrimp. Sprinkle with salt and pepper. Cook about 2 minutes, stirring frequently.
2. Stir in garlic and red pepper and cook over medium heat until shrimp is opaque and pink throughout - do not overcook. Remove from heat and add lemon juice.

Per serving: 222 Cal, 12g Fat, 27g Pro, <1g Sug, 1g Carb, 0g Fib, **NET CARBS: 1**

Easy Baked Shrimp

MAKES 4 SERVINGS

Jumbo size shrimp are quite expensive. For a more affordable dish, you can substitute medium shrimp for the jumbo.

2   pounds jumbo shrimp
⅓ cup butter, melted
2   tablespoons oil
¼ cup fresh lemon juice
3   medium garlic cloves, minced

1. Preheat oven to 450°F. Peel, devein and butterfly shrimp. Place in a 13x9-inch baking dish.
2. Combine remaining ingredients and pour over shrimp. Bake 6 to 10 minutes or until opaque and pink.

Per serving: 268 Cal, 12g Fat, 36g Pro, <1g Sug, 1g Carb, 0g Fib, **NET CARBS: 1**

Bacon Prawns

MAKES ONE SERVING

These are also delicious on the grill.

3   bacon slices
3   prawns
1   teaspoon butter, melted with parsley or desired herbs

1. Partially cook bacon to the just limp stage; drain.
2. Shell prawns except for the tails and devein.
3. Wrap a bacon slice around each prawn; secure with wooden toothpicks. Place on broiler rack in pan. Brush with butter mixture. Cook; turning once, until prawns turn opaque and pink, brushing occasionally with butter.

Per serving: 123 Cal, 8g Fat, 10g Pro, 0g Sug, 0g Carb, 0g Fib, **NET CARBS: 0**

Poultry

♜ Chicken
♜ Turkey

Teriyaki Chicken

Serve with Mock Mashed Potatoes, page 246.

4　chicken breast halves, skinned, boned
¼　cup chopped onions
1　medium garlic clove, minced
2　tablespoons Splenda®
½　teaspoon dried ginger
½　cup soy sauce

1. Place chicken in an 8x8-inch baking dish or re-sealable bag. Combine remaining ingredients with 1/4-cup water. Pour over chicken. Marinate, in refrigerator, for one hour.

2. Preheat oven to 350°F. Place chicken in a sprayed shallow roasting pan. Pour marinade over top. Bake 20 minutes; turn chicken and bake 10 to 15 minutes or until cooked through, basting frequently with the sauce.

Per serving: 155 Cal, 3g Fat, 24g Pro, <1g Sug, 2g Carb, <1g Fib, *NET CARBS: 2*

Mock Chicken Cordon Bleu

MAKES 4 SERVINGS

Most of us enjoy Cordon Bleu, but lack the time or patience to prepare it. This version is easier.

4　chicken breast halves, skinned, boned
1　cup low-carb white bread crumbs
1½　teaspoons seasoning salt
¼　cup sour cream
4　thin slices boiled ham
1　thin slice Swiss cheese, about 5x8-inches, cut into 4 rectangles

1. Preheat oven to 350°F. Combine bread crumbs and seasoning salt. Brush chicken with sour cream. Roll in crumbs to coat. Place on a sprayed shallow baking pan and bake 30 to 40 minutes or until cooked through.

2. Top each chicken breast with a ham slice folded to fit. Top with a cheese slice. Bake long enough to melt cheese.

Per serving: 248 Cal, 8g Fat, 36g Pro, 1g Sug, 5g Carb, 2g Fib, *NET CARBS: 3*

Pesto Stuffed Chicken

MAKES 4 SERVINGS

Use your favorite pesto sauce.

4　large chicken breasts, with skin, bone in
4　tablespoons pesto sauce
1　tablespoon oil
½　cup grated Parmesan cheese

1. Preheat oven to 350°F. Spread pesto under chicken skin, leaving skin attached. Place in a sprayed 13x9-inch baking dish. Brush with oil and bake 30 minutes.

2. Brush with drippings and sprinkle with cheese. Bake 10 to 15 minutes or until cooked through.

Per serving: 291 Cal, 16g Fat, 33g Pro, 0g Sug, 1g Carb, <1g Fib, *NET CARBS: 1*

Onion-Pepper Chicken

A nice blend of vegetables with the chicken.

4   chicken breast halves, skinned, boned
2   tablespoons oil
1   medium onion, sliced
½   medium red and green pepper, julienned
½   cup sliced fresh mushrooms
     Salt and pepper to taste

1. Heat oil in a medium skillet. Add chicken and cook until lightly browned, cooking each side 2 to 3 minutes or until cooked through. Remove and keep warm.

2. Add onion, peppers and mushrooms to skillet. Sprinkle with salt and pepper; cook until just crisp-tender. Serve over chicken.

Per serving: 220 Cal, 10g Fat, 27g Pro, 2g Sug, 5g Carb, 1g Fib, *NET CARBS: 4*

Diner's Chicken Plate

MAKES 4 SERVINGS

Substitute fat-free dressing for a low-fat recipe.

4   chicken breast halves, skinned, boned
2   tablespoons no-carb vinaigrette
4   (1-oz) slices Pepper Jack cheese
8   large lettuce leaves
8   tomato slices
8   thin onion slices

1. In a medium skillet, cook chicken in vinaigrette over medium heat until cooked through, turning once. Top with cheese and cook to melt.

2. Place chicken on lettuce on individual serving plates. Garnish with tomato and onion slices.

Per serving: 303 Cal, 16g Fat, 33g Pro, 2g Sug, 4g Carb, <1g Fib, *NET CARBS: 4*

Baked Fried Chicken

MAKES 8 SERVINGS

The easiest way there is to "fry" chicken.

8   chicken legs
     Salt and pepper
     Paprika
6   tablespoons butter

1. Preheat oven to 400°F. Sprinkle chicken with salt, pepper and paprika. Place, skin-side down, in a shallow baking pan. Dot with butter. Cover with foil and bake for 30 minutes.

2. Remove foil. Increase temperature to 425°, bake 30 minutes or until cooked through.

Per serving: 302 Cal, 19g Fat, 30g Pro, 0g Sug, 0g Carb, 0g Fib, *NET CARBS: 0*

MENU

Baked Fried Chicken
Broccoli Meringue
Berry-Berry Fruit Salad
Mocha Mousse

6 net carbs per meal.

Brunch Enchiladas

You don't have to make this for brunch; it's a great casserole for dinner. The servings are quite generous, so you won't go away hungry.

3   cups cubed cooked chicken
½   cup chopped green onions
8   (10-inch) low-carb white ortillas
3   cups (12-oz) Cheddar cheese, shredded
1   cup heavy cream
6   large eggs, lightly beaten

1. Preheat oven to 350°F. Combine chicken and onion. Spoon just a little over 1/3 cup down center of each tortilla. Sprinkle with 2 cups of the cheese divided among the tortillas. Roll up and place, seam-side down, in a sprayed 13x9-inch baking dish.

2. Combine cream with 1 cup water and the eggs; pour over tortillas. Cover with foil and bake 30 minutes.

3. Uncover; sprinkle with remaining cheese and bake 10 to 15 minutes or until custard is set. Let stand 10 minutes. For easier serving, cut lengthwise down center of casserole.

note: Casserole can be made ahead and refrigerated before baking. You may have to increase baking time.

Per serving: 371 Cal, 26g Fat, 27g Pro, 1g Sug, 17g Carb, 11g Fib, **NET CARBS: 6**

Candied Chicken

The high heat is to help prevent sauce from getting too thin.

4   chicken breast halves, bone-in
     Salt and pepper
1   cup no-carb maple syrup
½   cup low-carb ketchup
¼   cup white vinegar

1. Preheat oven to 425°F. Sprinkle chicken with salt and pepper. Place in a sprayed 13x9-inch baking dish.

2. Combine remaining ingredients and pour over chicken. Bake 30 to 45 minutes or until cooked through, basting every 15 minutes. Serve sauce with chicken.

Per serving: 181 Cal, 3g Fat, 25g Pro, 0g Sug, 3g Carb, 0g Fib, **NET CARBS: 3**

Chicken Italian

Dinner in about 30 minutes.

4   chicken breast halves, skinned, boned
2   tablespoons oil
1   medium garlic clove, minced
1   small onion, sliced, separated into rings
1   (14.5-oz) can Italian stewed whole
    tomatoes, with juice
¼   teaspoon salt

1. Lightly brown chicken in heated oil in a medium skillet. Remove chicken and set aside.

2. Add garlic and onion; cook over medium heat until onion is crisp-tender. Add tomatoes, chicken and salt. Cover and cook on low heat 15 to 20 minutes or until chicken is cooked through.

Per serving: 226 Cal, 10g Fat, 27g Pro, 3g Sug, 6g Carb, 1g Fib, *NET CARBS: 5*

Chicken Broccoli Supreme

A colorful dish for a special person.

1   chicken breast half, skinned, boned
1   tablespoon oil
    Salt and pepper
1   broccoli spear, cooked crisp-tender
½   slice Swiss cheese
    Paprika

1. Gently pound chicken to 1/4-inch thickness. Cook chicken in heated oil in a medium skillet, turning once. Sprinkle with salt and pepper.

2. Top with broccoli spear. Place cheese on top. Sprinkle with paprika. Cover and heat just long enough to melt the cheese.

note: Broccoli spears can be cooked quickly by steaming on top of the stove or in the microwave in a small amount of water.

Per serving: 247 Cal, 12g Fat, 31g Pro, 1g Sug, 3g Carb, 1g Fib, *NET CARBS: 2*

Lemon Pepper Chicken

An easy way to prepare chicken on those days when you have very little time to cook.

4   chicken breast halves, skinned, boned
1   tablespoon olive oil
    Lemon pepper

1. Preheat oven to 375°F. Place chicken, skin-side up, on a shallow baking pan. Brush with oil. Sprinkle lightly with lemon pepper. Bake 30 to 40 minutes or until cooked through.

note: Decrease cooking time if using boneless chicken breasts.

Per serving: 170 Cal, 6g Fat, 26g Pro, 0g Sug, 0g Carb, 0g Fib, *NET CARBS: 0*

Lemon Chicken Packet

MAKES 1 SERVING

*Be careful when you open the packet,
the steam is very hot.*

1   chicken breast half, skinned, boned
1   tablespoon fresh lemon juice
    Dried tarragon or rosemary
    Salt and pepper
1   green onion, sliced

1. Preheat oven to 375°F. Place chicken on a
large square of foil. Pour lemon juice over
chicken. Sprinkle lightly with tarragon, salt,
pepper, and then the onion. Cover chicken with
the foil and seal tightly. Bake 30 to 40 minutes or
until cooked through.

tip: Tarragon and rosemary are very strong
herbs and should be used with a light hand.

Per serving: 147 Cal, 3g Fat, 27g Pro, <1g Sug,
2g Carb, <1g Fib, **NET CARBS: 2**

Swiss Onion Chicken

MAKES 4 SERVINGS

A great fix-it and put it in the oven recipe.

4   chicken breast halves, skinned, boned
    Salt
2   tablespoons Dijon mustard
3   green onions, sliced
½   cup (2-oz) Swiss cheese, shredded
    Paprika

1. Preheat oven to 350°F. Place chicken in a
sprayed shallow baking pan. Sprinkle lightly
with salt. Brush with mustard. Sprinkle onions,
cheese, and then paprika over chicken. Bake 20
to 25 minutes or until cooked through.

Per serving: 207 Cal, 8g Fat, 31g Pro, <1g Sug,
2g Carb, <1g Fib, **NET CARBS: 2**

Lemon Roasted Chicken

MAKES 6 SERVINGS

*Nutritional analysis is based on
skin removed before serving.*

1   (4 -lb) roasting chicken
¾   cup butter, softened
1   tablespoon fresh lemon zest
    Salt and pepper

1. Preheat oven to 375°F. Place chicken on a
rack in roasting pan.
2. Combine butter with lemon zest. Add a little
salt and pepper. Loosen the skin from the breast
area and spread half the butter mixture under the
skin. Rub remaining mixture over the chicken.
Bake 1 to 1-1/2 hours or until leg-thigh registers
170°, brushing occasionally with pan juices.

Per 4 oz serving: 282 Cal, 16g Fat, 33g Pro, 0g Sug,
0g Carb, 0g Fib, **NET CARBS: 0**

Roast Chicken in Foil

*Chicken should be very tender and moist.
Also great for recipes requiring
cubed or sliced chicken.*

1   **(3 to 3½-lb) chicken**
½   **teaspoon salt**
¼   **teaspoon pepper**
¼   **teaspoon garlic powder**
¼   **teaspoon dried rosemary**

1. Preheat oven to 400°F. Place a large piece of heavy duty foil in a shallow baking pan. Place chicken on top.
2. Combine seasonings and sprinkle over chicken. Wrap foil tightly to seal. Bake 60 minutes; reduce heat and cook 20 to 30 minutes or until thigh registers 170°.

tip: If browned chicken is desired, open foil last 20 minutes of cooking time.

Per 4 oz serving: 271 Cal, 15g Fat, 31g Pro, 0g Sug, 0g Carb, 0g Fib, **NET CARBS: 0**

Creamy Chicken & Mushrooms

MAKES 4 SERVINGS

*To quote my daughter, "yummm." Also
good served over low-carb pasta.*

4   **chicken breast halves, skinned, boned**
⅓   **cup butter**
½   **cup chopped onion**
3   **cups sliced mushrooms**
1   **cup heavy cream**
¾   **cup grated Parmesan cheese**

1. Cut chicken cross-wise into narrow strips. Sauté in heated butter 3 to 4 minutes.
2. Add onion and mushrooms; cook about 3 minutes, stirring frequently.
3. Add cream and cook over medium heat until slightly thickened.
4. Lower heat; add cheese and cook until cheese is melted and sauce is smooth.

Per serving: 560 Cal, 44g Fat, 35g Pro, 2g Sug, 5g Carb, 1g Fib, **NET CARBS: 4**

Chicken Strips Stir-Fry

MAKES 4 SERVINGS

This marinade gives the chicken a subtle ginger flavor. Additional oil isn't needed for stir-frying.

4 chicken breast halves, skinned, boned
1 tablespoon oil
¼ teaspoon salt
5 thin slices fresh ginger

1. Cut chicken into narrow strips. Combine chicken with remaining ingredients. Cover and chill at least 1 hour.
2. Remove ginger slices and cook chicken in a medium skillet over medium-high heat. Cook quickly, stirring often, until cooked through. This doesn't take long. Remember that over-cooked chicken is dry and tough.

Per serving: 170 Cal, 6g Fat, 26g Pro, 0g Sug, 0g Carb, 0g Fib, *NET CARBS: 0*

Nice & Tender Chicken

MAKES 6 SERVINGS

Nutritional analysis based on skin being removed before serving.

1 chicken, cut up
   Seasoning salt
1 tablespoon flour
2 cups chicken broth, heated

1. Preheat oven to 350°F. Sprinkle chicken lightly with seasoning salt.

2. Sprinkle flour over bottom of a 13x9-inch baking dish. Place chicken in the dish and pour broth over top. Bake 45 to 60 minutes or until cooked through.

Per 4-oz serving: 278 Cal, 16g Fat, 31g Pro, 1g Sug, 1g Carb, 0g Fib, *NET CARBS: 1*

Chicken-Vegetable Dish

MAKES 4 SERVINGS

A nice colorful main dish.

4   chicken breast halves, skinned, boned
    Salt and pepper
2   tablespoons oil
1¼ cups chicken broth
2   cups broccoli florets
1   medium yellow squash, sliced

1. Sprinkle chicken with salt and pepper. Heat oil in a large skillet and brown chicken on both sides. Add chicken broth; cover and cook 15 to 20 minutes or until chicken is cooked through.
2. Add vegetables and sprinkle lightly with salt and pepper. Cover and cook 5 to 6 minutes or until vegetables are just crisp-tender.

Per serving: 191 Cal, 7g Fat, 28g Pro, <1g Sug, 3g Carb, 2g Fib, *NET CARBS: 1*

Bernstein's Baked Chicken

MAKES 6 SERVINGS

I hope your supermarket carries Bernstein dressings. They can be used in many chicken recipes, as well as your favorite salad combinations.

1   **chicken, cut up**
¼   **cup Bernstein's Cheese Fantastico Dressing**

1. Preheat oven to 400°F. Brush chicken with dressing. Place, skin-side up, on a baking pan. Bake 45 to 60 minutes, basting once or twice with dressing, until chicken is golden and cooked through.

Per 4-oz serving: 395 Cal, 20g Fat, 31g Pro, <1g Sug, <1g Carb, 0g Fib, **NET CARBS: <1**

Baked Chicken Roll-ups

MAKES 4 SERVINGS

Another great company dish.

4   **chicken breast halves, skinned, boned**
4   **thin slices deli boiled ham**
2   **thin slices Swiss cheese, halved**
¼   **cup whipped cream cheese**
4   **slices bacon**

1. Preheat oven to 350°F. Pound chicken to 1/4-inch thickness.
2. Roll ham slices and place off center on chicken. Top with Swiss cheese. Spread 1 tablespoon whipped cream cheese over top. Roll up to completely enclose the filling, tucking in

edges as needed. Use wooden toothpicks, if necessary.
3. Wrap bacon around chicken. Place in sprayed 8x8-inch baking dish and bake 35 to 45 minutes or until cooked through.

tip: Make sure ends of rolls are sealed to prevent melted cheese from spilling out.

Per serving: 283 Cal, 13g Fat, 37g Pro, <1g Sug, 2g Carb, 0g Fib, **NET CARBS: 2**

Garlic Butter Chicken

MAKES 6 SERVINGS

Another quick and easy recipe.

1   **chicken, cut up**
½   **cup butter**
1   **tablespoon garlic salt**
¼   **teaspoon pepper**

1. Preheat oven to 350°F. Place chicken, skin-side down, in a sprayed 13x9-inch baking dish.
2. Combine remaining ingredients. Brush chicken with some of the mixture and bake 30 minutes, basting twice. Turn chicken and bake 20 to 30 minutes or until cooked through, basting frequently.

Per 4-oz serving: 338 Cal, 23g Fat, 31g Pro, 0g Sug, 0g Carb, 0g Fib, **NET CARBS: 0**

Broccoli-Tomato Chicken

MAKES 4 SERVINGS

A colorful dish.

2   chicken breast halves, skinned, boned
2   tablespoons oil, divided
2   small onions, sliced
2   cups broccoli florets
1   medium tomato (wedges)
    Salt and pepper

1. Cut chicken into bite-size pieces and toss with 1 tablespoon of the oil. Add to a large skillet and cook over high heat, stirring frequently, until just tender.
2. Add remaining oil and onion. Cook over medium heat, about 2 minutes. Add broccoli and tomato. Sprinkle with salt and pepper. Cover and cook 4 minutes or until vegetables are just crisp-tender.

Per serving: 158 Cal, 8g Fat, 15g Pro, 2g Sug,
7g Carb, 2g Fib, *NET CARBS: 5*

Stir-Fry Chicken

MAKES 4 SERVINGS

Another way to get your vegetables for the day.

4   chicken breast halves, skinned boned
2   tablespoons oil
1   medium onion, sliced
1   red or green pepper, sliced
2   cups bean sprouts
2   tablespoons soy sauce

1. Cut chicken into bite-size pieces. Heat oil in a large skillet; add chicken and cook, stirring frequently, until just tender. Remove chicken.
2. Add onions and pepper; cook until crisp-tender, adding more oil if needed. Add sprouts, soy sauce and chicken. Heat through, but do not overcook.

Per serving: 253 Cal, 11g Fat, 33g Pro, 2g Sug,
7g Carb, 1g Fib, *NET CARBS: 6*

Chicken Hawaiian

MAKES 4 SERVINGS

Another company favorite.

4   large chicken breast halves, skinned, boned
2   canned pineapple rings, halved
¼   cup unsweetened shredded coconut
1   teaspoon salt
½   cup low-carb dry white bread crumbs
½   cup butter, melted

1. Preheat oven to 350°F. Place chicken between waxed paper and pound to 1/4-inch thickness.
2. Place a pineapple half toward one end of chicken. Sprinkle with 1 tablespoon coconut. Fold sides over and roll up to enclose filling. Secure with wooden toothpicks.
3. Combine salt and bread crumbs. Dip chicken in melted butter and coat with bread crumbs. Place on sprayed baking sheet. Bake 35 to 45 minutes or until golden and cooked through, brushing with butter if chicken appears dry.

Per serving: 402 Cal, 29g Fat, 30g Pro, <1g Sug,
5g Carb, 2g Fib, *NET CARBS: 3*

Curried Chicken Bake

MAKES 6 SERVINGS

Delight your palate with just a touch of curry.

1   chicken, cut up
½   cup mayonnaise
2   teaspoons curry powder
½   teaspoon prepared horseradish
½   teaspoon soy sauce
½   teaspoon Dijon mustard

1. Preheat oven to 350°F. Place chicken, skin-side down, in a sprayed 13x9-inch baking dish. Combine remaining ingredients and brush chicken; turn and brush with remaining sauce. Bake 50 to 60 minutes or until browned and cooked through.

Per 4-oz serving: 407 Cal, 20g Fat, 31g Pro, 0g Sug, <1g Carb, 0g Fib, *NET CARBS: <1*

Chicken-Bacon Rolls

MAKES 4 SERVINGS

The bacon keeps the chicken moist as well as adding lots of flavor.

4   chicken breast halves, skinned, boned
¼   cup drained oil-packed sun-dried tomatoes, chopped
    Salt and pepper
4   thin slices bacon

1. Preheat oven to 350°F. Pound chicken to 1/4-inch thickness.

2. Top each with 1 tablespoon sun-dried tomatoes. Roll up to enclose filling. Sprinkle with salt and pepper.

3. Stretch bacon by running a knife down the slice and pulling at the same time. Wrap around chicken; secure with a wooden toothpick. Bake 20 to 30 minutes or until cooked through.

Per serving: 189 Cal, 7g Fat, 30g Pro, 0g Sug, 2g Carb, <1g Fib, *NET CARBS: 2*

Company Chicken

MAKES 4 SERVINGS

When you reach maintenance level, you can place a sliced pineapple ring between the ham and cheese slices.

4   chicken breast halves, skinned, boned
¼   cup flour
2   tablespoons oil
2   slices deli ham, halved
2   slices Monterey Jack cheese, halved

1. Dip chicken in flour; shake off excess. Cook in heated oil over medium-high heat, turning once.

2. Top with a slice of ham and then the cheese. Cook until cheese is melted.

Per serving: 285 Cal, 14g Fat, 32g Pro, <1g Sug, 5g Carb, <1g Fib, *NET CARBS: 5*

Oven-Baked Herb Chicken

A delicious herb-flavored chicken that is easy to prepare for everyday fare or casual company dinners.

1   chicken, cut up
1   (0.7 oz) package Good Seasons Cheese Garlic salad dressing mix
2   tablespoons flour
¼   cup butter, melted
1   tablespoon fresh lemon juice

1. Preheat oven to 350°F. Place chicken, skin-side up, in a sprayed 13x9-inch baking dish.

2. Combine remaining ingredients; brush over chicken. Bake 50 to 60 minutes or until chicken is cooked through. Best served hot from the oven.

Per 4-oz serving: 355 Cal, 23g Fat, 31g Pro, <1g Sug, 4g Carb, 0g Fib, **NET CARBS: 4**

Chicken & Sausage Kabobs

Kabobs are made for grilling.

4   chicken breast halves, skinned, boned
    Salt and pepper
2   Italian sausages
12 small mushrooms
¼   cup butter, melted

1. Cut chicken into 1-1/2 inch pieces. Sprinkle with salt and pepper.

2. Cut sausage into 12 (1-inch) slices. Simmer sausage in a little water 5 to 6 minutes or until partially cooked.

3. Thread chicken, sausage and mushrooms on skewers. Grill 4 to 5 minutes on each side, or until cooked through, basting frequently with butter.

Per serving: 345 Cal, 19g Fat, 36g Pro, 1g Sug, 4g Carb, 1g Fib, **NET CARBS: 3**

Chicken Seafood Kabobs

MAKES 4 SERVINGS

A very low-carb recipe.

2   chicken breast halves, skinned, boned
8   small mushrooms
½   red pepper, cut into squares
8   jumbo shrimp, peeled, deveined
4   green onions, 4-inch lengths
¼   cup olive oil

1. Cut chicken into 1-1/2 inch pieces. Alternate food on skewers beginning and ending with chicken. Brush with oil.
2. Grill, turning several times and basting with oil until cooked through.

Per skewer: 258Cal, 10g Fat, 38g Pro, 2g Sug, 3g Carb, 1g Fib, *NET CARBS: 2*

Orange Chicken Kabobs

MAKES 4 SERVINGS

The kabobs can be grilled or broiled. This is an easy recipe for family meals or entertaining.

4   chicken breast halves, skinned, boned
⅓   cup low-carb apricot marmalade spread
1   tablespoon Grand Marnier

1. Cut chicken breasts into bite-size pieces. Thread on 4 skewers, leaving a small space between each piece of chicken. Place on a heated grill and cook, turning once, until chicken is almost cooked through.
2. Combine remaining ingredients and brush some of the sauce over the chicken. Cook one

side, turn and baste with sauce. Continue to cook until cooked through.

Per serving: 193 Cal, 1g Fat, 27g Pro, 1g Sug, 3g Carb, 0g Fib, *NET CARBS: 3*

Broccoli-Cheese Chicken

MAKES 4 SERVINGS

Can also be baked in the oven.

4   chicken breast halves, skinned, boned
2   tablespoons oil
4   thin tomato slices
4   small broccoli spears, cooked
4   slices Mozzarella cheese

1. Heat oil in a large skillet. Cook chicken 6 to 8 minutes or until cooked through, turning once.
2. Top chicken with remaining ingredients, cutting to fit if necessary. Cover skillet and cook to heat through and melt cheese.

Per serving: 271 Cal, 12g Fat, 35g Pro, 1g Sug, 4g Carb, 1g Fib, *NET CARBS: 3*

Quick Grill

Brush chicken pieces with Italian dressing and bake at 350°F for 30 to 45 minutes. If cooking for a crowd, I like to do this step ahead. Then place chicken on grill over medium coals. Brush with low-carb barbecue sauce and cook, basting frequently, until heated through.

Easy Baked Chicken

MAKES 6 SERVINGS

This is about as easy as it gets.

1 **chicken, cut up**
⅓ **cup butter**
  Paprika
  Salt and pepper

1. Preheat oven to 400°F. Place chicken, skin-side up, in a 13x9-inch baking dish. Dot with butter and sprinkle with paprika and salt and pepper. Bake 50 to 60 minutes or until cooked through, basting occasionally with the butter.

Per serving: 346 Cal, 24g Fat, 31g Pro, 0g Sug, 0g Carb, 0g Fib, **NET CARBS: 0**

Baked Garlic Chicken

MAKES 6 SERVINGS

A mild-flavored garlic chicken that is so tender it just falls off the bone.

1 **chicken, cut up**
  Salt and pepper
¼ **cup flour**
3 **tablespoons oil**
30 **large garlic cloves, for flavor only**
½ **teaspoon Italian seasoning**

1. Preheat oven to 350°F. Sprinkle chicken with salt and pepper. Lightly coat with flour and brown in heated oil in a large pot or Dutch oven.
2. Remove paper-like covering from garlic, but do not peel. Add to pot and sprinkle with season-ing. Add 1/2-cup water. Cover and bake 1-1/2 hours or until chicken is cooked through.

note: Count 1g of carbs per garlic clove. Keep this in mind if you would like to try one.

Per serving: 350 Cal, 22g Fat, 32g Pro, 0g Sug, 4g Carb, 0g Fib, **NET CARBS: 4**

Dilly Chicken

MAKES 4 SERVINGS

If you like the flavor of dill, you will enjoy this recipe.

4 **chicken breast halves, skinned, boned**
¾ **cup sour cream**
1 **cup chicken broth**
2 **tablespoons flour**
1 **teaspoon Splenda®**
1 **teaspoon dried dill weed**

1. Preheat oven to 350°F. Place chicken in a sprayed 13x9-inch baking dish.
2. Combine remaining ingredients in a small saucepan. Bring to a boil and cook, stirring frequently, until thickened. Pour over chicken and bake 30 minutes. Increase temperature to 375° and cook 15 minutes or until cooked through.

Per serving: 249 Cal, 12g Fat, 29g Pro, <1g Sug, 5g Carb, <1g Fib, **NET CARBS: 5**

Italiano Chicken

Your kitchen will smell "sooo" good!

4	chicken breast halves, skinned, boned
½	cup grated Parmesan cheese
½	teaspoon oregano
1	teaspoon garlic salt
¼	teaspoon pepper
¼	cup butter, melted

1. Preheat oven to 375°F. Rinse chicken and pat dry.
2. Combine next 4 ingredients. Dip chicken in melted butter; coat with cheese mixture and place in a shallow baking dish. Pour any remaining butter over top. Bake 30 to 40 minutes or until chicken is cooked through.

Per serving: 284 Cal, 17g Fat, 30g Pro, 0g Sug, 1g Carb, <1g Fib, *NET CARBS: 1*

Roasted Garlic Chicken

MAKES 6 SERVINGS

This imparts a wonderful garlic-herb flavor; but, to assure that, it must be marinated for 24 hours.

1	chicken, cut up
1½	cups oil
11	medium garlic cloves, divided
2	teaspoons dried thyme
1	tablespoon dried rosemary
	Salt and pepper

1. Place chicken in a shallow roasting pan. Pour oil over top. Flatten 8 of the garlic cloves and scatter over chicken. Cover and refrigerate for 24 hours, turning occasionally.
2. Preheat oven to 450°F. Remove chicken from pan. Save 1/3-cup of the marinade, discarding the rest. Return chicken to pan, skin-side up.
3. Mince the remaining 3 garlic cloves and add to marinade along with the thyme and rosemary. Pour over chicken. Sprinkle with salt and pepper. Bake 45 to 60 minutes or until nicely roasted and cooked through.

Per 4-oz serving: 356 Cal, 25g Fat, 31g Pro, 0g Sug, 1g Carb, <1g Fib, *NET CARBS: 1*

Glazed Chicken

MAKES 4 SERVINGS

This chicken is richly glazed, tender and delicious. A family favorite. If desired, garnish with sesame seeds.

4	chicken breast halves, skinned, boned
¼	cup flour
2	tablespoons olive oil
¼	cup soy sauce
2	tablespoons dry sherry
2	tablespoons Splenda®

1. Preheat oven to 350°F. Coat chicken with flour; shake off excess.
2. Heat oil in a large skillet and quickly brown chicken over high heat, turning once.
3. Place in a sprayed 11x7-inch baking dish. Bake 15 minutes. Combine remaining ingredients and baste chicken. Bake 15 minutes or until cooked through, basting every 5 minutes.

Per serving: 241 Cal, 10g Fat, 29g Pro, <1g Sug, 6g Carb, 0g Fib, *NET CARBS: 6*

Chicken Elegant

MAKES 8 SERVINGS

Such a simple recipe, but very "elegant." Serve with Lemon Broccoli, Mock Mashed Potatoes and Tossed Salad with Mushrooms.

4   whole chicken breasts
⅓   cup plus 3 tablespoons butter
1   cup chicken broth
¼   cup flour
6   tablespoons heavy cream
    Salt and pepper

1. Preheat oven to 375°F. Chicken breasts should be left whole with the bones removed, but do not remove the skin.

2. Heat the 1/3-cup butter in a heavy 12-inch skillet. Tuck chicken ends and skin under, shaping into a nice round. Brown bottom side first, then turn and brown top side.

3. Place in a sprayed 13x9-inch baking dish. Add broth. Cover with foil and bake 50 to 60 minutes or until cooked through. Remove chicken and keep hot, but reserve the broth.

4. Melt remaining butter in small saucepan. Stir in the flour until blended. Remove from heat and stir in the reserved broth, cream and 1/2-cup water. Cook, stirring frequently, until mixture boils and thickens. Season with salt and pepper. Place chicken on serving plates and top with sauce.

Per serving: 321 Cal, 20g Fat, 30g Pro, 0g Sug, 3g Carb, 0g Fib, **NET CARBS: 3**

Company Swiss Chicken

MAKES 6 SERVINGS

Everyone loves this recipe.

6   chicken breast halves, skinned
    Salt and pepper
¼   cup butter, melted, divided
12 slices bacon, cooked, crumbled
6   ounces mushrooms, sliced
1½ cups (6-oz) Swiss cheese, shredded

1. Preheat oven to 350°F. Place chicken, skin-side up, in a sprayed 13x9-inch baking dish. Sprinkle with salt and pepper. Drizzle 3 tablespoons of the butter over top. Bake 30 minutes.

2. Meanwhile, sauté mushrooms in remaining 1 tablespoon butter. Combine mushrooms with bacon and cheese. Spoon over chicken. Bake 15 to 20 minutes or until cooked through.

Per serving: 389 Cal, 14g Fat, 40g Pro, <1g Sug, 2g Carb, <1g Fib, **NET CARBS: 2**

Purchase Tips

Chicken at the supermarket has usually been frozen at least once and, if not sold right away, sometimes twice. This is usually okay, but if we take it home and freeze it again, we may be looking at one tough chicken. For best results, look for packages with the least amount of liquid in the tray, the more liquid the more times it's been frozen and thawed, and cook within one or two days of purchase.

Chicken Divine Casserole

This is a favorite casserole in our family. Serve with a tossed salad and fresh fruit.

4 chicken breast halves, cooked
2 cups broccoli florets
1 (8-oz) package cream cheese, softened
¼ cup heavy cream
¾ teaspoon garlic salt
¾ cup grated Parmesan cheese

1. Preheat oven to 350°F. Cut chicken lengthwise into 1/4-inch slices. Place in a sprayed 8x8-inch baking dish. Top with broccoli.

2. Beat cream cheese until smooth. Combine cream with 3/4 cup water and gradually add to cream cheese.

3. Spoon into a saucepan; add garlic salt and Parmesan. Cook, over low heat, until thickened. Pour over broccoli and bake 35 to 40 minutes.

Per serving: 464 Cal, 33g Fat, 38g Pro, <1g Sug, 4g Carb, 1g Fib, *NET CARBS: 3*

Chicken Curry

MAKES 6 SERVINGS

Serve with Brussels Sprouts and a fruit salad.

6 chicken breast halves, skinned, boned
6 tablespoons butter, divided
¼ cup flour
½ cup heavy cream
½ teaspoon salt
1½ teaspoons curry powder

1. Cube chicken and cook in 2 tablespoons of the butter.

2. Melt remaining butter in a 2-quart saucepan. Stir in flour until blended. Combine cream with 1-1/2 cups water and gradually add to flour mixture. Bring to a boil and cook 2 minutes. Reduce heat and cook, stirring frequently, until thickened.

3. Add salt, curry and chicken and heat through.

Per serving: 410 Cal, 26g Fat, 36g Pro, 0g Sug, 5g Carb, <1g Fib, *NET CARBS: 5*

Cook's Tip

Most curries are enhanced by sweet garnishes. Although limited on a low-carb diet, we can still use, in moderation, unsweetened coconut and chopped nuts.

Baked Chicken Curry

Add curry to taste.

1 chicken, cut up
½ cup butter, melted
1 teaspoon fresh lemon juice
2 garlic cloves, minced
1 teaspoon salt
2 teaspoons curry powder

1. Preheat oven to 350°F. Place chicken, skin-side down, in a sprayed 13x9-inch baking dish.

2. Combine remaining ingredients. Brush chicken with some of the sauce. Bake 30 minutes, basting once.

3. Turn chicken, bake 20 minutes or until cooked through, basting every 10 minutes.

Per 4-oz serving: 408 Cal, 30g Fat, 31g Pro, 0g Sug, 1g Carb, 0g Fib, **NET CARBS: 1**

Chicken Madeira

MAKES 4 SERVINGS

The sauce is so delicious you may be tempted to eat it with a spoon.

4 chicken breast halves, skinned, boned
   Lemon pepper
3 tablespoons butter
1¾ cup heavy cream, divided
¼ cup Madeira wine
2 cups sliced mushrooms

1. Sprinkle chicken with lemon pepper. Melt butter in a medium heavy skillet. Lightly brown chicken, turning once. Remove chicken.

2. Add 1 cup of the cream and the Madeira. Bring to a simmer; add chicken and cook 10 minutes. Add remaining 3/4 cup cream and mushrooms. Cook 8 to 10 minutes or until chicken is cooked through.

3. If sauce is on the thin side, remove chicken and cook over medium heat until thickened, about 3 to 4 minutes.

Per serving: 583 Cal, 50g Fat, 30g Pro, 1g Sug, 4g Carb, 0g Fib, **NET CARBS: 4**

When browning, frying or sautéing chicken (or meats), make sure you don't crowd the pieces in the pan. If you do, you end up steam cooking instead of browning. Ever wonder why you have all that liquid in the pan? This may be the reason.

Chicken & Gravy

MAKES 6 SERVINGS

Isn't it nice that we don't have to give up everything we like.

1	chicken, cut-up
3	tablespoons butter
	Seasoning salt
3	tablespoons flour
¼	cup sour cream

1. Brown chicken in heated butter in a large skillet. (If butter starts to burn, add a little oil.) Sprinkle with seasoning salt.
2. Add 1 cup water; bring to a boil. Reduce heat; cover and cook for 20 minutes. Turn chicken and cook 15 to 20 minutes or until cooked through. Remove chicken and keep warm.
3. Combine flour with 1/2 cup water. Gradually add to liquid in skillet. Cook until mixture comes to a boil and thickens. Stir in sour cream, but do not boil. Check for seasoning.

Per serving: 357 Cal, 23g Fat, 32g Pro, 0g Sug, 4g Carb, 0g Fib, *NET CARBS: 4*

Butterflied Grilled Chicken

MAKES 4 SERVINGS

Butterflying the chicken speeds up the cooking time.

1	(2½ to 3-lb) chicken
¼	cup butter, melted
1	tablespoon lemon juice
	Salt and pepper

1. Split chicken lengthwise all the way through the back. With 2 long metal skewers, skewer chicken diagonally to keep chicken flat.

2. Combine butter and lemon juice; baste chicken. Sprinkle with salt and pepper.

3. Place, skin-side up, on grill over medium coals. Cover and cook 45 to 60 minutes or until cooked through, basting with the butter mixture.

Per 4 oz serving: 322 Cal, 21g Fat, 31g Pro, 0g Sug, <1g Carb, 0g Fib, *NET CARBS: <1*

Shopper's Chicken

MAKES 6 SERVINGS

My customers have always enjoyed this recipe.

6   chicken breast halves
1   cup sour cream
2   tablespoons lemon juice
1   teaspoon salt
1   teaspoon paprika
½   cup butter, melted

1. Preheat oven to 350°F. Place chicken, skin-side up, in a sprayed 13x9-inch baking dish.

2. Combine remaining ingredients except butter, and spread over chicken. Dot with butter. Bake 30 to 40 minutes or until cooked through.

Per serving: 413 Cal, 30g Fat, 31g Pro, <1g Sug, 2g Carb, <1g Fib, *NET CARBS: 2*

Chinese Browned Chicken

MAKES 4 SERVINGS

Lots of flavor for so few ingredients.

4   chicken breast halves
2   tablespoons butter, melted
2   tablespoons Worcestershire sauce
1   tablespoon soy sauce

1. Preheat oven to 350°F. Line a shallow baking pan with foil for easier cleaning. Place chicken on foil, skin-side up.

2. Combine remaining ingredients. Brush chicken and bake 30 to 40 minutes, basting occasionally.

Per serving: 254 Cal, 13g Fat, 30g Pro, 1g Sug, 2g Carb, 0g Fib, *NET CARBS: 2*

Chicken Monterey

Picture perfect. A dish you will enjoy.

4   chicken breast halves, skinned, boned
    Lemon pepper
8   slices bacon, cooked
4   slices Monterey Jack cheese
½   cup diced tomatoes
3   tablespoons sliced green onions

1. Preheat oven to 350°F. Place chicken in a sprayed 8x8-inch baking dish. Sprinkle lightly with lemon pepper. Bake 20 to 30 minutes or until cooked through.

2. Place 2 slices bacon on top of each chicken breast, cutting to fit if necessary. Top with cheese. Return to oven to melt cheese. Place on serving plates and top with tomato and onion.

Per serving: 325 Cal, 17g Fat, 38g Pro, <1g Sug, 2g Carb, <1g Fib, **NET CARBS: 2**

Roquefort Chicken

MAKES 6 SERVINGS

Serve with Asparagus & Almonds, page 239.

6   chicken breast halves, skinned, boned
    Salt and pepper
¼   cup butter
4   ounces Roquefort cheese
1   garlic clove, minced
1   cup sour cream

1. Preheat oven to 350°F. Sprinkle chicken with salt and pepper. Heat butter in a large heavy skillet and lightly brown chicken. Place in a sprayed 13x9-inch baking dish.

2. Add remaining ingredients to skillet. Heat, but do not boil; pour over chicken. Bake 30 to 40 minutes or until cooked through.

Per serving: 360 Cal, 24g Fat, 32g Pro, 0g Sug, 2g Carb, 0g Fib, **NET CARBS: 2**

Swiss-Artichoke Chicken

MAKES 4 SERVINGS

Serve with Lemon Broccoli, page 245.

4   chicken breast halves, skinned, boned
2   tablespoons oil
1   (6.5-oz) jar marinated artichoke hearts, drained
4   slices Swiss cheese

1. Heat oil in a large skillet. Add chicken and cook 6 to 8 minutes or until cooked through, turning once.

2. Cut artichokes if too large and place on chicken. Top with cheese, trimming if necessary. Cover skillet and cook to melt cheese.

Per serving: 337 Cal, 19g Fat, 35g Pro, <1g Sug, 5g Carb, 1g Fib, **NET CARBS: 4**

Johnny's Chicken

MAKES 6 SERVINGS

I call this Johnny's Chicken because the seasoning is produced by a popular local restaurant by that name.

1   **chicken, cut up**
¼   **cup butter, melted**
    Johnny's Garlic Spread & Seasoning

1. Preheat oven to 400°F. Place chicken pieces, skin-side up, in a 13x9-inch baking dish. Pour butter over top. Sprinkle lightly with seasoning. Bake 45 to 60 minutes, basting occassionally.

variation: Use all chicken legs and keep some in the refrigerator for those mid-afternoon or late-night snacks.

note: The seasoning can usually be found in discount warehouse stores.

Per 4-oz serving: 338 Cal, 23g Fat, 31g Pro, 0g Sug, 0g Carb, 0g Fib, **NET CARBS: 0**

Chicken Delight

MAKES 4 SERVINGS

If you just happen to have Hollandaise sauce in the frig, that's great. Otherwise you be the judge as to whether you have time to make the sauce or not.

4   **chicken breast halves, skinned, boned**
2   **tablespoons oil**
4   **small slices deli ham**
8   **asparagus spears, cooked**
2   **slices Swiss cheese**
    Mock Hollandaise sauce, see page 210 (optional)

1. In a medium skillet, cook chicken in heated oil, turning once.
2. Place a slice of ham on chicken. Top each with 2 asparagus spears. Cut cheese in half diagonally and place over asparagus. Cover skillet and cook to melt the cheese. Top with Hollandaise. If using Mock Hollandaise, there are no added carbs.

Per serving: 280 Cal, 14g Fat, 35g Pro, 1g Sug, 2g Carb, 0g Fib, **NET CARBS: 2**

Cook's Tip

If you want to take the time to pound boneless chicken to an even thickness, the cooking will be more even and less dry. To do this, place chicken between plastic wrap and pound to 1/4-inch thickness.

Chicken Bundles

A great company dish.

10   chicken breast halves, skinned, boned
 2   cups sour cream
 1   tablespoon Worcestershire sauce
 2   teaspoons salt
1¼   teaspoons paprika
1½   cups low-carb dry white bread crumbs

1. Place chicken in a 13x9-inch baking dish. Combine next 4 ingredients and pour over chicken. Turn pieces to coat. Cover. Refrigerate overnight.

2. Drop chicken into bread crumbs to coat. Tuck ends under to make a nice round fillet. Place in sprayed shallow baking pan. Cover. Chill at least 1-1/2 hours.

3. Bake 45 to 60 minutes or until golden and cooked through. If coating appears dry, brush with melted butter.

Per serving: 259 Cal, 13g Fat, 30g Pro, <1g Sug, 5g Carb, 1g Fib, **NET CARBS: 4**

Fried Chicken

MAKES 6 SERVINGS

This is a popular recipe among southern cooks. Fried chicken just isn't the same without Cream Gravy as a side; see page 211.

 1   chicken, cut up
     Salt and pepper
 ¼   cup flour
     oil

1. Rinse chicken, but do not dry. Sprinkle with salt and pepper.

2. Roll chicken in flour and shake off excess.

3. Heat about 2-inches of oil in a deep 12-inch skillet (if possible, a black iron skillet or chicken fryer). Temperature of oil should be 350°F.

4. Add chicken, skin-side down. Cover and cook 10 minutes. Uncover and cook 5 minutes or until golden. Turn and cook, uncovered, 10 minutes or until golden and cooked through.

note: Chicken will be easier to coat if you use 1/2 cup flour, but there will be flour leftover. Amount of oil doesn't really matter. The chicken absorbs only 1 tablespoon or less.

Per serving: 282 Cal, 16g Fat, 30g Pro, 0g Sug, 3g Carb, 0g Fib, **NET CARBS: 3**

Chicken Divan

A very old, but still very good, recipe.

4   chicken breast halves, skinned, boned, cooked
8   small broccoli spears
1   cup mayonnaise
2   teaspoons prepared mustard
¼   cup finely chopped onion
1   cup (4 -oz) Cheddar cheese, shredded

1. Preheat oven to 350°F.   Slice each chicken breast lengthwise into 3 slices. Steam broccoli until just crisp-tender.

2. Place broccoli in a sprayed 8x8-inch baking dish. Add chicken.

3. Combine mayonnaise, mustard and onion and spread over chicken. Top with cheese. Bake 30 minutes or until heated through.

Per serving: 683 Cal, 57g Fat, 35g Pro, 1g Sug, 7g Carb, 3g Fib, **NET CARBS: 4**

Skillet Chicken with Sage

MAKES 4 SERVINGS

A very impressive dish.

4   chicken breast halves, skinned, boned
4   slices prosciutto
4   fresh sage leaves
3   tablespoons flour
¼   cup olive oil
½   cup dry white wine

1. Pound chicken to 1/4-inch thickness. Place prosciutto on chicken, folding to fit. Place a sage leaf in center and secure with wooden toothpicks. Coat with flour; shaking off excess.

2. Heat oil in a large skillet. Cook chicken, sage-side down, 2 to 3 minutes per side, turning once. Chicken should be slightly undercooked. Remove and set aside.

3. Add wine to skillet and stir into drippings. Return chicken; turn to coat both sides and cook about 2 minutes.

Per serving: 364 Cal, 20g Fat, 35g Pro, 0g Sug, 5g Carb, <1g Fib, **NET CARBS: 5**

Pesto Chicken Saltimbocca

Not your typical Saltimbocca recipe.

4   chicken breast halves, skinned, boned
4   tablespoons pesto
4   thin slices prosciutto
4   thin slices fontina cheese
    Salt and pepper
2   tablespoons oil

1. Pound chicken breasts between plastic wrap, to 1/4-inch thickness.

2. Spread chicken with pesto. Top with prosciutto and cheese. Fold in bottom and sides and roll up to enclose filling. Secure with wooden toothpicks. Sprinkle with salt and pepper.

3. Heat oil in large skillet over medium-high heat. Add chicken and cook 5 to 6 minutes, or until nicely browned, turning once. Reduce heat to medium-low, cover and cook 10 to 15 minutes or until cooked through.

variation: If desired, serve with Pesto-Mayonnaise Sauce, page 207.

Per serving: 451 Cal, 30g Fat, 43g Pro, <1g Sug, 1g Carb, <1g Fib, *NET CARBS: 1*

Chicken & Sun-Dried Tomatoes

MAKES 4 SERVINGS

The sun-dried tomatoes add a nice touch.

4   chicken breast halves, skinned, boned
⅓   cup chopped oil-packed sun-dried tomatoes, with 2 tablespoons of the oil
2   garlic cloves, finely chopped
¼   cup finely chopped onion
1   cup heavy cream

1. In a large skillet, cook chicken in 1 tablespoon of oil from the sun-dried tomatoes; turning once. Remove and keep warm.

2. Add remaining oil, garlic, onion and sun-dried tomatoes to skillet. Cook until onion is tender.

3. Add cream and simmer 4 to 5 minutes or until thickened. Spoon over chicken.

Per serving: 429Cal, 33g Fat, 28g Pro, <1g Sug, 5g Carb, 1g Fib, *NET CARBS: 4*

༄ Hint ༄

The secret to tender moist chicken is in not over-cooking. Watch carefully during the last few minutes of cooking time. Leaving the skin on the chicken will also contribute to moist chicken and in some recipes will contribute to more even browning.

Brined Roast Chicken

MAKES 8 SERVINGS

See Easy Brine recipe, page 213. Plan on 8 hours or overnight for the brining.

1   **(4-lb) roasting chicken**
1   **lemon, cut into 8 slices**
    Salt and pepper
¼   **cup coarsely chopped onion**
2   **large garlic cloves, halved**

1. Clean chicken and remove excess fat. Place in enough brining solution to cover chicken. Cover. Refrigerate 8 hours or overnight.

2. Preheat oven to 400°F. Remove chicken from brine and pat dry. Loosen skin from the breast. Place 4 lemon slices under skin. Sprinke with salt and pepper. Fill cavity with remaining lemon slices, onion and garlic. Place on rack in roasting pan and bake 60 to 70 minutes or until thigh registers 170°F. Let stand 15 minutes before carving.

Per 4-oz serving: 275 Cal, 7g Fat, 49g Pro, <1g Sug, 1g Carb, <1g Fib, *NET CARBS: 1*

Italian Chicken

MAKES 6 SERVINGS

A perfect busy day recipe.

1   **chicken, cut up**
    No-carb vinaigrette dressing

1. Marinate chicken several hours or overnight in the dressing.

2. Preheat oven to 350°F. Remove chicken from dressing and place in a 13x9-inch baking dish. Bake 50 to 60 minutes or until cooked through, basting frequently with additional dressing.

Per serving: 296 Cal, 18g Fat, 31g Pro, 0g Sug, 0g Carb, 0g Fib, *NET CARBS: 0*

Soy Chicken

MAKES 6 SERVINGS

Ready to bake in less than 10 minutes.

1   **chicken, cut up**
½   **cup brown Sugar Twin®**
½   **cup soy sauce**
¼   **cup butter, melted**

1. Preheat oven to 350°F. Place chicken, skin-side down, in a sprayed 13x9-inch baking dish.

2. Combine remaining ingredients and pour over chicken. Bake 30 minutes. Turn chicken and bake 20 to 30 minutes, basting occasionally, until cooked through. Serve sauce with chicken.

Per serving: 314 Cal, 19g Fat, 32g Pro, 2g Sug, 2g Carb, 0g Fib, *NET CARBS: 2*

Ben's Chicken Parmesan

MAKES 4 SERVINGS

Use remaining sauce in jar to serve over pasta.

4 chicken breast halves, skinned, boned
3 tablespoons grated Parmesan cheese
1¼ cups low-carb spaghetti sauce
1 cup (4-oz) Mozzarella cheese, shredded
   Parsley

1. Preheat oven to 350°F. Place chicken in a sprayed 11x7-inch baking dish.
2. Combine Parmesan and sauce; pour over chicken. Cover. Bake 30 minutes or until cooked through.
3. Top with cheese and a sprinkle of parsley. Bake 5 minutes to melt cheese.

Per serving: 292 Cal, 13g Fat, 36g Pro, 3g Sug, 5g Carb, 1g Fib, *NET CARBS: 4*

Maple Sauce Chicken

MAKES 6 SERVINGS

This is a family favorite.

1 chicken, cut up
1 small onion, sliced
½ cup no-carb maple syrup
½ cup low-carb ketchup
¼ cup white vinegar
2 tablespoons Mild & Creamy Dijon mustard

1. Preheat oven to 350°F. Clean chicken and pat dry.

2. Place onion in a sprayed 13x9-inch baking dish. Arrange chicken on top.
3. Combine remaining ingredients and spoon over chicken. Bake 50 to 60 minutes or until nicely glazed and cooked through, basting frequently.

Per serving: 302 Cal, 15g Fat, 31g Pro, <1g Sug, 4g Carb, <1g Fib, *NET CARBS: 4*

Chicken Quesadillas

MAKES 8 SERVINGS

Serve these as a light lunch, or as appetizers, served with additional salsa and/or sour cream, if desired.

1½ cups chopped cooked chicken
1 cup (4-oz) Cheddar cheese, shredded
¾ cup thick and chunky salsa
8 (7-inch) low-carb tortillas

1. Combine chicken, cheese and salsa. Place each tortilla in a sprayed heated skillet or griddle. Spread each with 1/4 of the chicken mixture. Top with a tortilla and cook until heated through, turning once. Cut in half and serve.

Per serving: 142 Cal, 7g Fat, 14g Pro, 1g Sug, 13g Carb, 8g Fib, *NET CARBS: 5*

Roast Cornish Hens

Just the right size for a serving.

4   Cornish hens
1   teaspoon seasoning salt
¼   teaspoon garlic powder
¼   teaspoon paprika

1. Preheat oven to 400°F. Combine seasoning salt, garlic powder and paprika. Sprinkle over hens. Place, breast-side down, in a sprayed shallow pan. Bake 30 minutes.

2. Turn, breast-side up, and bake 30 to 40 minutes or until cooked through, basting with drippings. Cut in half and serve.

Per serving: 398 Cal, 28g Fat, 34g Pro, 0g Sug, <1g Carb, 0g Fib, **NET CARBS: <1**

Roast Capon

MAKES 8 SERVINGS

A capon is one of the most delicious fowls you can buy. Today it is most often found frozen rather than fresh.

1   (7-lb) capon
    Melted butter
    Salt and pepper

1. Preheat oven to 325°F. Rinse capon and pat dry. Skewer or tie wings and legs, if desired, but it isn't ncecessary. Place on a rack in shallow roasting pan. Brush with butter and sprinkle with salt and pepper.

2. Bake 2 to 2-1/2 hours or until temperature in leg-thigh area reaches 170°. If skin browns too quickly, cover loosely with foil. Let stand 20 minutes before slicing.

tip: Makes a good substitute for a small turkey.

Per 4 oz serving: 260 Cal, 13g Fat, 33g Pro, 0g Sug, 0g Carb, 0g Fib, **NET CARBS: 0**

Paulina's Turkey Meatballs

These are great to have on hand in the freezer. Just pull out the number you need for a variety of dishes or for between meal snacks.

1   **pound ground turkey**
¼   **cup low-carb soft white bread crumbs**
1   **egg**
2   **tablespoons finely chopped onions**
½   **teaspoon prepared horseradish**
½   **teaspoon salt**

1. Preheat oven to 400°F. Combine ingredients, mixing lightly.

2. Shape into walnut-size meatballs. Place in a sprayed shallow baking pan and bake 18 to 20 minutes or until cooked through.

tip: You'll reach 1 gram of carbohydrates when you've eaten 8 meatballs.

Per 8 meatballs: 288 Cal, 16g Fat, 33g Pro, 0g Sug, 2g Carb, 1g Fib, **NET CARBS: 1**

Cook's Tip For safety reasons, wear plastic gloves when mixing ground meat by hand. Actually you only need one, because you can mix it with one hand. Check your discount warehouse stores for the best prices.

Pizza Turkey Loaf

MAKES 10 SERVINGS

Lots of flavor packed in a small loaf.

2   **pounds ground turkey**
¾   **cup low-carb soft white bread crumbs**
1   **cup finely chopped onions**
1   **large egg**
1   **(15.5-oz) jar low-carb pizza sauce, divided**
2   **cups (8-oz) Mozzarella cheese, shredded, divided**

1. Preheat oven to 350°F. Combine first 4 ingredients.

2. Add 1-1/2 cups of the pizza sauce and 1-1/2 cups of the cheese, mixing gently to blend. Spoon into a sprayed 9x5-inch loaf pan. Bake 45 minutes.

3. Spread remaining pizza sauce on top. Bake 15 minutes. Sprinkle with remaining cheese and bake 15 minutes or until cooked through. The loaf should feel quite firm to the touch. Pour off any fat, cover with foil and let stand 10 minutes for easier slicing.

Per serving: 268Cal, 15g Fat, 26g Pro, 2g Sug, 5g Carb, 1g Fib, **NET CARBS: 4**

Taco Burger Patties

*This is a great recipe if you
are also watching your fat intake.*

1½   **pounds ground turkey**
1   **(1.25-oz) package taco seasoning mix**
⅓   **cup low-carb soft white bread crumbs**
1   **egg, lightly beaten**

1. Gently combine the ingredients and shape
into 8 patties, about 1/4-inch thick. Shaping will
be easier if you wet your hands with a little
water.

2. Cook in a sprayed nonstick skillet, turning
once. Cook 3 to 4 minutes on each side or until
lightly browned and cooked through.

Per serving: 170 Cal, 9g Fat, 18g Pro, 0g Sug,
3g Carb, <1g Fib, **NET CARBS: 3**

Teriyaki Turkey Burgers

MAKES 6 PATTIES

A delicious burger, even without the bun.

1   **pound ground turkey**
3   **tablespoons soy sauce**
1   **tablespoon pineapple juice**
¼   **cup low-carb white bread crumbs**
⅛   **teaspoon ground ginger**

1. Gently combine all ingredients; form into 6
patties. Cook in a sprayed nonstick skillet, grill
or broiler until browned and cooked through.

Per serving: 138 Cal, 7g Fat, 16g Pro, 1g Sug,
2g Carb, <1g Fib, **NET CARBS: 2**

Turkey-Bacon Burgers

MAKES 6 SERVINGS

*The bacon keeps the patties moist and adds
flavor.*

1   **pound ground turkey**
⅓   **cup low-carb soft white bread crumbs**
1   **egg, lightly beaten**
1   **tablespoon Worcestershire sauce**
     Salt and pepper to taste
6   **slices of bacon**

1. Gently mix the first 5 ingredients (this is
easier to do with your hands). Form into 6
patties. Carefully wrap a slice of bacon around
outer edge of each patty and secure with a
wooden toothpick.

2. Cook patties in a large nonstick skillet, or
broil or grill until cooked through, turning once.
Remove bacon and discard.

Per serving: 181 Cal, 11g Fat, 19g Pro, <1g Sug,
1g Carb, <1g Fib, **NET CARBS: 1**

Orange Glazed Turkey Breast

A wonderful marmalade glaze and black pepper add a nice touch to the finished dish.

1   (6-lb) whole turkey breast
2   teaspoons oil
⅓   cup low-carb orange marmalade spread
1   tablespoon prepared mustard
2   teaspoons Worcestershire sauce
½   teaspoon cracked pepper

1. Preheat oven to 350°F. Place turkey breast, breast-side up, on a rack in a roasting pan. Brush with oil. Cover with foil or pan lid and bake 1-1/2 to 2 hours.

2. Combine remaining ingredients and brush over turkey. Cook 30 to 40 minutes or until temperature reaches 160°, basting frequently with the pan drippings. Cover and let stand 15 minutes before slicing.

Per 4 oz serving: 242 Cal, 9g Fat, 33g Pro, 0g Sug, 1g Carb, 0g Fib, **NET CARBS: 1**

Roasted Turkey

This is one of the simplest and best ways to cook that Thanksgiving turkey.

1   (16-lb) turkey
2   tablespoons oil

1. Preheat oven to 325°F. Remove giblets and neck from cavities. Rinse and pat dry. Turn the wing tip back and tie leg ends together.

2. Place turkey, breast-side up, on rack in a deep roasting pan. Insert thermometer into thickest part of thigh. Brush oil over skin. Bake about 3½ to 4 hours or to 170°. Cover loosely with foil if skin is browning too quickly. Let stand 20 to 30 minutes before carving. If desired, use this time to make the gravy.

Per 4 oz serving: 138 Cal, 4g Fat, 25g Pro, 0g Sug, 0g Carb, 0g Fib, **NET CARBS: 0**

Need Ideas for Leftover Turkey?

Soup
Sandwiches
Turkey Salad
Curry
Casseroles
Hot Turkey Sandwiches
Creamed Turkey over Toast
Stir-Fry
Chef Salad

Pasta

- Side Dishes
- Main Dishes
- Casseroles
- Sauces
- Slow Cooker

Chicken Pasta Soup

MAKES 6 SERVINGS

A light refreshing soup.

6   cups chicken broth
½   cup diced cooked chicken
3   ounces low-carb spaghetti, 1-inch pieces
½   cup green onion, 1-inch slices

1. Combine broth and chicken in a large saucepan. Bring to a boil; add spaghetti and cook about 7 minutes or until almost done.

2. Add onion and cook until pasta is tender.

Per serving: 68 Cal, 1g Fat, 5g Pro,<1g Sug, 2g Carb, <1g Fib, *NET CARBS: 2*

Chicken Noodle Soup

MAKES 10 SERVINGS

Your mom is right, chicken soup is good for you.

4   ounces low-carb linguine
7   cups chicken broth
1   small carrot, shredded
½   cup sliced celery
1   cup cubed cooked chicken
¼   cup frozen peas

1. Break pasta into 2-inch lengths and cook according to package directions. Drain and rinse.

2. In a large pot, combine broth, carrots and celery. Bring to a boil, reduce heat and simmer until vegetables are tender, about 5 to 6 minutes. Add peas, chicken and pasta. Cook until heated through.

Per serving: 60 Cal, <1g Fat, 5g Pro, <1g Sug, 2g Carb, <1g Fib, *NET CARBS: 2*

Pasta

Dreamfields makes a delicious pasta that is low in fat and very low in net carbohydrates, since they deduct their specific fiber blend from the total carbs. If you have any questions call them at 800-250-1917 and they can give you up-to-date information.

Sample Label

Per 2 ounce serving

Calories	190
Fat	1g
S. Fat	0g
Chol	0mg
Sodium	0mg
Fiber	4g
Sugars	1g
Protein	7g
Net Carbs	5

Pesto Salad

A rather simple salad with a lot of flavor.

8	ounces low-carb penne
¼	cup sliced black olives
½	cup diced red bell pepper
¼	cup pesto, or to taste
½	cup mayonnaise
	Dash pepper

1. Cook pasta according to package directions. Rinse to cool, then drain. Combine with remaining ingredients. Cover and chill at least 2 hours.

Per serving: 323 Cal, 21g Fat, 6g Pro, 1g Sug, 5g Carb, <1g Fib, **NET CARBS: 5**

Broccoli Pasta Salad

For a main course, add leftover chicken, ham, pepperoni or shrimp.

2	cups low-carb elbow macaroni
2½	cups broccoli florets
½	cup cherry tomatoes, halved
½	cup (2-oz) Monterey Jack cheese, diced
½	cup no-carb vinaigrette dressing

1. Cook pasta according to package directions. Rinse to cool, then drain.
2. Combine ingredients in a large bowl, using just enough dressing to lightly coat. Cover and chill about 2 hours.

Per serving: 172 Cal, 11g Fat, 5g Pro, <1g Sug, 3g Carb, <1g Fib, **NET CARBS: 3**

Pepperoni Cheese Salad

Just a small amount of pepperoni is all you need.

8	ounces low-carb penne
⅓	cup no-carb vinaigrette dressing
1½	ounces thinly sliced pizza pepperoni, (18 small)
1	cup (4-oz) Mozzarella cheese, cubed
⅓	cup sliced green onions, green part
¼	cup grated Parmesan cheese

1. Cook pasta according to package directions. Rinse to cool, then drain. Place in a large bowl and toss with about 3 tablespoons of the dressing. Add pepperoni, cheese cubes and green onion. Cover and chill at least 2 hours.
2. Just before serving, toss with additional dressing, if needed, and the Parmesan cheese.

Per serving: 299 Cal, 16g Fat, 12g Pro, 1g Sug, 5g Carb, <1g Fib, **NET CARBS: 5**

Quick Pasta Sauce

Cook heavy cream until thickened. It should be thick enough to lightly coat the pasta. This works nicely as a side dish.

Nutty Butter Sauce

MAKES 4 CUPS

This is wonderful on pasta and equally as good served on grilled beef tenderloin, sirloin or New York steaks. Make enough for several recipes.

1   **pound butter, softened**
⅓   **cup whipping cream**
3   **egg yolks**
1   **cup grated Parmesan cheese**
3   **medium garlic cloves, minced**
1   **cup toasted pecans, finely chopped**

1. Cream the butter in a mixer bowl. Add cream and egg yolks.
2. Add remaining ingredients and beat until well mixed. If using immediately, add 1/2 cup to 8 ounces cooked spaghetti. Sprinkle with a little Parmesan cheese. Store the remainder in the refrigerator. Let stand at room temperature to soften.

note: The garlic is more pronounced when freshly made but mellows after the first day. If you are concerned about uncooked eggs, either avoid the recipe or use an egg substitute.

Per 2 tablespoons: 152 Cal, 16g Fat, 2g Pro, <1g Sug, <1g Carb, <1g Fib, *NET CARBS: < 1*

Pesto Sauce

MAKES 1-1/4 CUPS

Pesto sauce can be frozen in desired size batches.

1½   **cups packed fresh basil leaves**
⅓   **cup pine nuts**
2   **medium garlic cloves**
½   **cup grated Parmesan cheese**
¾   **cup oil**

1. Combine all the ingredients in a blender or food processor and blend until fairly smooth. Cover and store in refrigerator until ready to use. Sauce will thicken as it stands.

Per tablespoon: 97 Cal, 10g Fat, 1g Pro, <1g Sug, <1g Carb, <1g Fib, *NET CARBS: <1*

Cream

Whipping Cream
30-36% butter fat

Heavy Whipping Cream
36-50% butter fat

Half-and-Half
10-12% butter fat,

Ultrapasteurized Cream
Processed to dramatically increase shelf-life. Doesn't always whip well and doesn't work in all recipes. Seen more and more in stores.

Gorgonzola Cheese Sauce

MAKES 8 SERVINGS

An excellent sauce for Gorgonzola fans.

1½ cups whipping cream
12   ounces Gorgonzola cheese, crumbled

1. In a medium saucepan, bring cream to a boil; reduce heat and bring to a simmer.
2. Add cheese and stir until melted and sauce has thickened (lumps remaining in sauce is okay, even better).
note: Makes enough sauce for 16 ounces pasta.

Per serving: 304 Cal, 30g Fat, 10g Pro, 0g Sug, 3g Carb, 0g Fib, ***NET CARBS: 3***

Easy Alfredo

MAKES 8 SERVINGS

This makes a filling meatless meal.

16   ounces low-carb linguine
½   cup butter, softened
¾   cup grated Parmesan cheese
¼   cup whipping cream
     Freshly ground black pepper

1. Cook pasta according to package directions. Rinse pasta and drain.
2. Meanwhile, in a mixer bowl, beat butter and then add the Parmesan cheese. Add cream until blended. Toss with hot pasta. Season with pepper.

Per serving: 350 Cal, 17g Fat, 10g Pro, 1g Sug, 10g Carb, 4g Fib, ***NET CARBS: 6***

Classic Alfredo Sauce

MAKES 3-1/2 CUPS

This versatile pasta sauce can be tossed with pasta (enough for about 1-1/2 pounds), then sprinkled with Parmesan and freshly ground black pepper. Add variety by tossing in meats and vegetables of your choice, but watch the carbs.

¾   cup butter
1½   cups whipping cream
1¼   cups grated Parmesan cheese

1. Heat butter and cream in a medium heavy saucepan. Cook over medium heat until hot and butter melts. Reduce heat to low; gradually add Parmesan cheese and cook until melted and smooth, stirring constantly.

Per 1/2 cup: 409 Cal, 42g Fat, 7g Pro, <1g Sug, 2g Carb, 0g Fib, ***NET CARBS: 2***

Buttered Cheesy Pasta

MAKES 6 SERVINGS

Great side dish with your favorite meats.

12   ounces low-carb spaghetti
½   cup butter, sliced
½   cup grated Parmesan cheese
     Freshly ground black pepper, to taste

1. Cook pasta according to package directions. Quickly rinse, drain and return to pot.
2. Add butter and toss to melt. Add Parmesan and pepper and toss until cheese is melted.

Per serving: 354 Cal, 18g Fat, 10g Pro, 1g Sug, 9g Carb, 4g Fib, ***NET CARBS: 5***

Stove Top Macaroni & Cheese

This makes a simple and delicious side dish.

1½   cups (6-oz) low-carb elbow macaroni
¾   cup heavy cream
2   light dashes nutmeg (not too much)
3   tablespoons grated Parmesan cheese

1. Cook macaroni according to package directions. Rinse and drain thoroughly. Pour into a medium saucepan. Add cream, 3/4 cup water and nutmeg. Bring to a boil and cook, over medium heat, about 6 to 8 minutes or until liquid is absorbed, stirring frequently.
2. Pour into a sprayed 8x8-inch baking dish and sprinkle with Parmesan cheese. Place under a broiler and broil just until cheese is golden.

Per serving: 208 Cal, 12g Fat, 5g Pro, 1g Sug, 5g Carb, 2g Fib, **NET CARBS: 3**

Browned Butter & Myzithra

This delicious recipe is similar to a pasta dish served at the Spaghetti Factory.

8   ounces low-carb spaghetti
⅓   cup butter
1   large garlic clove, minced
½   cup grated Myzithra cheese

1. Cook pasta according to pasta directions. Rinse pasta and drain.

2. Melt butter in a small heavy skillet, over medium-low heat. Add garlic and cook until butter turns a light brown; watch carefully at this point. Toss butter with pasta. Place on serving plates and sprinkle with cheese.

Per serving: 424 Cal, 23g Fat, 14g Pro, 1g Sug, 10g Carb, 4g Fib, **NET CARBS: 6**

Baked Pasta & Cream

If I weren't counting carbs, I could make a whole meal out of this dish. The chewy cheese is a nice contrast to the creamy pasta.

8   ounces low-carb penne
1   cup heavy cream, divided
1   cup (4-oz) Mozzarella cheese, softened
2   tablespoons grated Parmesan cheese

1. Preheat oven to 350° F. Cook pasta according to package directions; rinse and drain.
2. Meanwhile, heat 1/2 cup of the cream in a large saucepan. Add pasta and cook, stirring frequently, until cream is absorbed.
3. Sprinkle half the Mozzarella cheese in a sprayed 8x8-inch baking dish. Add half the pasta, remaining cheese, then remaining pasta. Pour remaining cream over top. Sprinkle with Parmesan cheese. Bake 25 to 30 minutes or until most of the liquid is absorbed. Let stand 5 minutes.

Per serving: 217 Cal, 13g Fat, 7g Pro,<1g Sug, 5g Carb, 2g Fib, **NET CARBS: 3**

Asparagus Pasta Dish

At the first sign of fresh asparagus, try this quick and flavorful vegetable dish.

8   ounces low-carb penne
1   pound asparagus, trimmed, sliced
¼   cup finely chopped oil-packed sun-dried tomatoes
3   tablespoons oil
    Salt and pepper to taste

1. Cook pasta according to package directions. Rinse and drain.

2. Meanwhile, microwave or steam asparagus until just crisp-tender.

3. In a large skillet, heat sun-dried tomatoes in the oil, 2 to 3 minutes. Watch carefully to prevent burning. Add pasta and asparagus, tossing to coat.

Per serving: 157 Cal, 6g Fat, 5g Pro, 2g Sug, 8g Carb, 3g Fib, **NET CARBS: 5**

MENU

Asparagus Pasta Dish
1/2 small tomato
Green Salad & Pecans
7 net carbs per meal.

Broccoli-Tomato Pasta Dish

A delicious and colorful way to use up leftover broccoli, asparagus or zucchini.

8   ounces low-carb linguine
2   tablespoons oil
1½   cups broccoli florets, cooked crisp-tender
    Freshly ground black pepper to taste
⅓   cup plus 1 tablespoon grated Parmesan cheese
2   small Plum tomatoes

1. Cook pasta according to package directions. Rinse, drain and return to pot.

2. Meanwhile, heat oil in a medium skillet. Add broccoli and cook quickly to heat through. Pour over pasta and toss to coat. Add pepper and the 1/3 cup of Parmesan cheese; toss to melt cheese. Spoon onto a large serving platter.

3. Cut tomatoes crosswise into narrow slices and place around outer edge of pasta. Sprinkle with remaining cheese.

Per serving: 150 Cal, 5g Fat, 6g Pro, 1g Sug, 6g Carb, 3g Fib, **NET CARBS: 3**

Colorful Red Pepper Pasta

MAKES 6 SERVINGS

Can be made in less than 20 minutes.

8   ounces low-carb penne
3   tablespoons butter
1   small red bell pepper, julienned
¼   cup coarsely chopped pecans

1. Cook pasta according to package directions. Rinse and drain.
2. Meanwhile, during last five minutes of cooking time for pasta, melt the butter in a medium skillet. Add peppers and pecans and quickly sauté until peppers are just crisp-tender (this doesn't take long). Add pasta and mix well.

Per serving: 216 Cal, 10g Fat, 5g Pro, 1g Sug, 7g Carb, 3g Fib, **NET CARBS: 4**

Basil-Nut Linguine

MAKES 6 SERVINGS

Rich enough for a main meal.

12   ounces linguine
¼   cup oil, divided
1   large garlic clove, minced
½   cup chopped walnuts
¼   cup chopped fresh basil
⅔   cup grated Parmesan cheese

1. Cook pasta according to package directions. Rinse, drain and return to pot.
2. Meanwhile, lightly toast garlic and walnuts in 1 tablespoon oil. Remove from heat and add remaining 3 tablespoons oil and basil.
3. Add Parmesan cheese to pasta, then the nut mixture and serve immediately.

Per serving: 373 Cal, 19g Fat, 12g Pro, 1g Sug, 11g Carb, 5g Fib, **NET CARBS: 6**

Linguine with Mascarpone

MAKES 8 SERVINGS

These convenient "on hand" ingredients can be thrown together for a quick, yet delectable meal. Does reheat nicely in the microwave.

16 ounces linguine
1   (8-oz) container Mascarpone cheese, softened
¼   cup parsley
½   cup grated Parmesan cheese

1. Cook pasta according to package directions. Rinse and drain. Return to pot.
2. Add Mascarpone cheese and parsley. Place on serving plates and sprinkle with Parmesan.

Per serving: 340 Cal, 16g Fat, 11g Pro, 1g Sug, 10g Carb, 4g Fib, **NET CARBS: 6**

Cauliflower Pasta Dish

MAKES 6 SERVINGS

Not a lot of color so I suggest serving it with a bright green vegetable and a colorful salad.

6   ounces low-carb penne
2   teaspoons dried rosemary
2   cups small cauliflower florets
¼   cup slivered almonds, toasted
2   teaspoons oil
    Salt and pepper to taste

1. Cook pasta according to package directions, adding rosemary to the water. Add cauliflower during last 4 minutes of cooking time. Cook until pasta tests done and cauliflower is tender. Rinse and drain well. Return to pot.
2. Add almonds, oil, salt and pepper.

note: It is easy to overcook the cauliflower. If desired, steam or microwave instead of cooking with the pasta.

Per serving: 144 Cal, 5g Fat, 5g Pro, 1g Sug, 7g Carb, 4g Fib, **NET CARBS: 3**

Zucchini Linguine Pasta

MAKES 8 SERVINGS

A colorful vegetable pasta dish.

12 ounces low-carb linguine
2   tablespoons oil
2   medium garlic cloves, minced
2   medium-small zucchini, julienned
½   cup diced red bell pepper
½   cup grated Parmesan cheese

1. Cook pasta according to package directions. Rinse, drain and return to pot.
2. Meanwhile, heat oil and garlic in a large skillet. Add zucchini and pepper and cook about 4 minutes or until just crisp-tender. Add to pasta and mix well. Pour onto a serving platter and sprinkle with Parmesan cheese.

Per serving: 202 Cal, 6g Fat, 8g Pro, 1g Sug, 8g Carb, 3g Fib, **NET CARBS: 5**

Cook's Tip To increase the amount of food in a serving without adding carbs, just add cooked chicken, beef, pork or salmon.

Swiss Noodles with Pecans

MAKES 6 SERVINGS

Serve on your most attractive serving dish.

12 ounces low-carb linguine
6 tablespoons butter, melted
2 cups (8-oz) Swiss cheese, shredded
   Ground black pepper to taste
1 tablespoon finely chopped pecans
1 tablespoon chopped parsley

1. Cook pasta according to package directions.
Rinse, drain and return to pot. Add butter and
gradually stir in the cheese. Add pepper to taste.
2. Spoon pasta onto a serving platter. Sprinkle
with pecans, then parsley.

Per serving: 448 Cal, 24g Fat, 18g Pro, 1g Sug,
10g Carb, 4g Fib, *NET CARBS: 6*

Penne with Broccoli & Mushrooms

MAKES 6 SERVINGS

*Using a nonstick skillet is important in
this recipe. Otherwise, you will be scrubbing
cheese off the pan until kingdom come.*

5 ounces low-carb penne
2 cups coarsely chopped broccoli
4 ounces mushrooms, sliced
½ cup butter, divided
1 cup grated Parmesan cheese

1. Cook pasta according to package directions.
Rinse, drain and return to pot.
2. Meanwhile, cook broccoli in a small amount
of water until just crisp-tender. Drain and add to
pasta.
3. In a large nonstick skillet, sauté the mushrooms in 3 tablespoons of the butter, cooking
until tender. Add pasta, the remaining butter and
the Parmesan cheese. Return to burner and heat
just long enough to melt the butter and cheese.

Per serving: 282 Cal, 19g Fat, 9g Pro, 1g Sug,
7g Carb, 3g Fib, *NET CARBS: 4*

Pasta with Sun-Dried Tomatoes

MAKES 6 SERVINGS

The sun-dried tomatoes lend a slightly tart flavor to the pasta dish. This recipe re-heats better than most recipes.

10   ounces low-carb penne
¼   cup chopped oil-packed sun-dried
     tomatoes, plus 3 tablespoons of the oil
¼   cup sliced green onions
¼   cup chopped walnuts
½   cup whipping cream
⅓   cup grated Parmesan cheese

1. Cook pasta according to package directions. Rinse and drain.

2. Meanwhile, heat oil from tomatoes in a large deep skillet. Add onion and walnuts and cook until onions begin to soften, stirring frequently. Add sun-dried tomatoes and cream and heat through.

3. Add pasta; sprinkle with cheese and toss until melted.

Per serving: 348 Cal, 20g Fat, 9g Pro, 1g Sug, 10g Carb, 4g Fib, **NET CARBS: 6**

Herbed-Tomato Spaghetti

MAKES 6 SERVINGS

Slivered almonds can be substituted for the pine nuts.

8   ounces low-carb spaghetti
¼   cup oil
¼   cup pine nuts
1   tablespoon chopped fresh basil
2   Plum tomatoes, coarsely chopped
¾   cup grated Parmesan cheese

1. Cook pasta according to package directions. Rinse, drain and return to pot.

2. Meanwhile, heat oil and pine nuts until nuts are lightly toasted. Add to pasta along with basil and tomatoes. This is somewhat hard to mix and you may have to re-arrange some of the tomatoes on the serving plates so that everyone gets their share. Sprinkle each serving with 2 tablespoons Parmesan cheese.

Per serving: 293 Cal, 17g Fat, 10g Pro, 2g Sug, 8g Carb, 3g Fib, **NET CARBS: 5**

Light Dinner Pasta

MAKES 6 SERVINGS

Delicious served as a meatless dish for a light lunch or dinner.

8   ounces low-carb linguine
⅓   cup oil-packed sun-dried tomatoes, plus 4
     tablespoons of the oil
2   small garlic cloves, minced
¼   teaspoon crushed red pepper flakes
½   cup grated Parmesan cheese
¼   cup toasted pine nuts

1. Cook pasta according to package directions. Drain, rinse and return to pot.

2. Meanwhile, coarsely chop the sun-dried tomatoes. Heat the oil in a small skillet. Add tomatoes, garlic and red pepper and sauté about 2 minutes or until garlic is just soft. Add to pasta and mix well. Add Parmesan cheese and nuts.

note: If you have continued to add olive oil to the jar to keep the sun-dried tomatoes covered, you should have 4 tablespoons oil. If not, you will need to add additional oil to the recipe.

Per serving: 291 Cal, 16g Fat, 9g Pro, 1g Sug, 9g Carb, 3g Fib, **NET CARBS: 6**

Pasta with Brie & Shrimp

MAKES 6 SERVINGS

Serve this versatile dish topped with shrimp, crab or chicken.

8 ounces low-carb linguine
8 ounces Brie cheese, diced
½ cup whipping cream
2 tablespoons finely chopped parsley
   Freshly ground pepper to taste
8 ounces cooked shrimp (should be hot)

1. Cook pasta according to package directions. Rinse and drain thoroughly. Return to pot and add Brie, stirring to melt. Add cream, parsley and pepper.

2. Place on serving plate and top with shrimp.

note: Crust should be removed from Brie before dicing.

Per serving: 363 Cal, 19g Fat, 21g Pro, 1g Sug, 7g Carb, 3g Fib, **NET CARBS: 4**

Baked Salmon & Pasta

MAKES 4 SERVINGS

If desired, grill the salmon and serve the pasta on the side.

8 ounces low-carb linguine
4 (6-oz) salmon fillets
1 tablespoon butter, melted
   Salt and pepper
¼ cup pesto, or to taste

1. Preheat oven to 450°F. Cook pasta according to package directions. Rinse and drain.

2. Meanwhile, place salmon in a sprayed shallow baking pan. Brush with butter. Sprinkle with salt and pepper. Bake 8 to 10 minutes or until cooked through.

3. Toss pasta with pesto. Spoon onto a large serving platter and arrange fillets over top.

Per serving: 496 Cal, 18g Fat, 43g Pro, 1g Sug, 9g Carb, 4g Fib, **NET CARBS: 5**

Noodles & Ham Casserole

This is somewhat on the dry side, but a nice change from our much-loved cream pastas.

6   ounces low-carb penne
⅓   cup green onions, sliced
1   teaspoon oil
1   cup (4-oz) diced ham
2   tablespoons sliced almonds
½   cup plus 2 tablespoons grated Parmesan cheese

1. Cook pasta according to package directions. Rinse and drain.
2. Preheat oven to 350°F. Toss onion with oil in a large skillet and cook until soft. Add ham and almonds; heat through. Add pasta and 1/2 cup of Parmesan. Pour into a sprayed 1-1/2-quart deep casserole. Sprinkle with remaining cheese. Bake about 15 minutes or until heated through.

Per serving: 258 Cal, 8g Fat, 16g Pro, 1g Sug, 9g Carb, 4g Fib, **NET CARBS: 5**

Chicken Linguine

Serve with toasted bread triangles.

8   ounces low-carb linguine
4   chicken breast halves, skinned, boned
1   tablespoon oil
½   cup chopped green onion
1   cup whipping cream
½   cup grated Parmesan cheese

1. Cook pasta according to package directions. Rinse and drain.
2. Meanwhile, slice chicken crosswise into narrow strips. Toss with oil. Add to a heated large skillet and cook over medium heat until cooked through, adding onions during last couple minutes of cooking time. (May have to cook chicken in 2 batches.)
3. Add cream and cook 4 to 5 minutes or until slightly thickened. Add Parmesan and cook until melted. Place pasta on serving plates and top with chicken mixture.

Per serving: 403 Cal, 22g Fat, 26g Pro, 1g Sug, 8g Carb, 3g Fib, **NET CARBS: 5**

Chicken Linguine with Pesto

Lots of color in this pasta dish.

8   ounces low-carb linguine
2   chicken breast halves, skinned, boned
1   tablespoon oil
¼   cup pesto, or to taste
1   Plum tomato, coarsely chopped
¼   cup grated Parmesan cheese

1. Cook pasta according to package directions. Rinse and drain.
2. Meanwhile, cut chicken crosswise into narrow strips. Heat oil in a large skillet and cook chicken, over medium-high heat, stirring frequently.
3. Add pesto and tomatoes. Add pasta and heat through. Sprinkle with Parmesan cheese.

Per serving: 394 Cal, 15g Fat, 24g Pro, 2g Sug, 10g Carb, 4g Fib, **NET CARBS: 6**

Linguine with Smoked Salmon

MAKES 8 SERVINGS

*Try this recipe when you want a great meal,
but have very little time to cook.*

16 ounces low-carb linguine
¼ cup butter
1 cup whipping cream
¾ cup grated Parmesan cheese
    Freshly ground black pepper
8 ounces smoked salmon, cubed or flaked

1. Cook pasta according to package directions. Rinse, drain and return to pot.
2. Melt butter in a small saucepan. Add cream and heat through. Gradually add the Parmesan cheese, stirring to melt. Add to the pasta. Season with pepper to taste and add salmon. Cook over low heat about 2 minutes. There will be quite a bit of sauce in the pan, but the pasta will gradually absorb most of it.

Per serving: 410 Cal, 21g Fat, 16g Pro, 1g Sug, 10g Carb, 4g Fib, **NET CARBS: 6**

Crab & Spinach with Linguine

MAKES 4 SERVINGS

*A quick and easy pasta dish with a
creamy mild-flavored cheese sauce.*

8 ounces low-carb linguine
½ cup whipping cream
5 ounces Brie cheese, skin removed, diced
½ cup shredded fresh spinach
8 ounces cooked crab, flaked, heated
2 tablespoons grated Parmesan cheese

1. Cook pasta according to package directions. Rinse and drain.
2. Meanwhile, during the last 5 minutes of cooking time, heat whipping cream in a small saucepan. Slowly add the Brie, stirring after each addition, until melted.
3. Place pasta in a large bowl. Add cheese sauce and spinach and toss quickly to coat. Spoon onto a serving platter and top with crab. Sprinkle with Parmesan cheese.

Per serving: 476 Cal, 28g Fat, 28g Pro, 1g Sug, 10g Carb, 4g Fib, **NET CARBS: 6**

Creamy Chicken Pesto Linguine

MAKES 6 SERVINGS

This recipe has several steps, but it is well worth the effort.

12 ounces low-carb linguine
 4 chicken breast halves, skinned, boned
 2 tablespoons plus ½ cup butter
 1 tablespoon plus ¼ cup pesto
 ½ cup heavy cream
 ⅓ cup grated Parmesan cheese

1. Cook pasta according to package directions. Rinse and drain. Return to pot and keep warm.

2. Meanwhile, cut chicken into bite-size pieces and cook in 2 tablespoons butter, stirring frequently. May have to do in 2 batches. Remove and toss with 1 tablespoon pesto.

3. In a small saucepan, heat the cream. Add the 1/2 cup butter and heat until melted. Gradually add the Parmesan cheese, stirring after each addition until melted.

4. Combine pasta, cream mixture and the 1/4 cup pesto. Spoon onto a large serving platter and top with the chicken.

Per serving: 604 Cal, 36g Fat, 28g Pro, 1g Sug, 10g Carb, 4g Fib, **NET CARBS: 6**

MENU

Creamy Chicken Pesto Linguine
Crisp Green Salad
Chocolate Pots De Créme
8 net carbs per meal.

Cook's Tip There are several brands of pesto on the market. Experiment to find the one you like best or better yet, make your own. See recipe on page 210.

Chicken & Pasta Stir-Fry

MAKES 6 SERVINGS

A colorful pasta dish.

12 ounces low-carb spaghetti, broken into thirds
 3 chicken breast halves, skinned, boned
 ¼ cup soy sauce
 ½ small red and green bell pepper, julienned
    Freshly ground black pepper

1. Cook pasta according to package directions. Rinse and drain.

2. Cut chicken crosswise into narrow strips. Cook in a sprayed nonstick skillet over medium-high heat until cooked through, stirring frequently.

3. Add soy sauce and peppers. Cook until vegetables are just crisp-tender. Season with pepper to taste. Toss with pasta.

Per serving: 270 Cal, 3g Fat, 21g Pro, 3g Sug, 10g Carb, 4g Fib, **NET CARBS: 6**

Cornish Hens & Pasta

MAKES 4 SERVINGS

*The pasta is served as a side dish
with the Cornish hens.*

2   Cornish hens, halved
2   tablespoons oil, divided
½   teaspoon dried rosemary, crushed
¼   teaspoon paprika
8   ounces low-carb linguine

1. Preheat oven to 350°F. Place Cornish hens,
cut-side down, in a sprayed shallow baking pan.
Combine 1 tablespoon of the oil with the
rosemary and paprika and brush over hens. Bake
45 to 60 minutes or until cooked through.
2. Meanwhile, cook pasta according to package
directions. Rinse and drain. Toss with the
remaining 1 tablespoon oil. Spoon onto a
serving platter and top with Cornish hens.

Per serving: 651 Cal, 36g Fat, 41g Pro, 1g Sug,
9g Carb, 4g Fib, *NET CARBS: 5*

Linguine with Chicken Mustard Sauce

MAKES 8 SERVINGS

*The Mild & Creamy Dijon mustard is
milder than regular Dijon and lower in carbs.*

8   ounces low-carb linguine
¾   cup heavy cream
1   tablespoon Mild & Creamy Dijon
     mustard, or to taste
2   cups cubed cooked chicken
2   tablespoons chopped parsley

1. Cook pasta according to package directions.
Rinse, drain and return to pot.
2. Add cream, mustard, and chicken to pasta.
Cook until heated through and most of the liquid
is absorbed, about 3 to 4 minutes. Spoon onto a
serving platter and sprinkle with parsley.

Per serving: 209Cal, 10g Fat, 11g Pro, 1g Sug,
6g Carb, 2g Fib, *NET CARBS: 4*

Stove-Top Ground Beef & Pasta

MAKES 8 SERVINGS

I love this recipe. It is quick, easy and filling.

8   ounces low-carb penne
1   pound lean ground beef
1   cup thick & chunky salsa
1   cup (4-oz) Cheddar cheese, shredded

1. Cook pasta according to package directions.
Rinse and drain well.
2. Meanwhile, brown ground beef in a large
skillet; drain. Add salsa and simmer about 5
minutes or until some of the liquid is reduced.
Add pasta and mix well. Cook until heated
through. Sprinkle cheese over top. Cover and
cook briefly to melt the cheese.

Per serving: 258 Cal, 12g Fat, 16g Pro, 2g Sug,
7g Carb, 2g Fib, *NET CARBS: 5*

Chicken Wings & Pasta

Whole chicken wings should be cut into 3 parts discarding the wing tip section.

30 chicken drummettes
½ teaspoon dry mustard
½ cup brown Sugar Twin®
¼ cup butter, plus 2 tablespoons
½ cup soy sauce
8 ounces low-carb penne

1. If frozen, thaw chicken wings, clean and trim excess fat.
2. Combine mustard, brown sugar, the 1/4 cup butter and soy sauce in a small saucepan. Heat until butter is just melted. Let cool. Put chicken in a large resealable bag and add sauce. Marinate, in refrigerator at least 2 hours, turning bag occasionally.
3. Preheat oven to 350°F. Save 1/4 cup marinade discarding the rest. Place wings, skin-side down, in a large foil-lined shallow baking pan. Pour marinade over chicken. Bake 30 minutes. Turn chicken and bake 15 minutes. Baste with drippings in pan and bake 15 to 20 minutes or until nicely browned.
4. Meanwhile, cook pasta, drain and toss with remaining butter. Serve with chicken wings.

Per serving: 583 Cal, 38g Fat, 29g Pro, 4g Sug, 9g Carb, 3g Fib, **NET CARBS: 6**

Italian Sausage Pasta

This is quite a large recipe. If desired, the recipe can be cut in half.

16 ounces low-carb linguine
1 pound Italian sausage links
½ cup chopped green onion
4 ounces fresh mushrooms, sliced
1 cup whipping cream
½ cup grated Parmesan cheese

1. Cook pasta according to package directions. Rinse, drain and return to pot.
2. Meanwhile, remove casings from sausage and crumble into a large skillet. Cook until almost cooked through. Drain off excess fat. Add onion and mushrooms and cook through. Add cream and bring to a boil. Pour mixture over the pasta. Add Parmesan cheese and toss until well-mixed.

Per serving: 335 Cal, 17g Fat, 12g Pro, 1g Sug, 10g Carb, 4g Fib, **NET CARBS: 6**

Penne & Sun-Dried Tomatoes

This pasta dish should be served immediately or serve chilled as a delicious pasta salad. Not as good reheated.

8 ounces low-carb penne
¼ cup oil-packed sun-dried tomatoes, plus 1 tablespoon of the oil
1 (6.5-oz) jar marinated artichoke hearts, drained

1. Cook pasta according to package directions. Rinse, drain and return to pot.

2. Chop tomatoes and coarsely chop the artichokes. Add to pasta along with the oil.

Per serving: 175 Cal, 5g Fat, 6g Pro, <1g Sug, 9g Carb, 4g Fib, **NET CARBS: 5**

Ham-Noodle Casserole

MAKES 8 SERVINGS

A quick economical meal.

8   ounces low-carb penne
½   cup sliced green onions
2   large eggs, lightly beaten
1   cup sour cream
¾   cup (3-oz) Swiss cheese, shredded
1½ cups cubed ham

1. Cook pasta according to package directions. Rinse and drain.

2. Preheat oven to 350°F. Cook onion in a small sprayed skillet until just tender.

3. Combine eggs and sour cream. Add onion, cheese and ham. Add pasta and mix well. Pour into a sprayed 2-quart casserole. Cover and bake 30 minutes. Uncover and bake 10 to 15 minutes or until heated through.

Per serving: 258 Cal, 12g Fat, 15g Pro, 1g Sug, 7g Carb, 2g Fib, **NET CARBS: 5**

Sausage-Pasta Casserole

MAKES 8 SERVINGS

A great tasting casserole that can be ready to eat in less than an hour.

6   ounces low-carb penne
1   (12-oz) package sausage
4   ounces fresh mushrooms, sliced
1   cup low-carb spaghetti sauce
1   cup (4-oz) Mozzarella cheese, shredded

1. Preheat oven to 350°F. Cook pasta according to package directions. Rinse and drain.

2. Meanwhile, brown the sausage in a large skillet. Add mushrooms toward the end of cooking time and cook 2 or 3 more minutes; drain.

3. Add spaghetti sauce and bring to a boil. Reduce heat and simmer about 5 minutes. Add pasta and mix well. Pour into a sprayed 8x8-inch baking dish and sprinkle with cheese. Bake 15 to 20 minutes or until cheese is lightly browned.

Per serving: 223 Cal, 12g Fat, 10g Pro, 2g Sug, 7g Carb, 2g Fib, **NET CARBS: 5**

Spaghetti Cheese Casserole

Thank goodness there is a good low-carb pasta on the market. We can now enjoy some of our favorite pasta dishes. This easy family casserole makes at least 12 generous servings.

12   **ounces low-carb spaghetti**
1   **pound lean ground beef**
2½   **cups low-carb spaghetti sauce**
2   **cups (8-oz) Cheddar cheese, shredded**
2   **cups (8-oz) Mozzarella cheese, shredded**

1. Cook pasta according to package directions. Rinse, drain and return to pot.

2. Preheat oven to 350°F. Meanwhile, cook ground beef in a large skillet; drain. Add spaghetti sauce and bring to a boil. Reduce heat and simmer 10 to 15 minutes to blend flavors.

3. Combine meat mixture with the pasta. This doesn't mix very well so you will need to rearrange some of the meat in the casserole.

4. Spoon half the pasta in a sprayed deep 13x9-inch baking dish. Top with half of each cheese. Add remaining pasta. Sprinkle with remaining cheese. Dish will be quite full. Bake 20 to 30 minutes or until heated through.

Per serving: 359 Cal, 20g Fat, 20g Pro, 2g Sug, 8g Carb, 3g Fib, ***NET CARBS: 5***

Pesto Pasta Frittata

This recipe reminds me of a good quiche, but made with pasta. Serve as a brunch, lunch or supper dish.

6   **ounces low-carb spaghetti**
6   **large eggs, lightly beaten**
3   **tablespoons pesto, or to taste**
1   **cup (4-oz) Mozzarella cheese, shredded**
⅓   **cup grated Parmesan cheese**

1. Preheat oven to 350°F. Cook pasta according to package directions. Rinse, drain and spoon into a sprayed 10-inch quiche dish or pie dish.

2. Combine eggs, pesto, and Mozzarella cheese; pour over pasta. Sprinkle with Parmesan and bake 20 minutes or until set.

Per serving: 283Cal, 14g Fat, 18g Pro, 1g Sug, 6g Carb, 2g Fib, ***NET CARBS: 4***

Casserole Dish or Baking Dish Do you know the difference?

A **Casserole Dish** is usually a round, square or oval deep dish and is referred to in quart sizes such as a 2-quart casserole dish.

A **Baking Dish** is usually rectangle, square or oval and is a shallow dish no more than 2 to 3 inches deep. They are usually referred to in measurements such as a 13x9-inch baking dish or pan.

Ham-Penne Casserole

*A little bit of ham goes a long way
in this easy dinner casserole.*

16 ounces low-carb penne
½ cup butter, divided
3 tablespoons flour
½ cup heavy cream
½ pound ham, diced
¾ cup grated Parmesan cheese, divided

1. Preheat oven to 350°F. Cook pasta according to package directions. Rinse, drain and return to pot.

2. Meanwhile, melt 2 tablespoons of the butter in a medium saucepan. Add flour and stir until smooth. Cook about 1 minute, stirring frequently. Remove from heat; add cream and 1 cup water. Cook over low heat until thickened, stirring frequently.

3. Add the remaining butter to the sauce and stir to melt. Add ham and 1/2 cup of the Parmesan cheese. Add to pasta and mix thoroughly. Pour into a sprayed 13x9-inch baking dish. Sprinkle with remaining 1/4 cup Parmesan cheese. Bake 20 to 30 minutes or until heated through.

Per serving: 301 Cal, 15g Fat, 14g Pro, 1g Sug, 8g Carb, 3g Fib, **NET CARBS: 5**

Spaghetti-Sausage Dish

*There aren't too many pasta dishes
that reheat well, but this one is an exception.*

8 ounces low-carb spaghetti
1 (12-oz) package sausage
¼ cup heavy cream
2 tablespoons canned diced green chilies
1 cup (4-oz) Monterey Jack cheese, shredded

1. Cook pasta according to package directions. Rinse and drain.

2. Meanwhile, brown sausage in a large skillet; drain off fat.

3. Add cream and 1/4 cup water and bring to a boil. Remove from heat and add green chilies and cheese. Add pasta and toss to mix.

Per serving: 509 Cal, 27g Fat, 26g Pro, 1g Sug, 10g Carb, 4g Fib, **NET CARBS: 6**

Slow Cooker Macaroni & Cheese

Prepare and keep hot in your slow cooker.

2½ cups low-carb elbow macaroni
2   large eggs, lightly beaten
1   tablespoon prepared mustard
⅛   teaspoon pepper
1   cup heavy cream
4   cups (16-oz) Cheddar cheese, shredded

1. Cook pasta according to package directions. Rinse and drain. Add to a sprayed slow cooker.

2. Combine eggs, mustard, pepper, cream, and 1 cup water. Add to pasta and mix well. Add cheese. Cover. Cook on HIGH 2 hours or until heated through and the cheese has melted. Stir after 1 to 1-1/2 hours, stirring the outer edges into the center.

3. Cook just until hot in the center and the mixture is nice and creamy. After that, the cheese might separate somewhat. It will still taste good, but it may not look as good.

Per serving: 345 Cal, 25g Fat, 15g Pro, <1g Sug, 4g Carb, 1g Fib, *NET CARBS: 3*

Slow Cooker Carbonara

By cooking the final stages of this recipe in a slow cooker, you can rest assured the eggs will be cooked through.

12 ounces low-carb spaghetti
12 slices bacon, cooked, crumbled
½   cup butter
3   large eggs, lightly beaten
¾   cup grated Parmesan cheese

1. Cook pasta according to package directions. Rinse and drain, but save 1/2 cup of the liquid. Place pasta in a sprayed slow cooker.

2. Add remaining ingredients and mix well. If mixture seems a little dry, add some of the reserved pasta water. Cover. Cook on LOW to finish cooking the eggs and to keep the pasta hot, about 1 hour.

Per serving: 471 Cal, 26g Fat, 19g Pro, 1g Sug, 10g Carb, 4g Fib, *NET CARBS: 6*

Slow Cooker Chicken Linguine

MAKES 6 SERVINGS

Such an easy recipe. Aren't slow cookers wonderful for our busy lifestyles!

½   **cup butter, plus 3 tablespoons**
1   **cup heavy cream**
1   **cup grated Parmesan cheese**
¼   **teaspoon pepper**
3   **chicken breast halves, skinned, boned**
8   **ounces low-carb linguine**

1. Place the 1/2 cup butter, cream, Parmesan cheese and pepper in a sprayed slow cooker. Cover. Cook on LOW about 45 minutes. All you really need to do is melt and blend the ingredients together.

2. Meanwhile, cut chicken into bite-size pieces and cook in the 3 tablespoons butter in a large skillet (may have to do in 2 batches). Drain and set aside.

3. Cook pasta according to package directions. Rinse and drain. Add to slow cooker along with the chicken. Serve or keep hot until ready to serve.

Per serving: 575 Cal, 41g Fat, 24g Pro, 1g Sug, 8g Carb, 3g Fib, *NET CARBS: 5*

Slow Cooker Spaghetti & Chicken

MAKES 8 SERVINGS

There's only one thing to say about this recipe. Delicious! You use the slow cooker to keep the pasta hot until ready to serve.

16   **ounces low-carb spaghetti**
4   **chicken breast halves, skinned, boned**
½   **cup oil, divided**
2   **large garlic cloves, minced**
¼   **cup chopped parsley**
½   **cup grated Parmesan cheese**

1. Cook pasta according to package directions. Rinse, drain and place in a sprayed slow cooker.

2. Meanwhile, cut chicken into 1/2-inch slices. Toss with 1 tablespoon oil. Heat remaining oil in a large skillet. Sauté chicken over medium-high heat, stirring almost constantly. Do in 2 batches. Just before chicken is cooked through, add the garlic and parsley. When cooked, pour into slow cooker. (Also, include oil from chicken.)

3. Add cheese and mix well. If mixture seems somewhat dry, add a little oil. Cover and keep hot on LOW until ready to serve. Should be able to keep at least an hour.

Per serving: 401 Cal, 17g Fat, 23g Pro, 1g Sug, 10g Carb, 4g Fib, *NET CARBS: 6*

Slow Cooker Ham & Pasta

MAKES 6 SERVINGS

The most time consuming part of this recipe is cooking the pasta. The rest is easy.

12   ounces low-carb linguine
¼   cup butter
½   cup heavy cream
⅓   cup sliced green onions, green part
1   cup diced ham
½   cup grated Parmesan cheese

1. Cook pasta according to package directions. Rinse and drain. Add pasta and butter to sprayed slow cooker and toss to melt the butter. Add remaining ingredients along with 1/2-cup water.
2. Cover. Cook on LOW until heated through but probably no longer than an hour, or it will tend to get a little dry. If this should happen, stir in additional cream.

Per serving: 391 Cal, 19g Fat, 16g Pro, 1g Sug, 10g Carb, 4g Fib, *NET CARBS: 6*

Slow Cooker Broccoli Pasta

MAKES 6 SERVINGS

Serve recipe as a side dish.

8   ounces penne
4   cups frozen broccoli florets, do not thaw
¼   cup olive oil
1   small garlic clove, minced
¼   teaspoon crushed red pepper
½   cup plus 2 tablespoons grated Parmesan cheese

1. Add pasta and broccoli to boiling water and cook pasta according to package directions. Rinse and drain. Place in a sprayed slow cooker along with the oil, garlic, red pepper and the 1/2-cup Parmesan cheese. Sprinkle with remaining 2 tablespoons cheese. Cover. Cook on LOW, at the most, 2 hours.

Per serving: 256 Cal, 12g Fat, 9g Pro, 1g Sug, 9g Carb, 4g Fib, *NET CARBS: 5*

Slow Cooker

Slow Cooker Tips

One thing I have learned about slow cookers is that each one has its own personality. I have 4 slow cookers and each one cooks at a different temperature, even identical models made by the same company. Today's slow cookers cook much faster than the models of the 70's and 80's. If you have purchased a new slow cooker, check the temperature and if it cooks too hot, return it and try another one.

You can check your slow cooker by using the water method. Fill with 2 quarts of water. Cover and heat on LOW for 8 hours. Then use on accurate thermometer to check the temperature. The ranges of my slow cookers are 185° to 218° with the 185° slow cooker being the one I like best. If you are happy with your slow cooker, use the recipes here as a guideline. When you make a recipe for the first time, jot down the cooking time. This will be very helpful the next time you make the recipe.

Since slow cookers come in various sizes, you have to be the judge as to what size best fits your needs. Most of these recipes were done in a 4-quart or a 5-quart slow cooker. They weren't always full so some recipes could accommodate a smaller size. If you haven't yet purchased a slow cooker or are thinking of buying a new one, I would suggest a 5-quart oval-shaped slow cooker. That size will cover most of your cooking needs and the recipes in this book.

Remember

1 hour on HIGH = 2 hours on LOW

Don't peek! We are curious creatures, but valuable heat is lost each time we lift the lid, extending the cooking time by about 20 minutes.

Easy Chocolate Sauce

MAKES 3 CUPS

About the most delicious chocolate sauce there is. If possible, use a 3-1/2 quart or smaller slow cooker.

2   cups whipping cream
12 ounces low-carb dark chocolate

1. Place ingredients in slow cooker. Cover. Cook on LOW 1 to 1-1/2 hours. Stir until smooth. Pour into a container and chill. Mixture will thicken as it cools.

Per tablespoon: 65 Cal, 6g Fat, <1g Pro, 0g Sug, 1g Carb, <1g Fib, *NET CARBS: 1*

White Hot Chocolate

MAKES 10 SERVINGS

By using a slow cooker, you don't have to worry about the white chocolate getting too hot.

3½ cups heavy cream
12 ounces low-carb white chocolate, broken up
1   teaspoon vanilla extract

1. Place ingredients in slow cooker along with 4-1/2 cups of water. Cover. Heat on LOW 2 to 2-1/2 hours or until chocolate has melted and mixture is hot. Stir well to blend.

variation: Just before serving, add 1 to 2 cups hot coffee.

Per serving: 327 Cal, 34g Fat, 2g Pro, 0g Sug, 2g Carb, 0g Fib, *NET CARBS: 2*

Hot Cocoa

MAKES 8 CUPS

Prepare a pot of cocoa and serve toppings on the side.

½   cup unsweetened cocoa
18 packets Splenda®
1½ cups heavy cream
1   teaspoon vanilla extract

1. Combine cocoa and Splenda in slow cooker.
2. Combine cream with 6-1/2 cups water. Gradually stir into sugar mixture. Cover. Cook on LOW 3 to 4 hours. Stir in vanilla.

Per cup: 180 Cal, 18g Fat, 2g Pro, 0g Sug, 7g Carb, 1g Fib, *NET CARBS: 6*

Hot Artichoke Dip

MAKES ABOUT 2-1/4 CUPS

This is good.

1   (14-oz) can artichoke hearts, drained
1   (4-oz) can chopped green chilies
1   cup mayonnaise
1   cup grated Parmesan cheese

1. Combine ingredients in a small slow cooker. Cover. Cook on LOW 1 hour or until heated through. Watch carefully after 30 minutes; if over-heated the mixture can separate.

note: If you don't have a small slow cooker, double the recipe or heat in a saucepan.

Per 1/4 cup: 230 Cal, 22g Fat, 4g Pro, <1g Sug, 3g Carb, <1g Fib, *NET CARBS: 3*

Beefy-Cheese Dip

MAKES 4 CUPS

This is good, too!

1   pound lean ground beef
1   teaspoon chili powder
1   teaspoon Worcestershire sauce
½   cup chopped green onion
1   (16-oz) package American cheese, shredded
1   (10-oz) can diced tomatoes & green chilies

1. Brown ground beef; drain. In slow cooker stir beef, chili powder and Worcestershire sauce.

2. Stir in remaining ingredients. Cover. Cook on LOW 2 to 2-1/2 hours. Do not allow to get too thick.

Per 1/4 cup: 148 Cal, 10g Fat, 10g Pro, <1g Sug, 3g Carb, <1g Fib, **NET CARBS: 3**

Raspberry Almond Brie

MAKES 20 SERVINGS

This appetizer will wow your guests.

1   (19.6-oz) round Brie cheese
1½   tablespoons low-carb raspberry spread
2   tablespoons brown Sugar Twin®
1   tablespoon sliced almonds

1. Remove top rind only from Brie. Place in a shallow dish as close to the size of the Brie as possible. A 7-inch pie tin is perfect.

2. Spread preserves on top of Brie. Sprinkle with brown sugar, then almonds. Place in slow cooker. Cover. Cook on LOW 1 to 1-1/2 hours or until heated through. Do not overcook or cheese will be too runny. Serve with low-carb crackers or tortillas.

Per 2 tablespoons: 98 Cal, 9g Fat, 6g Pro, <1g Sug, <1g Carb, 0g Fib, **NET CARBS: <1**

Nacho Cheese Sauce

MAKES 8 CUPS

*We almost always have a cool July 4th',
so this is a popular hot dip.*

16   ounces processed cheese spread, cubed
2   cups (8-oz) Cheddar cheese, shredded
3½   cups thick and chunky salsa
1   cup sliced ripe olives

1. Combine ingredients in slow cooker. Cover; cook on LOW 3 to 4 hours or until heated through.

Per 1/4 cup: 78 Cal, 6g Fat, 4g Pro, 0g Sug, 2g Carb, <1g Fib, **NET CARBS: 2**

Texas Chili

MAKES 6 SERVINGS

Delicious served over hot dogs.

2   pounds lean ground beef
1   cup chopped onion
2   small green peppers, chopped
1   (28-oz) can diced tomatoes
1½ teaspoons chili powder
2   teaspoons salt

1. Brown ground beef and onion; drain. Place in slow cooker along with remaining ingredients. Cover; cook on LOW 4 to 5 hours.

Per serving: 304 Cal, 19g Fat, 25g Pro, <1g Sug, 8g Carb, 2g Fib, *NET CARBS: 6*

Ground Beef & Vegetable Soup

MAKES 12 CUPS

My favorite ground beef soup.

1   pound lean ground beef
½   cup chopped onion
2   (14.5-oz) cans Italian stewed tomatoes
2   cups frozen low-carb vegetables
    Salt and pepper to taste

1. Brown ground beef and onion; drain. Add to slow cooker along with remaining ingredients and 2-1/2 cups water. Cover. Cook on LOW 3 to 4 hours to blend flavors.

Per cup: 129 Cal, 8g Fat, 8g Pro, 4g Sug, 6g Carb, 2g Fib, *NET CARBS: 4*

Ground Beef & CabbageSoup

MAKES 10 CUPS

Don't forget to make your favorite soups in a slow cooker.

1   pound lean ground beef
½   cup chopped onion
2   (14.5-oz) cans diced stewed tomatoes
½   small cabbage, thinly sliced
    Salt and pepper to taste

1. Brown ground beef and onion; drain. Add to slow cooker along with remaining ingredients and enough water to cover, or to a soup consistency. Cover. Cook on LOW 7 to 8 hours or until cabbage is tender. Add salt and pepper.

Per cup: 155 Cal, 10g Fat, 9g Pro, 4g Sug, 8g Carb, 2g Fib, *NET CARBS: 6*

Southwestern Chili

MAKES 6 CUPS

This is good -- but very hot!

2   pounds lean ground beef
2   (10-oz) cans Diced Tomatoes & Green
    Chiles
1½ teaspoons salt
1   tablespoon chili powder, or to taste
½   cup water

1. Brown ground beef; drain. Add remaining ingredients and add to slow cooker. Cover. Cook on LOW 4 to 5 hours.

Per cup: 417 Cal, 31g Fat, 27g Pro, 0g Sug, 4g Carb, 3g Fib, *NET CARBS: 1*

Ground Beef Stew

A hearty flavorful stew.

2   **pounds lean ground beef**
1   **(14.5-oz) can Italian stewed tomatoes, cut-up**
4   **ounces tiny pearl onions, about 20**
4   **ounces small whole mushrooms, halved**
½   **teaspoon dried basil**
    Salt and pepper, to taste

1. Brown ground beef; drain. Add to slow cooker along with remaining ingredients. Cover. Cook on LOW 2-1/2 to 3 hours.

Per serving: 300 Cal, 19g Fat, 25g Pro, 3g Sug, 6g Carb, 1g Fib, **NET CARBS: 5**

Asparagus Cheese Soup

MAKES 5 SERVINGS

This soup is too good to reserve for just special occasions. Can make ahead and reheat.

8   **ounces asparagus, trimmed**
½   **cup butter**
¼   **cup flour**
2   **(14-oz) cans chicken broth**
    Pepper to taste
8   **ounces Brie cheese**

1. Cut asparagus into 1-inch pieces. Cook asparagus in melted butter in a large saucepan. Stir in flour and cook 2 minutes. Gradually add broth, mixing until smooth. Add pepper. Bring to a boil, reduce heat and simmer 15 minutes.

2. Blend half the soup at a time in blender; watch carefully, soup is very hot. Also, make sure the lid is on tight.

3. Pour into slow cooker. Remove rind from Brie, cube and add to slowcooker. Cover. Cook on LOW 1 to 1-1/2 hours or until cheese has melted.

tip: In this recipe, very little time is spent in the slow cooker, but the cheese melts nicely without the chance of it separating.

Per serving: 351 Cal, 31g Fat, 12g Pro, 1g Sug, 7g Carb, 1g Fib, **NET CARBS: 6**

Italian Sausage Soup

MAKES 7 CUPS

Chock full of meat and vegetables.

1   **pound Italian sausage**
⅓   **cup chopped onion**
1   **small green pepper, diced**
1   **(14.5-oz) can diced tomatoes**
2   **(14-oz) cans beef broth**
1   **cup frozen green beans**

1. Brown sausage, onion and pepper; drain. Place in slow cooker along with tomatoes and broth. Last hour of cooking time, add green beans. Cover. Cook on LOW 7 to 8 hours.

Per cup: 76 Cal, 4g Fat, 7g Pro, 2g Sug, 5g Carb, 1g Fib, **NET CARBS: 4**

Beef Chuck Steak

MAKES 10 SERVINGS

This recipe is for times when we are gone all day.

1   (4-lb) beef chuck steak
½   cup chopped onion
1   (14.5-oz) can stewed tomatoes
1   medium carrot, thinly sliced
    Salt and Pepper

1. Trim roast of excess fat. Add onion to slow cooker, then beef, tomatoes and carrot slices. Sprinkle with salt and pepper. Cover. Cook on LOW 14 to 16 hours or HIGH 7 to 8 hours.

Per 4 oz serving: 369 Cal, 23g Fat, 36g Pro, 2g Sug, 3g Carb, <1g Fib, *NET CARBS: 3*

BBQ Roast Beef

MAKES 8 SERVINGS

I haven't found a purchased low-carb barbecue sauce that is nearly as good as the barbecue sauce recipe on page 209.

1   (3-lb) beef chuck roast
¾   cup low-carb barbecue sauce
½   cup chopped onion

1. Trim roast of excess fat and place in slow cooker. Add barbecue sauce and onion. Cover. Cook on LOW 10 to 12 hours or until meat is very tender.

Per 4 oz serving: 382 Cal, 26g Fat, 30g Pro, 1g Sug, 3g Carb, 0g Fib, *NET CARBS: 3*

Beef Chuck Roast

MAKES 8 SERVINGS

Leftover meat makes a great sandwich.

1   (3-lb) beef chuck roast
1   cup chopped onion
¼   cup cider vinegar
2   medium garlic cloves, minced
1   teaspoon salt
¼   teaspoon pepper

1. Trim roast of excess fat and place in slow cooker. Combine remaining ingredients and pour over roast. Add 1/2-cup water. Cover. Cook on LOW 10 to 12 hours or until tender. When serving, use broth to moisten.

Per 4 oz serving: 338 Cal, 22g Fat, 33g Pro, <1g Sug, <1g Carb, 0g Fib, *NET CARBS: <1*

Barbecue Ribs

MAKES 3 SERVINGS

Ribs are tender, moist and delicious.

1½   racks of baby back ribs
¾   cup low-carb Barbecue Sauce, see page 209

1. Cut ribs into 2-rib sections. Brush with barbecue sauce and place as many of the ribs as you can, meaty-side out, around the pot. Place remaining ribs in the center. Cover. Cook on LOW 8 to 9 hours Serve with sauce, if desired.

Per 8 oz serving: 409 Cal, 31g Fat, 25g Pro, 2g Sug, 5g Carb, 0g Fib, *NET CARBS: 5*

Barbecued Pot Roast

A nice slow-cooking roast.

1   (3-lb) beef chuck roast
1   cup low-carb ketchup
½   cup chopped onion
2   teaspoons Worcestershire sauce
2   tablespoons brown Sugar Twin®

1. Trim roast of excess fat and place in slow cooker.
2. Combine remaining ingredients with 1/2 cup water and pour over roast. Cover. Cook on LOW 10 to 12 hours.

Per 4 oz serving: 344 Cal, 22g Fat, 33g Pro, <1g Sug, 1g Carb, 0g Fib, **NET CARBS: 1**

Dilly Pot Roast

MAKES 8 SERVINGS

Save money and make broth from bouillon.

1   (3-lb) beef chuck roast
1   teaspoon garlic salt
1   teaspoon paprika
½   teaspoon dill weed
¼   cup beef broth
1   small onion, sliced

1. Trim roast of excess fat and place in slow cooker. Sprinkle with seasonings. Add broth. Scatter onion around sides of roast. Cover. Cook on LOW 9 to 10 hours.

Per 4 oz serving: 342 Cal, 22g Fat, 33g Pro, <1g Sug, 1g Carb, <1g Fib, **NET CARBS: 1**

Slow Cooker Swiss Steak

MAKES 8 SERVINGS

Nice for a casual dinner.

1   (3-lb) beef round steak
1   cup chopped onion
1   (14.5-oz) can diced tomatoes
½   green pepper, cubed
1   teaspoon salt
½   teaspoon Worcestershire sauce

1. Trim meat of excess fat and cut into 6 serving size pieces. Add meat along with remaining ingredients to slow cooker. Cover. Cook on LOW 8 to 10 hours.

Per 4 oz serving: 256 Cal, 10g Fat, 37g Pro, 2g Sug, 3g Carb, <1g Fib, **NET CARBS: 3**

Spicy Pot Roast

MAKES 10 SERVINGS

Serve with Mock Mashed Potatoes, page 246.

1   (4-lb) beef chuck shoulder roast
¾   teaspoon salt
¾   teaspoon pepper
2   teaspoons paprika
¼   teaspoon dry mustard

1. Rinse roast and pat dry. Combine remaining ingredients and rub over meat, coating all sides. Place in slow cooker and add 1/2 cup water. Cover. Cook on LOW 10 to 12 hours.

Per 4 oz serving: 350 Cal, 23g Fat, 34g Pro, 0g Sug, 0g Carb, 0g Fib, **NET CARBS: 0**

Medium-Rare Roast Beef

MAKES 8 SERVINGS

Yes, you can cook a medium-rare roast in a slow cooker. Don't pour wine over meat or baste with drippings. Why? The top of the meat will turn an odd off-white color. This may not happen with all wines, but will with a merlot-type wine.

1   **(3-lb) sirloin tip roast**
½   **cup coarsely chopped onion**
1   **garlic clove, chopped**
½   **cup dry red wine**
    Salt and pepper

1. Rinse roast and pat dry. Add onion, garlic and wine to slow cooker.
2. Add roast and sprinkle with salt and pepper. Cover. Cook on LOW 7 to 8 hours or to 140°F. Remove and cover lightly with foil. Let stand 10 to 15 minutes before slicing.

Per 4 oz serving: 246 Cal, 11g Fat, 33g Pro, <1g Sug, 1g Carb, 0g Fib, *NET CARBS: 1*

Slow Cooker Tri-Tip Roast

MAKES 8 SERVINGS

A popular roast whether cooked in the slow cooker or in the oven.

1   **(2½-lb) Tri-Tip roast**
    Salt and pepper
1   **medium onion, sliced**
¼   **cup beef broth**

1. Trim roast of excess fat and place in slow cooker. Sprinkle with salt and pepper. Add onion and broth. Cover. Cook on LOW 8 to 9 hours or until very tender.

Per 4 oz serving: 212 Cal, 9g Fat, 30g Pro, <1g Sug, 1g Carb, <1g Fib, *NET CARBS: 1*

Beef Round Tip Roast

MAKES ABOUT 8 SERVINGS

This recipe can be in the slow cooker in less than 10 minutes.

1   **(3½-lb) beef round tip roast**
1   **(0.7-oz) package Italian dressing mix**
1   **(1.1-oz) package Au Jus mix**
1   **(14-oz) can beef broth**

1. Place roast in slow cooker.
2. Combine remaining ingredients and add to slow cooker. Cover. Cook on LOW 9 to 10 hours or until meat is tender.

note: If desired, the broth can be thickened with a little cornstarch.

Per 4 oz serving: 199 Cal, 7g Fat, 31g Pro, <1g Sug, 0g Carb, 0g Fib, *NET CARBS: 0*

Busy Day Roast

MAKES 8 SERVINGS

If you are on maintenance and can afford the carbs, strain the broth and use it for French Dip sandwiches.

1   (3½-lb) beef bottom round roast
1   cup chopped onion
½   cup dry white wine
1   (1.1 oz) package Au Jus mix
2   cups beef broth

1. Trim fat from roast. Place in slow cooker and add onion.
2. Combine wine, Au Jus mix and broth. Pour over meat. Cover. Cook on LOW 9 to 10 hours or until meat is tender.

Per 4 oz serving: 263 Cal, 10g Fat, 38g Pro, <1g Sug, 2g Carb, <1g Fib, *NET CARBS: 2*

Sirloin Tip Roast

MAKES 10 SERVINGS

Serve with a gravy, if desired.

1   (4-lb) sirloin tip roast
1   teaspoon salt
½   cup chopped onion
½   cup dry red wine
1   (14.5-oz) can diced tomatoes

1. Trim roast of excess fat and place in slow cooker along with remaining ingredients. Cover. Cook on LOW 10 to 12 hours.

Per 4 oz serving: 248 Cal, 11g Fat, 31g Pro, 2g Sug, 3g Carb, <1g Fib, *NET CARBS: 3*

Ribs for Two

MAKES 2 SERVINGS

These come out nicely browned and very tasty.

1   small rack baby back ribs, about 12 ribs
    Salt and pepper

1. Sprinkle ribs generously with salt and pepper. Place, meat-side up, in one layer in slow cooker. Cover. Cook on LOW 7 to 8 hours or until tender and browned.

Per 8 oz serving: 387 Cal, 31g Fat, 25g Pro, 0g Sug, 0g Carb, 0g Fib, *NET CARBS: 0*

Ribs and Sauerkraut

MAKES 2 SERVINGS

I've put just about everything else with sauerkraut, so we might as well do ribs too.

1   small rack baby back ribs, about 12 ribs
    Salt and pepper
1   (14-oz) can sauerkraut, drained
¼   cup chopped onion
2½ tablespoons brown Sugar Twin®
½   teaspoon caraway seeds

1. Trim ribs of excess fat. Sprinkle with salt and pepper. Cut in half, crosswise.
2. Add remaining ingredients to slow cooker. Arrange ribs on top, meaty-side up. Add 1/4-cup water. Cover. Cook on LOW 5 to 6 hours.

Per serving: 428 Cal, 31g Fat, 27g Pro, 4g Sug, 10g Carb, 5g Fib, *NET CARBS: 5*

Meatloaf Dijon

MAKES 6 SERVINGS

Meat must be cooked to 160°.

1½   pounds lean ground beef
⅓   cup low-carb soft white bread crumbs
½   cup finely chopped onion
⅓   cup low-carb ketchup
1   tablespoon Mild & Creamy Dijon mustard
1   large egg, lightly beaten

1. Gently combine all ingredients until well mixed. Place in slow cooker and form into a loaf about the size of bottom of pot. Cook on LOW 5 to 6 hours or until meat reaches 160°.

Per serving: 230 Cal, 15g Fat, 19g Pro, 1g Sug, 4g Carb, 1g Fib, **NET CARBS: 3**

Beefy Squash Boats

MAKES 4 SERVINGS

A nice light meal, all in one.

1   pound lean ground beef
½   cup chopped onion
½   cup coarsely chopped green pepper
1   teaspoon salt
1   cup (4-oz) Cheddar cheese, shredded
2   (8-oz) yellow crookneck squash

1. Brown ground beef, onion and pepper; drain. Sprinkle with salt and half the cheese.
2. Cut squash in half lengthwise. Scoop out centers. Place in slow cooker and fill with meat mixture. Spoon extra meat around squash. Cover. Cook on LOW 3-1/2 to 4 hours or until squash is just tender.
3. Sprinkle with remaining cheese. Cover and cook until melted, about 5 minutes.

Per serving: 346 Cal, 23g Fat, 26g Pro, <1g Sug, 8g Carb, 2g Fib, **NET CARBS: 6**

Soft Taco Casserole

MAKES 8 SERVINGS

Instead of baking in the oven you can bake in the slow cooker. Cooking time is short.

1   pound lean ground beef
1   small green pepper, cubed
½   cup thick and chunky salsa
8   (7-inch) low-carb white tortillas
½   cup sour cream
1½   cups (6-oz) Cheddar cheese, shredded

1. Brown ground beef and green pepper in a medium skillet; drain. Add salsa.
2. Spread each tortilla with 1 tablespoon sour cream. Spoon 2 tablespoons meat mixture on each tortilla and roll to secure filling. Place seam-side down in slow cooker.
3. Spoon remaining meat mixture over tortillas. Sprinkle with cheese making sure tortillas are completely covered. Cover. Cook on LOW 1-1/2 to 2 hours or until heated through.

Per serving: 270 Cal, 19g Fat, 20g Pro, <1g Sug, 13g Carb, 8g Fib, **NET CARBS: 5**

Beef Stroganoff

MAKES 4 SERVINGS

*We can now have stroganoff served
over delicious low-carb pasta.*

1   (1½-lb) top sirloin steak
1   cup chopped onion
1   (14-oz) can beef broth
¼   teaspoon salt
¼   teaspoon pepper
1   cup sour cream

1. Cut meat crosswise into slightly less than
1/4-inch slices. If slices are too long, cut in half.
Place in slow cooker along with onion, broth, salt
and pepper. Cover. Cook on HIGH 3-1/2 to 4
hours or until meat is tender. Watch carefully last
half hour of cooking time.
2. Add sour cream and cook until heated
through.

Per serving: 398 Cal, 25g Fat, 37g Pro, 2g Sug,
7g Carb, 1g Fib, **NET CARBS: 6**

Sweet-Sour Meatballs

MAKES 60 MEATBALLS

*In order for the sauce to thicken, this recipe
must be cooked on HIGH.*

2   pounds lean ground beef
2   cups low-carb ketchup
1   cup brown Sugar Twin®
1   tablespoon prepared mustard
2   teaspoons Worcestershire sauce
2   teaspoons soy sauce

1. Preheat oven to 425°F. Shape meat into 1-
inch balls and place in a shallow baking pan.
Bake 15 minutes or until lightly browned. Drain
on paper towels and place in slow cooker.
2. Combine remaining ingredients and pour
over meatballs. Cover. Cook on HIGH 1-1/2 to
2 hours or until sauce has thickened.

Per 5 meatballs: 155 Cal, 9g Fat, 12g Pro, 2g Sug,
4g Carb, 0g Fib, **NET CARBS: 4**

Country Style Ribs

MAKES 6 SERVINGS

*A relatively inexpensive cut of meat that is
flavorful and tender when slow cooked.*

2½   pounds country style pork ribs with bone
½   cup brown Sugar Twin®
1   cup low-carb ketchup
1   tablespoon Worcestershire sauce
1   tablespoon prepared mustard
¼   cup lemon juice

1. Place ribs in slow cooker. Combine remaining ingredients and pour over ribs. Cover. Cook
on LOW 6 to 7 hours. Serve the sauce over the
meat.

Per serving: 316 Cal, 22g Fat, 24g Pro, 1g Sug,
4g Carb, 0g Fib, **NET CARBS: 4**

Pork Roast

*This cut of pork has more fat in it,
but it is also very flavorful.*

1   **(3-lb) Boston pork butt roast**
     Salt and pepper
     Garlic salt
     Paprika

1. Place roast in slow cooker (no liquid).
Sprinkle with remaining ingredients. Cover.
Cook on LOW 10 to 12 hours or until meat is
tender enough to slice or cook a little longer if
you want to shred the meat.

Per 4 oz serving: 264 Cal, 16g Fat, 27g Pro, 0g Sug,
0g Carb, 0g Fib, **NET CARBS: 0**

Ham & Cheese Casserole

MAKES 8 SERVINGS

Serve for brunch or dinner.

2   **cups cubed ham**
¼   **cup sliced green onions**
1   **cup (4-oz) Pepper Jack cheese, shredded**
12   **large eggs, lightly beaten**
1   **cup heavy cream**

1. Place ham, onion and cheese in slow cooker.
Combine eggs, cream and 1 cup water. Pour
over cheese. Cover. Cook on HIGH 2-1/2 to 3
hours or until center is set.

Per serving: 324 Cal, 25g Fat, 22g Pro, 1g Sug,
2g Carb, <1g Fib, **NET CARBS: 2**

Pork & Sauerkraut

MAKES 6 SERVINGS

*For a milder sauerkraut flavor,
rinse well and drain.*

1   **(3-lb) boneless pork loin**
     Salt and pepper
1   **(32-oz) jar sauerkraut, well drained**
1½   **teaspoons caraway seeds**
1½   **cups (6-oz) Swiss cheese, shredded**

1. Remove fat and silver skin from pork.
Sprinkle with salt and pepper. Place in slow
cooker and add 1/2-cup water. Cover. Cook on
LOW 4 hours. Remove meat and discard liquid.

2. Combine remaining ingredients. Add all but
1 cup to slow cooker. Add pork and spoon
remaining mixture over top of meat. Cover. Cook
on LOW 1 to 2 hours or until meat reaches 140°.
It should be tender at this point, and not over-
cooked.

Per 4 oz serving: 324 Cal, 14g Fat, 41g Pro, 3g Sug, 8g
Carb, 4g Fib, **NET CARBS: 4**

Swiss Dogs & Sauerkraut

MAKES 4 SERVINGS

This could become a family favorite.

1   (32-oz) jar sauerkraut, well drained
1½ teaspoons caraway seeds
8   hot dogs
1½ cups (6-oz) Swiss cheese, shredded

1. Combine sauerkraut and caraway seeds in slow cooker. Add hot dogs and sprinkle with cheese. Cover. Cook on LOW 3-1/2 to 4 hours.

Per serving: 605 Cal, 48g Fat, 33g Pro, 4g Sug, 10g Carb, 5g Fib, **NET CARBS: 5**

Slow Cooked Ham

MAKES ABOUT 8-10 SERVINGS

If you can't get the lid on, cover slowcooker with heavy-duty foil, pressing around edges to seal.

1   (5 to 6-lb) ham
½   cup brown Sugar Twin®
½   teaspoon dry mustard
2   tablespoons orange juice

1. Place ham, cut-side down, in slow cooker. Cover. Cook on LOW 4 to 5 hours or until temperature reaches 130°F.
2. Combine remaining ingredients and brush over ham. Cover. (The carbs in the orange juice aren't counted because most of it ends up in the liquid in the pot.) Cook on HIGH 20 to 30 minutes or until meat reaches 140°.

Per 4 oz serving: 183 Cal, 6g Fat, 28g Pro, <1g Sug, 1g Carb, 0g Fib, **NET CARBS: 1**

Barbecued Pork Chops

MAKES 4 SERVINGS

Easy!

4   (½-inch thick) pork chops
½   cup Barbecue Sauce, page 209

1. Place pork chops in slow cooker. Pour sauce over top. Cover. Cook on LOW 6 to 7 hours.

Per serving: 222 Cal, 11g Fat, 24g Pro, 2g Sug, 4g Carb, 0g Fib, **NET CARBS: 4**

Corned Beef Brisket

MAKES 6 SERVINGS

So tender.

1   (3-lb) corned beef brisket
    Seasoning salt
½   cup onion, chopped
3   Plum tomatoes, chopped
1   cup beef broth

1. Sprinkle meat generously with seasoning salt. Brown, fat-side down, in a large skillet, turning once.
2. Add onion and tomatoes to slow cooker. Add meat, then the broth. Cover. Cook on HIGH 6 to 7 hours. Thinly slice across the grain.

Per 4-oz serving: 297 Cal, 22g Fat, 21g Pro, 1g Sug, 3g Carb, 1g Fib, **NET CARBS: 2**

Paprika Drumsticks

MAKES 8 SERVINGS

Drumsticks are great between meal snacks.

8   **chicken legs, skinned**
1   **medium onion, sliced**
2   **teaspoons oil**
1   **teaspoon salt**
½   **teaspoon pepper**
2   **teaspoons paprika**

1. Add onion to slow cooker. Top with chicken legs, in one layer as much as possible.
2. Combine remaining ingredients with 1 teaspoon water and brush on chicken. Cover. Cook on LOW 7 to 8 hours.

Per serving: 126 Cal, 6g Fat, 16g Pro, 1g Sug, 2g Carb, 1g Fib, *NET CARBS: 1*

Busy Day Chicken Legs

MAKES 8 SERVINGS

If desired, substitute 8 large chicken thighs.

8   **chicken legs, skinned**
    Paprika
    Garlic salt
    Lemon pepper

1. Place chicken in slow cooker in one layer as much as possible. Sprinkle with seasonings (do not add liquid). Cover. Cook on LOW 7 to 8 hours. The chicken should be nicely browned.

Per serving: 265 Cal, 15g Fat, 30g Pro, 0g Sug, 0g Carb, 0g Fib, *NET CARBS: 0*

Slow Cooker Chicken

MAKES 6 SERVINGS

If desired, substitute chicken parts for the whole chicken.

1   **(4-lb) chicken**
⅔   **cup coarsely chopped onion**
½   **cup coarsely chopped celery**
½   **cup sliced carrots**
    Salt and pepper

1. Place chicken in slow cooker. Add 1 cup water. Place vegetables around chicken. Sprinkle with salt and pepper.
2. Cover. Cook on LOW 7 to 8 hours or until thigh temperature reaches 170°. Remove skin before serving.

Per 4 oz serving: 214 Cal, 8g Fat, 31g Pro, 1g Sug, 3g Carb, 1g Fib, *NET CARBS: 2*

Roast Chicken

MAKES 8 SERVINGS

1   **(5-lb) chicken**
1   **teaspoon oil**
1   **teaspoon Italian herbs**
¼   **teaspoon pepper**

1. Brush chicken with oil. Sprinkle with herbs and pepper. Place in slow cooker and add 1/4-cup water. Cover. Cook on LOW 8 to 10 hours or until thigh temperature reaches 170°. Remove skin before serving.

Per 4 oz serving: 215 Cal, 8g Fat, 31g Pro, 0g Sug, 0g Carb, 0g Fib, *NET CARBS: 0*

Roast Chicken Pesto

MAKES 6 SERVINGS

I think pesto goes with almost anything.

1   (4-lb) chicken
½   cup pesto
    Salt and Pepper

1. Carefully loosen skin covering breast and leg area.
2. Spread pesto under skin. If desired, tie legs with kitchen string. Place chicken in slow cooker and sprinkle with salt and pepper. Cover. Cook on LOW 7 to 8 hours or until thigh temperature reaches 170°.

Per 4 oz serving: 291 Cal, 18g Fat, 30g Pro, <1g Sug, <1g Carb, <1g Fib, *NET CARBS: <1*

Quick Chicken Legs

MAKES 8 SERVINGS

Quick means you have it in the pot in just minutes. For low-carbers, keep these in the refrigerator for a great between meal treat.

8   chicken legs, skinned
    Seasoning salt

1. Place chicken in one layer, if possible, in slow cooker. Sprinkle with seasoning salt. Cover. Cook on LOW 7 to 8 hours.
note: Do not add liquid to slow cooker.

Per serving: 108 Cal, 5g Fat, 15g Pro, 0g Sug, 0g Carb, 0g Fib, *NET CARBS: 0*

Tarragon Chicken

MAKES 4 SERVINGS

Basil or oregano could also be used.

8   small chicken thighs, skinned
⅓   cup chopped onion
4   Plum tomatoes, chopped
1   large garlic clove, minced
½   teaspoon dried tarragon
½   teaspoon salt

1. Place chicken in slow cooker. Add remaining ingredients. Cover. Cook on LOW 6 hours.

Per serving: 236 Cal, 11g Fat, 28g Pro, 2g Sug, 4g Carb, 1g Fib, *NET CARBS: 3*

Barbecue Chicken Legs

MAKES 8 SERVINGS

Flavorful and must be eaten with a fork.

8   chicken legs, skinned
½   cup brown Sugar Twin®
½   cup low-carb ketchup
1   tablespoon Worcestershire sauce
1½   teaspoons prepared mustard
2   tablespoons lemon juice

1. Place chicken in one layer, if possible, in slow cooker. Combine remaining ingredients. Remove 1/3 cup of the mixture and brush over chicken. Save remaining sauce to serve with chicken. Cover. Cook on LOW 7 to 8 hours.

Per serving: 195 Cal, 8g Fat, 26g Pro, 1g Sug, 3g Carb, 0g Fib, *NET CARBS: 3*

Italian Chicken Legs

The brown sugar reduces the acid in the tomato sauce.

8   chicken legs, skinned
1   teaspoon Italian seasoning
1   tablespoon brown Sugar Twin®
1   (8-oz) can tomato sauce
½   cup coarsely chopped onion

1. Place chicken in slow cooker. Add remaining ingredients. Cover. Cook on LOW 7 to 8 hours.

Per serving: 196 Cal, 8g Fat, 26g Pro, 2g Sug, 3g Carb, 1g Fib, *NET CARBS: 2*

Wined Chicken Thighs

MAKES 4 SERVINGS

The brown meat is tender and moist.

4   leg-thigh quarters
1   small onion, sliced
    Salt and pepper
1   (4-oz) can sliced mushrooms, drained
½   cup dry white wine

1. Trim chicken, rinse and pat dry.
2. Place onion in slow cooker. Add chicken. Sprinkle with salt and pepper. Add remaining ingredients. Cover. Cook on LOW 8 to 9 hours or until cooked through.

Per serving: 323 Cal, 14g Fat, 40g Pro, 1g Sug, 3g Carb, 1g Fib, *NET CARBS: 2*

Herb Roast Chicken

MAKES 8 SERVINGS

Use leftovers for salads.

. 1   (5-lb) chicken
1   teaspoon mixed herbs
¼   teaspoon pepper
2   garlic cloves, minced
1   medium onion, sliced, separated

1. Carefully loosen skin covering the breast and leg area (this really isn't difficult). Combine herbs, pepper and garlic. Carefully spread under skin.
2. Place onion in a large (about 5 quart) slow cooker. Add chicken. Cover. Cook on LOW 8 to 10 hours or until thigh temperature reaches 170°.

Per 4 oz serving: 215 Cal, 5g Fat, 33g Pro, 0g Sug, 0g Carb, 0g Fib, *NET CARBS: 0*

Sherried Chicken

MAKES 10 SERVINGS

The sherry adds a lot of flavor.

10 chicken legs
1   medium onion, sliced
4   ounces fresh mushrooms, sliced
½   cup dry sherry
1   teaspoon Italian seasoning

1. Place onion and mushrooms in slow cooker. Top with chicken; add sherry and sprinkle with seasoning. Cover. Cook on LOW 7 to 8 hours.

Per serving: 197 Cal, 8g Fat, 26g Pro, 1g Sug, 2g Carb, <1g Fib, *NET CARBS: 2*

Teriyaki Chicken Thighs

MAKES 8 SERVINGS

A nice change from chicken legs.

8   large chicken thighs
½   cup soy sauce
¼   cup brown Sugar Twin®
1   tablespoon grated fresh ginger
2   medium garlic cloves, minced

1. Place chicken in slow cooker. Combine remaining ingredients and pour over chicken. Cover. Cook on LOW 7 to 8 hours. Strain broth and spoon over top. Remove skin before serving.

Per serving: 116 Cal, 6g Fat, 14g Pro, 0g Sug, 1g Carb, 0g Fib, *NET CARBS: 1*

Sweet-Hot Chicken Thighs

MAKES 8 SERVINGS

Hopefully, more supermarkets will soon be carrying low-carb ketchup.

8   large chicken thighs
½   cup low-carb apricot spread
¼   cup low-carb ketchup
2   tablespoons soy sauce
½   teaspoon hot sauce

1. Place chicken in one layer, in slow cooker.
2. Combine remaining ingredients and spoon over chicken. Cover. Cook on LOW 7 to 8 hours.

Per serving: 176 Cal, 10g Fat, 16g Pro, 0g Sug, 1g Carb, 0g Fib, *NET CARBS: 1*

Curried Chicken Legs

MAKES 8 SERVINGS

The marmalade spread can be found in most supermarkets.

8   chicken legs
¾   cup chopped onion
½   teaspoon curry powder
1   tablespoon butter, melted
¼   cup low-carb apricot spread

1. Place chicken in one layer, if possible, in slow cooker. Sprinkle onion over top.
2. Combine remaining ingredients and spoon over chicken. Cover. Cook on LOW 7 to 8 hours.

Per serving: 297 Cal, 17g Fat, 30g Pro, 0g Sug, 1g Carb, 0g Fib, *NET CARBS: 1*

Slow Cooker Roast Chicken

MAKES 8 SERVINGS

Nice when your cupboard is getting low.

1   (4-lb) chicken
1   medium onion, quartered
    Lemon pepper

1. Place about 1/4 of the onion in cavity of chicken. Place remaining onion in bottom of slow cooker. Add chicken and 1/4 cup water. Sprinkle chicken with lemon pepper. Cover. Cook on LOW 7 to 8 hours or until thigh temperature reaches 170°.

Per 4 oz serving: 215 Cal, 5g Fat, 33g Pro, 0g Sug, 0g Carb, 0g Fib, *NET CARBS: 0*

Apricot Turkey Breast

MAKES 6 SERVINGS

The apricot spread adds few carbs,
but a lot of flavor.

1	(2½-lb) turkey breast half
½	cup low-carb apricot spread
1	tablespoon prepared mustard
2	teaspoons Worcestershire sauce
¼	teaspoon ground pepper

1. Place turkey breast, skin-side up, in slow cooker.

2. Combine remaining ingredients and spread over turkey. Cover. Cook on LOW 8 to 9 hours or until temperature reaches 160°. Remove skin before serving.

Per 4 oz serving: 156 Cal, 3g Fat, 22g Pro, <1g Sug, 1g Carb, 0g Fib, **NET CARBS: 1**

Saucy Chicken Thighs

MAKES 4 SERVINGS

A flavorful slow cooker recipe.

4	large chicken thighs
1	large garlic clove, minced
⅓	cup soy sauce
1½	tablespoons low-carb ketchup

1. Place chicken in slow cooker. Combine remaining ingredients and pour over top. Cover. Cook on LOW 7 to 8 hours. If possible, baste chicken twice during cooking time.

Per serving: 201 Cal, 14g Fat, 16g Pro, 0g Sug, <1g Carb, 0g Fib, **NET CARBS: <1**

Chicken Wings

MAKES 5 SERVINGS

So easy!

10	chicken wings, split
½	cup soy sauce
24	packets Splenda®
¼	teaspoon ground ginger
½	teaspoon hot pepper sauce

1. Place chicken wings in slow cooker. Combine remaining ingredients and pour over top. Cover. Cook on LOW 3-1/2 to 4 hours. If possible, stir wings 2 to 3 times while cooking. This will make for more even browning.

Per serving: 234 Cal, 13g Fat, 21g Pro, 1g Sug, 6g Carb, <1g Fib, **NET CARBS: 6**

Turkey Legs

BASED ON 4-OUNCE SERVINGS

To reduce cooking time, cook on
HIGH 5-1/2 to 6 hours.

3	turkey legs
1	teaspoon oil
	Paprika
	Seasoning salt
	Garlic salt
	Mixed herbs

1. Place turkey legs in slow cooker. Brush with oil. Sprinkle lightly with seasonings. Cover. Cook on LOW 10 to 12 hours.

Per 4 oz serving: 216 Cal, 9g Fat, 32g Pro, 0g Sug, 0g Carb, 0g Fib, **NET CARBS: 0**

Slow Cooker Turkey Thighs

MAKES 6 SERVINGS

If you can't find the turkey thighs, use turkey legs. Use the meat for sandwiches and soups or serve with vegetables and a salad for an easy dinner meal.

3 **pounds turkey thighs, skinned**
   Salt and Pepper

1. Place turkey in slow cooker. Sprinkle with salt and pepper. Cover. Cook on LOW heat 7 to 8 hours.

Per 4oz serving: 212 Cal, 8g Fat, 32g Pro, 0g Sug, 1g Carb, 0g Fib, **NET CARBS: 1**

Turkey Meatloaf

MAKES 8 SERVINGS

You can't fool everyone, but some don't even realize this is ground turkey.

2 **pounds ground turkey**
⅓ **cup finely chopped celery**
½ **cup finely chopped onion**
6 **tablespoons chopped Plum tomatoes**
1 **large egg, lightly beaten**
½ **teaspoon dried Italian herbs**

1. Combine ingredients until blended. Add to slow cooker and form into an 8-inch loaf. Cover. Cook on LOW 5-1/2 to 6 hours or until firm.

Per serving: 207 Cal, 11g Fat, 23g Pro, 1g Sug, 2g Carb, <1g Fib, **NET CARBS: 2**

> ### ☙ Hint ❧
> Fish cooks rather quickly in a slow cooker. The advantage of this method of cooking is that it eliminates last minute watching, freeing you to do other things. Fish that is a thicker cut, and somewhat firm, works best in a slow cooker.

Halibut with Roasted Peppers

MAKES 4 SERVINGS

Easy, tasty, and looks great!

1 **pound halibut fillets**
½ **cup canned roasted red peppers, drained**
2 **tablespoons oil**
3 **to 4 dashes hot pepper sauce**
2 **tablespoons chopped fresh basil**
⅓ **cup grated Parmesan cheese**

1. Place halibut in slow cooker.
2. Place roasted peppers, oil and pepper sauce in a blender and blend until almost smooth (it's nice to have a few small bits of pepper.) Spoon over fish.
3. Combine basil and Parmesan; sprinkle over fish. You may or may not use all the mixture. Cover. Cook on LOW 1-1/2 to 2 hours.

Per serving: 254 Cal, 11g Fat, 28g Pro, 0g Sug, 5g Carb, 0g Fib, **NET CARBS: 5**

Company Salmon Pesto

Here's that pesto again, but it teams well with salmon.

4   (6-oz) salmon fillets
¼   cup pesto

1. Place fillets in slow cooker and brush with pesto. Cover. Cook on LOW 1-1/2 to 2 hours.

Per serving: 278 Cal, 13g Fat, 37g Pro, 0g Sug, 1g Carb, <1g Fib, **NET CARBS: 1**

Salmon in a Pot

MAKES 6 SERVINGS

Cook in a slow cooker while you are preparing the rest of the meal.

1   (1½ to 2-lb) salmon fillet
¼   cup dry white wine
2   tablespoons butter, melted
2   tablespoons fresh lemon juice
1   teaspoon light soy sauce

1. Check for bones before placing salmon in a slow cooker. Combine remaining ingredients and pour over fish. Cover. Cook on LOW 1-1/2 to 2 hours. After first hour of cooking time, watch carefully so as not to overcook.
note: If you don't want to use wine, omit and add 1 minced garlic clove and 2 tablespoons finely chopped fresh basil.

Per serving: 175 Cal, 8g Fat, 23g Pro, <1g Sug, <1g Carb, <1g Fib, **NET CARBS: <1**

Florentine Salmon

MAKES 4 SERVINGS

Fancy enough for company.

4   (6-oz) salmon fillets
2   tablespoons butter
¾   cup sliced mushrooms
⅓   cup sliced green onions
½   bunch fresh spinach
⅓   cup dry white wine

1. Cut a long slit in top of each fillet and spread slightly.
2. Heat butter in a large skillet and quickly cook mushrooms and onion. Add spinach and cook until spinach is just slightly wilted.
3. Fill fillets with spinach mixture. Place in slow cooker and add wine. Cover. Cook on LOW 1-1/2 to 2 hours.

Per serving: 280 Cal, 12g Fat, 36g Pro, 1g Sug, 3g Carb, 1g Fib, **NET CARBS: 2**

Fillet of Sole

MAKES 4 SERVINGS

Lots of flavor from the mushrooms and cheese.

4   sole fillets, about 1 pound
1   medium onion, sliced
2   tablespoons butter
8   ounces mushrooms, sliced
1   cup (4-oz) Swiss cheese, shredded

1. Cook onion in butter until just soft. Add mushrooms and cook until soft. Place half the mixture in slow cooker. Sprinkle with half the cheese.

2. Fold fillets in half or thirds and place over cheese. Top with remaining vegetables and cheese. Cover. Cook on LOW 2 to 2-1/2 hours.

Per serving: 273 Cal, 15g Fat, 29g Pro, 3g Sug, 6g Carb, 1g Fib, **NET CARBS: 5**

Orange Roughy

MAKES 4 SERVINGS

This is a mild white fish similar to cod.

4   **(4-oz) Orange Roughy fillets**
3   **tablespoons fresh lemon juice**
1   **medium garlic clove, minced**
½   **teaspoon dried dill weed**
    Salt and pepper to taste

1. Place fish in one layer in slow cooker. Combine lemon juice, garlic and dill weed; brush over fish. Lightly sprinkle with salt and pepper. Cover. Cook on LOW 1 hour.

note: If using fresh dill weed, sprinkle over fish during last half hour of cooking time.

Per serving: 87 Cal, 1g Fat, 18g Pro, <1g Sug, 1g Carb, 0g Fib, **NET CARBS: 1**

Fajita Vegetables

MAKES 6 SERVINGS

Add beef or chicken and serve in tortillas. Also good served over grilled steaks and hamburgers or as a vegetable tortilla wrap.

2   **medium peppers, 1 red & 1 green, julienned**
2   **medium onions, thinly sliced**
2   **tablespoons oil**
½   **teaspoon paprika**
    Salt and pepper to taste

1. Combine ingredients in slow cooker. Cover. Cook on HIGH 3-1/2 to 4 hours or until vegetables are crisp tender.

Per serving: 65 Cal, 5g Fat, 1g Pro, 3g Sug, 6g Carb, 1g Fib, **NET CARBS: 5**

Green Bean Dish

MAKES 8 SERVINGS

This dish can also be baked in the oven.

3 (14.5-oz) cans green beans, drained
¼ cup finely chopped onion
¼ cup butter, melted
4 teaspoons prepared mustard
2 teaspoons prepared horseradish
3 tablespoons brown Sugar Twin®

1. Place green beans in slow cooker.
2. Heat remaining ingredients in small sauce-pan cooking just until onion is soft. Pour over beans. Cover. Cook on LOW 2-1/2 to 3 hours.
note: My family doesn't like tomatoes added to this dish, but I like to top the beans with 3 to 4 tomato slices and then the sauce.

Per serving: 85 Cal, 6g Fat, 2g Pro, 2g Sug,
7g Carb, 3g Fib, **NET CARBS: 4**

Cheesy Green Beans

MAKES 8 SERVINGS

The flour adds very little to the carb count.

3 (14.5-oz) cans green beans, drained
½ cup finely chopped onion
2 tablespoons butter, melted
1 tablespoon flour
2 cups (8-oz) Monterey Jack cheese, shredded

1. Place green beans and onion in slow cooker. Combine butter and flour and toss with beans.

Add cheese and toss to mix. Cover. Cook on HIGH 3 to 3-1/2 hours, stirring ingredients half-way through, if possible.
note: It is possible to overcook this recipe. Watch carefully last hour of cooking time.

Per serving: 169 Cal, 12g Fat, 8g Pro, 2g Sug,
9g Carb, 3g Fib, **NET CARBS: 6**

Zucchini Casserole

MAKES 8 SERVINGS

Watch carefully to avoid overcooking.

4 medium zucchini
   Salt and pepper
1   medium onion, sliced
1 medium green pepper, sliced
6 Plum tomatoes, sliced
1½ cups (6-oz) Pepper Jack cheese

1. Cut zucchini into 1/2 inch slices. Place in slow cooker. Sprinkle with salt and pepper.
2. Layer onion, green pepper and then toma-toes, sprinkling each layer lightly with salt and pepper. Cover. Cook on LOW 5 to 6 hours or until almost tender.
3. Sprinkle with cheese. Cover and cook until vegetables are tender and cheese is melted, about 30 minutes.

Per serving: 101 Cal, 7g Fat, 5g Pro, 2g Sug,
5g Carb, 1g Fib, **NET CARBS: 4**

Salads, Dressings & Sauces

♟ Green Salads
♟ Spinach Salads
♟ Chicken Salads
♟ Jell-o Salads
♟ Dressings
♟ Sauces
♟ Gravies
♟ Marinades

Artichoke-Olive Salad

MAKES 4 SERVINGS

*Don't have time to boil the eggs?
That's okay, just leave them out.*

8   cups mixed greens
1   (6.5-oz) jar marinated artichokes, drained
¾   cup sliced fresh mushrooms
½   cup sliced ripe olives
⅓   cup no-carb vinaigrette dressing
2   large hard-boiled eggs

1. Combine first 4 ingredients in large bowl. (cut artichokes if too large). Toss with just enough dressing to lightly coat.
2. Cut each egg lengthwise into 4 quarters. Garnish each salad with 2 egg slices.

Per serving: 206 Cal, 18g Fat, 7g Pro, 1g Sug, 8g Carb, 4g Fib, *NET CARBS: 4*

Asparagus-Tomato Salad

MAKES 4 SERVINGS

Simple but good.

4   cups romaine, torn
2   small Plum tomatoes, sliced crosswise
1   pound asparagus, cooked, chilled
½   cup no-carb vinaigrette dressing

1. Place romaine on 4 salad plates. Place asparagus spears on top. Garnish with tomatoes. Drizzle with dressing.

Per serving: 184 Cal, 17g Fat, 3g Pro, 2g Sug, 6g Carb, 3g Fib, *NET CARBS: 3*

Asparagus Salad

MAKES 4 SERVINGS

Three vegetables all in one salad.

8   medium romaine leaves
8   thin tomato slices
8   ounces asparagus, cooked, chilled
2   hard-boiled eggs, quartered
4   tablespoons no-carb vinaigrette

1. Arrange romaine and tomato slices on salad plates. Top with asparagus and eggs and drizzle each with 1 tablespoon vinaigrette.

Per serving: 128 Cal, 11g Fat, 4g Pro, 2g Sug, 3g Carb, 1g Fib, *NET CARBS: 2*

Brie Salad

Other cheeses can be substituted for the Brie.

8   **cups mixed greens**
2   **tablespoons sliced almonds**
⅓   **cup no-carb vinaigrette dressing**
4   **(1-inch) wedges Brie cheese**

1. Preheat oven to 350°F. Combine greens and almonds in a large mixing bowl. Toss with just enough dressing to lightly coat.
2. Place salad on serving plates. Place Brie on a baking sheet and bake about 1 minute, or until warm, but not runny. Top each salad with cheese.

Per serving: 229 Cal, 21g Fat, 8 Pro, 1g Sug, 4g Carb, 3g Fib, **NET CARBS: 1**

Tomato-Tarragon Salad

MAKES 4 SERVINGS

Use a light hand with tarragon.

2   **medium tomatoes, sliced**
1   **tablespoon olive oil**
¼   **cup tarragon wine vinegar**
2   **teaspoons chopped fresh tarragon**
    Freshly ground black pepper

1. Place tomatoes in an 11x7-inch baking dish. Combine oil, vinegar and tarragon and pour over tomatoes. Sprinkle with pepper. Cover. Refrigerate at least 2 hours to blend flavors.

Per serving: 48 Cal, 4g Fat, 1g Pro, 2g Sug, 4g Carb, 1g Fib, **NET CARBS: 3**

Romaine Salad

MAKES 6 SERVINGS

There are times when what you really want is a rather simple, but tasty salad. This one will go with almost any meal.

2   **bunches romaine**
6   **tablespoons oil**
2   **tablespoons apple cider vinegar**
1   **garlic clove, thinly sliced**
½   **teaspoon salt**
⅛   **teaspoon pepper**

1. Tear romaine into bite-size pieces; you should have about 8 cups. Cover and chill.
2. Combine remaining ingredients; let stand at room temperature 1 to 2 hours to blend flavors.
3. Remove garlic and toss romaine with just enough dressing to lightly coat.

Per serving: 133 Cal, 14g Fat, 1g Pro, 1g Sug, 3g Carb, 2g Fib, **NET CARBS: 1**

Green Salad & Pecans

MAKES 4 SERVINGS

For variety top each salad with a few cooked shrimp.

6   **cups assorted greens**
½   **cup coarsely chopped pecans**
1   **tablespoon butter**
½   **cup oil**
¼   **cup red wine vinegar**
    Salt and pepper to taste

1. Place greens in a large salad bowl.
2. In a small skillet, lightly toast pecans in

melted butter; cool slightly. Add to greens.

3. Combine remaining ingredients and toss salad with just enough dressing to lightly coat.

Per serving: 380 Cal, 41g Fat, 3g Pro, 1g Sug, 4g Carb, 3g Fib, **NET CARBS: 1**

Broccoli Salad

MAKES 6 SERVINGS

Splenda® can be substituted for Xylitol, but you will need to add 2 net carbs per serving.

5   **cups small broccoli florets**
1   **cup (4-oz) Monterey Jack cheese, cubed**
½   **cup Xylitol**
1   **cup mayonnaise**
2   **tablespoons white wine vinegar**
8   **slices bacon, cooked, crumbled**

1. Place broccoli and cheese in a large bowl.

2. Combine Xylitol, mayonnaise and vinegar. Let stand a few minutes. The Xylitol will only partially dissolve, but unless you are looking for it, you won't notice it in the salad. Add to broccoli and mix well. Cover and chill 2 to 3 hours, stirring occasionally.

3. Add bacon just before serving.

Per serving: 439 Cal, 39g Fat, 10g Pro, 0g Sug, 4g Carb, 2g Fib, **NET CARBS: 2**

Romaine-Articho

MAKES 8 SERVINGS

A perfect salad with almost any meal.

8   **cups romaine**
1   **(6.5-oz) jar marinated artichoke hearts, drained**
6   **tablespoons oil**
2   **tablespoons garlic red wine vinegar**
¼   **cup grated Parmesan cheese, divided**
8   **cherry tomatoes, halved**

1. Place romaine in a large salad bowl. Cut artichokes into smaller pieces and add to bowl.

2. Combine oil, vinegar and 2 tablespoons of the Parmesan. Toss salad with just enough dressing to lightly coat. Serve on salad plates. Sprinkle with remaining Parmesan and garnish with tomatoes.

Per serving: 128 Cal, 12g Fat, 2g Pro, 1g Sug, 4g Carb, 2g Fib, **NET CARBS: 2**

Mini Chef Salad

MAKES 1 SALAD

Use purchased dressing (no more than 2 carbs per 2 tablespoons) or make recipe on page 203.

3 cups assorted greens
¼ cup sliced mushrooms
2 slices deli ham, julienned
½ cup (2-oz) Cheddar cheese, shredded
¼ cup low-carb Thousand Island dressing

1. Place greens on a dinner plate. Top with ingredients in order given.

Per salad: 548 Cal, 43g Fat, 32g Pro, 2g Sug, 8g Carb, 4g Fib, **NET CARBS: 4**

Spring Shrimp Salad

MAKES 4 SERVINGS

A nice and filling low-carb salad.

6 cups spring greens
4 ounces cooked small shrimp
½ small red onion, thinly sliced
½ cup sugar snap peas
⅓ cup no-carb vinaigrette dressing

1. Combine first 4 ingredients in a salad bowl. Toss with just enough dressing to lightly coat.

Per serving: 149 Cal, 11g Fat, 7g Pro, 2g Sug, 5g Carb, 2g Fib, **NET CARBS: 3**

Italian Tuna Salad

MAKES 4 SERVINGS

Can substitute other vegetables, if desired.

8 cups mixed greens
½ small cucumber, thinly sliced
1 cup small cauliflower florets
1 (6-oz) can tuna in water, drained
½ cup no-carb vinaigrette dressing

1. Place first 4 ingredients in a large salad bowl and toss with just enough dressing to lightly coat.

Per serving: 224 Cal, 18g Fat, 13g Pro, 1g Sug, 5g Carb, 3g Fib, **NET CARBS: 2**

Tuna-Pineapple Salad

MAKES 4 SERVINGS

When your diet is ready for a little pineapple, this makes a nice salad or sandwich.

2 (6-oz) cans tuna, drained
1 (8-oz) can crushed pineapple, drained
½ cup finely chopped celery
2 large hard-boiled eggs, chopped
⅓ cup mayonnaise

1. Combine first 4 ingredients and toss with just enough mayonnaise to lightly coat. Cover and chill before serving.

Per serving: 283 Cal, 19g Fat, 20g Pro, 5g Sug, 6g Carb, 1g Fib, **NET CARBS: 5**

Bacon-Spinach Salad

This is a nice salad served with almost any type of low-carb dressing.

8   cups fresh spinach
8   slices bacon, cooked, crumbled
⅓   cup crumbled Feta cheese
½   cup Ranch-style dressing

1. Combine first 3 ingredients and toss with just enough dressing to lightly coat.

Per serving: 286 Cal, 26g Fat, 10g Pro, 2g Sug, 4g Carb, 1g Fib, **NET CARBS: 3**

Taco Salad with Sour Cream

A quick easy way to serve a salad.

1   pound lean ground beef
1   cup thick and chunky salsa
8   cups shredded lettuce
1   cup (4-oz) Cheddar cheese, shredded
¼   cup Plum tomatoes, chopped
¼   cup sour cream

1. Brown ground beef in medium skillet; drain. Add the salsa. Bring to a boil, reduce heat and simmer 5 to 10 minutes, or until liquid is absorbed.
2. Place meat mixture, lettuce, cheese and tomatoes in a mixing bowl. Toss lightly and serve with a dollop of sour cream.

Per serving: 384 Cal, 27g Fat, 26g Pro, 2g Sug, 7g Carb, 2g Fib, **NET CARBS: 5**

Easy Taco Salad

Who doesn't like a good taco salad.

1   pound lean ground beef
1   cup thick and chunky salsa, divided
8   cups shredded lettuce
1   cup (4-oz) Cheddar cheese, shredded
⅓   cup ripe olives

1. Brown ground beef; drain. Add 3/4 cup salsa. Bring to a boil, reduce heat and simmer 5 to 10 minutes or until liquid is absorbed.
2. Spread 2 cups lettuce on each plate. Top with meat, cheese, remaining salsa and olives.

Per serving: 264 Cal, 25g Fat, 26g Pro, 1g Sug, 7g Carb, 3g Fib, **NET CARBS: 4**

Crisp Green Salad

A very vegetable salad.

4   cups assorted salad greens
8   cherry tomatoes, halved
1   cup small cauliflower florets
½   small green pepper, sliced
½   small cucumber, sliced
¼   cup no-carb vinaigrette dressing

1. Combine first 5 ingredients with just enough dressing to lightly coat.

Per serving: 67 Cal, 6g Fat, 1g Pro, 2g Sug, 3g Carb, 2g Fib, **NET CARBS: 1**

Caesar Salad

Homemade is almost always better, but if using a purchased dressing, watch the carb count.

2   bunches romaine (about 8 cups)
½   cup jicama, julienned
½   cup Caesar Salad Dressing, page 201
3   tablespoons grated Parmesan cheese

1. Tear romaine into bite-size pieces. Place romaine and jicama in a large salad bowl. Toss with just enough dressing to lightly coat. Spoon onto salad plates and sprinkle with cheese.

Per serving: 106 Cal, 9g Fat, 3g Pro, 1g Sug, 4g Carb, 2g Fib, **NET CARBS: 2**

Coleslaw

Don't leave out the cranberries; they add color as well as flavor.

6   cups shredded cabbage
⅓   cup dried cranberries
1   cup mayonnaise
⅓   cup Xylitol, or to taste
2   tablespoons heavy cream

1. Combine cabbage and cranberries.
2. Combine mayonnaise, Xylitol, cream and 1/4 cup water.
3. Toss 3/4 of the mayonnaise mixture with the cabbage. Cover. Chill 1 hour to blend flavors.
4. When ready to serve, add remaining mayonnaise mixture, if cabbage appears dry.

Per serving: 208 Cal, 19g Fat, 1g Pro, 3g Sug, 6g Carb, 1g Fib, **NET CARBS: 5**

Caesar Salads

Although not exactly traditional, you can enhance these wonderful salads by adding your choice of the following items: chicken, turkey, salmon, shrimp, fried oysters, bacon, sun-dried tomatoes, and low-carb penne pasta.

Tossed Salad with Mushrooms

There is a lot of crunch in this salad.

6 cups mixed greens
8 slices bacon, cooked, crumbled
½ cup cubed jicama
½ cup sliced mushrooms
½ cup no-carb vinaigrette dressing
2 tablespoons grated Parmesan cheese

1. Combine first 4 ingredients in a large bowl. Toss with just enough dressing to lightly coat. Arrange on salad plates and sprinkle lightly with Parmesan.

Per serving: 167 Cal, 15g Fat, 5g Pro, 1g Sug, 3g Carb, 2g Fib, *NET CARBS: 1*

Pine Nut-Strawberry Salad

MAKES 6 SERVINGS

Thank goodness, we can now have strawberries.

8 cups fresh spinach
1 cup sliced strawberries
⅓ cup sliced green onion
3 tablespoons pine nuts
½ cup Poppy Seed Dressing, page 203.

1. Combine first 4 ingredients and toss with just enough dressing to lightly coat.

Per serving: 185 Cal, 18g Fat, 2g Pro, 2g Sug, 6g Carb, 2g Fib, *NET CARBS: 4*

Feta Cheese Salad

MAKES 4 SERVINGS

Do try the Raspberry Vinaigrette.

8 cups assorted salad greens
½ small red onion, thinly sliced
½ cup pecan halves, toasted
⅓ cup jicama, julienned
⅓ cup Raspberry Vinaigrette, see page 201
4 tablespoons crumbled Feta cheese

1. Combine first 4 ingredients. Toss with just enough dressing to lightly coat. Place on salad plates and top with cheese.

Per serving: 225 Cal, 21g Fat, 5g Pro, 2g Sug, 8g Carb, 4g Fib, *NET CARBS: 4*

Ham Salad

MAKES 4 SERVINGS

Serve as salad or a sandwich spread.

2 cups (8-oz) cooked ham, ground
1 teaspoon prepared mustard
3 tablespoons finely chopped dill pickles
½ cup (2-oz) Cheddar cheese, diced
½ cup mayonnaise (approximately)

1. Combine first 4 ingredients with just enough mayonnaise to lightly moisten.

Per serving: 349 Cal, 30g Fat, 18g Pro, 0g Sug, 1g Carb, 0g Fib, *NET CARBS: 1*

Raspberry-Spinach Salad

MAKES 4 SERVINGS

The dressing must be chilled before serving.

4   cups fresh spinach
1   cup fresh raspberries
½   cup chopped macadamia nuts
¼   cup Raspberry Vinaigrette, page 201

1. Combine ingredients in salad bowl and toss with just enough dressing to lightly coat.

Per serving: 224 Cal, 22g Fat, 3g Pro, 2g Sug, 8g Carb, 4g Fib, **NET CARBS: 4**

Sweet-Sour Spinach Salad

MAKES 4 SERVINGS

Dressing can be made ahead and chilled. For variety add sliced fresh mushrooms.

8   cups fresh spinach
8   slices bacon, cooked, crumbled
½   of a small red onion, sliced
½   cup mayonnaise
2   packets Splenda®
2   tablespoons white vinegar

1. Place spinach, bacon and onion in a large salad bowl. Combine remaining ingredients and toss salad with just enough dressing to lightly coat. You may not need all the dressing. Do not allow to stand too long before serving.

Per serving: 288 Cal, 28g Fat, 6g Pro, 1g Sug, 4g Carb, 1g Fib, **NET CARBS: 3**

Spinach-Tomato Salad

MAKES 6 SERVINGS

If desired, the eggs can be omitted.

8   cups fresh spinach
2   hardboiled eggs, sliced
12 cherry tomatoes, halved
8   bacon slices, cooked, crumbled
½   cup Ranch dressing

1. Place first 4 ingredients in a salad bowl and toss with just enough dressing to lightly coat.

Per serving: 184 Cal, 16g Fat, 7g Pro, 2g Sug, 4g Carb, 1g Fib, **NET CARBS: 3**

Spinach-Orange Salad

The orange peel adds a lot of flavor.

8   cups fresh spinach
½   cup jicama, julienned
⅓   cup toasted pecan halves
2   teaspoons grated orange peel
⅓   cup no-carb vinaigrette dressing

1. Place first 4 ingredients in a large bowl. Toss with just enough dressing to lightly coat.

Per serving: 121 Cal, 12g Fat, 2g Pro, < 1g Sug, 3g Carb, 2g Fib, **NET CARBS: 1**

Company Spinach Salad

MAKES 6 SERVINGS

A nice touch of color for a special company dinner.

8   cups fresh spinach
½   cup toasted pecan halves
¾   cup strawberries, sliced
½   cup Poppy Seed Dressing, see page 203

1. Combine first 3 ingredients in a large salad bowl. Toss with just enough dressing to lightly coat.

variation: Substitute 1/4 cup pomegranate seeds for the strawberries.

Per serving: 214 Cal, 21g Fat, 2g Pro, 2g Sug, 6g Carb, 2g Fib, **NET CARBS: 4**

Almond-Spinach Salad

MAKES 4 SERVINGS

Don't tell kids there is spinach in this salad and you won't have any problems getting them to eat it.

8   cups fresh spinach
⅓   cup sliced or slivered almonds, toasted
8   slices bacon, cooked, crumbled
½   small red onion, thinly sliced
⅓   cup no-carb vinaigrette dressing

1. Combine first 4 ingredients with just enough dressing to lightly coat.

Per serving: 232 Cal, 21g Fat, 8g Pro, 1g Sug, 5g Carb, 2g Fib, **NET CARBS: 3**

Italian Pepperoni Salad

MAKES 2 SERVINGS

A nice Italian salad.

4   cups mixed greens
½   cup (2-oz) Mozzarella cheese, shredded
⅓   cup small pepperoni slices, halved
¼   cup sliced black olives
¼   cup no-carb vinaigrette dressing

1. Combine first 4 ingredients. Toss with just enough dressing to lightly coat.

Per serving: 440 Cal, 39g Fat, 17g Pro, 1g Sug, 7g Carb, 3g Fib, **NET CARBS: 4**

Coconut Chicken Salad

*If you can afford the carbs, add
1/2 cup drained crushed pineapple.*

4   **cups diced cooked chicken**
½   **cup thinly sliced celery**
½   **cup unsweetened shredded coconut**
½   **teaspoon curry, or to taste**
1   **cup mayonnaise**

1. Combine first 3 ingredients in mixing bowl.
2. Combine curry and mayonnaise. Add just enough mayonnaise to chicken to lightly moisten.

Per serving: 670 Cal, 55g Fat, 36g Pro, 1g Sug, 3g Carb, 2g Fib, **NET CARBS: 1**

Easy Club Salad

Tastes like a club sandwich minus the bread.

   Lettuce leaves
3   **thin slices cooked chicken**
3   **thin slices tomato**
3   **slices bacon, cooked, crumbled**
2   **tablespoons Thousand Island dressing, page 203**

1. Arrange lettuce leaves on salad plate. Top with chicken, tomato slices, then bacon. Drizzle with dressing.

Per serving: 348 Cal, 21g Fat, 34g Pro, 2g Sug, 4g Carb, 1g Fib, **NET CARBS: 3**

Spinach Salad with Chicken

*For variety, add shredded cheese
or sliced mushrooms.*

8   **cups spinach**
1   **cup cubed cooked chicken**
2   **hard-boiled eggs, chopped**
¼   **cup sliced almonds**
½   **cup Sweet Onion Dressing, page 200**

1. Combine first 4 ingredients with just enough dressing to lightly coat.

Per serving: 244 Cal, 20g Fat, 13g Pro, 1g Sug, 5g Carb, 2g Fib, **NET CARBS: 3**

Waldorf Chicken Salad

*Jicama is a very good substitute for the
apples traditionally found in Waldorf salads.*

3   **cups cubed cooked chicken**
⅓   **cup chopped celery**
¾   **cup chopped jicama**
⅓   **cup chopped walnuts**
½   **cup mayonnaise**

1. Combine first 4 ingredients with just enough mayonnaise to moisten. Cover and chill before serving.

Per serving: 253 Cal, 20g Fat, 15g Pro, 0g Sug, 2g Carb, 1g Fib, **NET CARBS: 1**

Chicken-Jicama Salad

Chicken and cabbage combine well to make this delicious salad. If you can afford the carbs, add an 8-oz can crushed pineapple, drained.

1   cup cubed cooked chicken
2   cups shredded cabbage
½   cup cubed jicama
¾   cup coarsely chopped pecans
⅓   cup chopped celery
⅔   cup mayonnaise

1. Combine first 5 ingredients with enough mayonnaise to lightly coat. Cover and chill at least 1 hour before serving.

Per serving: 469 Cal, 47g Fat, 9g Pro, 1g Sug, 7g Carb, 4g Fib, **NET CARBS: 3**

Grilled Chicken Salad

Ranch is a versatile dressing and low in carbs.

4   chicken breast halves, skinned, boned
8   cups romaine lettuce
½   yellow pepper, cut into strips
½   cup jicama, julienned
½   cup Ranch dressing

1. Grill or broil chicken until cooked through.
2. Meanwhile, place lettuce, pepper strips and jicama in a large bowl. Toss with just enough dressing to lightly coat. Place on individual salad plates and top with chicken breasts sliced on the diagonal.

Per serving: 317 Cal, 19g Fat, 28g Pro, 3g Sug, 7g Carb, 3g Fib, **NET CARBS: 4**

Cook's Tip
Leftover cooked chicken can be used for salads, soups, casseroles and sandwiches.

Chicken Pecan Salad

MAKES 3 SERVINGS

This has got to be my favorite chicken salad. Use as a salad on a bed of lettuce, as a sandwich or as a snack on low-carb crackers.

2   **cups cubed cooked chicken**
½   **cup coarsely chopped pecans**
⅓   **cup chopped celery**
½   **cup mayonnaise**

1. Combine first 3 ingredients adding just enough mayonnaise to lightly coat. Chill before serving.

Per serving: 499 Cal, 46g Fat, 20g Pro, 1g Sug, 3g Carb, 2g Fib, *NET CARBS: 1*

Cashew Chicken Salad

MAKES 4 SERVINGS

The cashews add flavor as well as crunch.

2½   **cups cubed cooked chicken**
¼   **cup cashews, chopped**
⅓   **cup thinly sliced celery**
2   **tablespoons finely chopped onion**
    Salt and pepper to taste
⅓   **cup mayonnaise**

1. Combine ingredients, stirring gently to mix. Cover and chill before serving.

Per serving: 276 Cal, 20g Fat, 19g Pro, 1g Sug, 3g Carb, <1g Fib, *NET CARBS: 3*

Club Salad

MAKES 4 SERVINGS

Also good with a low-carb Thousand Island dressing. See page 203.

1½   **cups cubed cooked chicken, white meat**
6   **cups mixed salad greens**
3   **Plum tomatoes, chopped**
⅓   **cup no-carb vinaigrette dressing**
2   **hard-boiled eggs, halved**

1. Place first 3 ingredients in a large salad bowl. Toss with just enough dressing to lightly coat. Garnish with eggs.

Per serving: 218 Cal, 15g Fat, 16g Pro, 2g Sug, 5g Carb, 2g Fib, *NET CARBS: 3*

Swiss Chicken Salad

MAKES 4 SERVINGS

Serve as a salad, a grilled sandwich with low-carb bread or as a low-carb tortilla wrap.

2   **cups cubed cooked chicken**
¼   **cup chopped celery**
½   **cup (2-oz) Swiss cheese, shredded**
⅓   **cup mayonnaise**

1. Combine first 3 ingredients and toss with just enough mayonnaise to lightly coat.

Per serving: 257 Cal, 20g Fat, 17g Pro, <1g Sug, 1g Carb, 0g Fib, *NET CARBS: 1*

Macadamia Chicken Salad

MAKES 6 SERVINGS

If you can afford the carbs, add a few pineapple tidbits to the salad.

4 cups cubed cooked chicken
¾ cup chopped macadamia nuts
½ cup chopped celery
¼ teaspoon ground ginger
1 cup mayonnaise

1. Combine first 3 ingredients.
2. Combine ginger and mayonnaise. Add just enough dressing to chicken mixture to lightly moisten. Cover and chill before serving.

Per serving: 481 Cal, 44g Fat, 19g Pro, 1g Sug, 3g Carb, 2g Fib, *NET CARBS: 1*

Romaine-Hazelnut Salad

MAKES 4 SERVINGS

A nice luncheon salad

1 bunch romaine, bite-size pieces
½ cup cubed cooked chicken
8 slices bacon, cooked, crumbled
½ cup coarsely chopped hazelnuts
½ cup no-carb vinaigrette dressing

1. Combine first 4 ingredients with just enough dressing to lightly coat.

Per serving: 342 Cal, 32g Fat, 12g Pro, 1g Sug, 4g Carb, 3g Fib, *NET CARBS: 1*

Cheesy Chicken Salad

MAKES 4 SERVINGS

Substitute Cheddar with Monterey Jack.

2 cups cubed cooked chicken
½ cup chopped celery
½ cup chopped walnuts
½ cup chopped jicama
½ cup (2-oz) Cheddar cheese, cubed
¾ cup mayonnaise

1. Combine first 5 ingredients with enough mayonnaise to lightly coat. Cover and chill before serving.

Per serving: 534 Cal, 49g Fat, 19g Pro, 1g Sug, 4g Carb, 2g Fib, *NET CARBS: 2*

Cobb Salad

MAKES 4 SERVINGS

Ranch dressing is very low in carbs.

8 cups shredded lettuce
2 cups cubed cooked chicken
1 medium tomato, chopped
2 hard-boiled eggs, chopped
8 slices bacon, cooked, crumbled
½ cup Ranch dressing

1. Arrange lettuce on four plates. Divide rows of chicken, tomato and egg on plates. Sprinkle with bacon and drizzle with dressing.

Per serving: 346 Cal, 24g Fat, 24g Pro, 4g Sug, 7g Carb, 2g Fib, *NET CARBS: 5*

Stuffed Tomatoes

It isn't possible to do the carb count for this recipe-just keep all the carbs low.

Medium tomatoes
Desired filling
Lettuce leaves

1. Remove top from tomatoes and carefully scoop out seeds and meat. Drain on paper towels. Fill with any of the following fillings, or those of your choice. Set tomatoes on lettuce leaves to serve.

- Chicken Salad
- Tuna Salad
- Crab Salad
- Egg Salad
- Cooked vegetables

Tomato only: 33 Cal, <1g Fat, 2g Pro, 5g Sug, 7g Carb, 2g Fib, **NET CARBS: 5**

Mixed Green Salad with Chicken

MAKES 4 SERVINGS

Carbs in purchased dressing should be no more than 2 grams per 2 tablespoons.

8   **cups mixed greens**
1   **cup cubed cooked chicken**
¼   **cup jicama, julienned**
½   **cup no-carb vinaigrette dressing**

1. Combine first 3 ingredients and toss with just enough dressing to lightly coat.

Per serving: 206 Cal, 18g Fat, 8g Pro, 1g Sug, 4g Carb, 3g Fib, **NET CARBS: 1**

Mixed Vegetable Salad

MAKES 6 SERVINGS

I used broccoli, red onion and red peppers but you can choose your own vegetables.

8   **cups mixed greens**
2   **cups mixed fresh vegetables**
1½   **cups cubed cooked chicken**
1   **cup (4-oz) Monterey Jack cheese, cubed**
⅓   **cup Ranch dressing**

1. Combine first 4 ingredients in a large mixing bowl. Toss with just enough dressing to lightly coat.

Per serving: 220 Cal, 14g Fat, 16g Pro, 3g Sug, 8g Carb, 3g Fib, **NET CARBS: 5**

Lemon Fruit Salad

MAKES 8 SERVINGS

*The celery adds a nice crunch,
but can be omitted.*

1   (0.6-oz) package sugar-free lemon gelatin
2   cups diet lemon-lime soda
½   cup raspberries
½   cup sliced strawberries
⅓   cup thinly sliced celery

1. Thoroughly dissolve gelatin in 1 cup boiling water. Add soda. Chill until consistency of unbeaten egg white.
2. Fold in fruit and celery. Pour into an 11x7-inch baking dish. Chill until set.

Per serving: 15 Cal, 0g Fat, 1g Pro, 1g Sug, 2g Carb, 1g Fib, *NET CARBS: 1*

Berry-Berry Fruit Salad

MAKES 8 SERVINGS

Serve as a salad or light dessert.

1   (0.6-oz) package sugar-free strawberry gelatin
1   cup sliced strawberries
1   cup raspberries

1. Prepare gelatin as directed on package. Pour into an 11x7-inch baking dish. Chill until consistency of unbeaten egg whites.
2. Gently fold in berries. Pour into a mold or keep in dish. Chill until set.

Per serving: 23 Cal, <1g Fat, 1g Pro, 2g Sug, 3g Carb, 1g Fib, *NET CARBS: 2*

Strawberry Fruit Salad

MAKES 6 SERVINGS

Use as a dessert or salad.

1   (0.6-oz) package sugarfree strawberry gelatin
1   cup sour cream, room temperature
1   cup chopped strawberries

1. Thoroughly dissolve gelatin in 1 cup boiling water.
2. Add sour cream and whisk until smooth.
3. Add strawberries and pour into an 8x8-inch baking dish. Chill until set.

note: The sour cream may be difficult to blend in. If so, use a rotary beater or mixer on low speed.

Per serving: 102 Cal, 8g Fat, 3g Pro, 1g Sug, 4g Carb, 1g Fib, *NET CARBS: 3*

Lemon-Mayonnaise Dressing

MAKES 1/2 CUP

This is wonderful on a salad of romaine, mushrooms, croutons, and Parmesan cheese.

¼ cup mayonnaise
¼ cup sour cream
1 teaspoon fresh lemon juice
1½ teaspoons Dijon mustard
½ teaspoon dried dill weed

1. Combine ingredients, cover and chill to blend flavors. If too thick, thin with a small amount of cream.

Per 2 tablespoons: 133 Cal, 14g Fat, 1g Pro, 0g Sug, 1g Carb, 0g Fib, **NET CARBS: 1**

Chicken Salad Dressing

MAKES 1 CUP

This is a wonderful dressing for almost any chunky style chicken salad.

⅔ cup mayonnaise
⅓ cup sour cream
1 teaspoon lemon juice
½ teaspoon salt
¼ teaspoon pepper

1. Combine ingredients and mix well.

Per 2 tablespoons: 154 Cal, 17g Fat, <1g Pro, 0g Sug, <1g Carb, 0g Fib, **NET CARBS: <1**

Creamy Mustard Dressing

MAKES 1-1/2 CUPS

A very low-carb dressing.

¼ cup Dijon mustard
¾ teaspoon dried dill weed
¼ cup tarragon wine vinegar
1 cup oil
1 tablespoon Half & Half
1 tablespoon grated Parmesan cheese

1. Combine mustard, dill weed and vinegar. Gradually add oil, whisking after each addition until blended. Stir in Half & Half and Parmesan.

Per 2 tablespoons: 170 Cal, 19g Fat, 1g Pro, 0g Sug, 1g Carb, 0g Fib, **NET CARBS: 1**

Sweet Onion Dressing

MAKES 1 CUP

Especially good on spinach salads and has an added bonus of keeping several days in the refrigerator.

½ cup olive oil
¼ cup cider vinegar
¼ cup finely chopped onion
½ teaspoon prepared mustard
½ teaspoon salt
2 packets Splenda®

1. Combine ingredients, mixing well to blend. Chill until ready to use.

Per 2 tablespoons: 123 Cal, 14g Fat, 0g Pro, 1g Sug, 1g Carb, 0g Fib, **NET CARBS: 1**

Caesar Salad Dressing

MAKES 1-1/4 CUPS

I've narrowed my favorite Caesar dressings down to two. This one and the Creamy Ceasar Dressing.

2   large garlic cloves
1   tablespoon stone ground or Dijon Mustard
1   teaspoon Worcestershire sauce
¼   cup fresh lemon juice
½   cup oil
½   cup grated Parmesan cheese

1. Combine first 4 ingredients in a blender or small food processor, blending until smooth.
2. Slowly add oil until blended.
3. Add cheese and briefly blend. Chill at least one hour to allow flavors to blend.

Per 2 tablespoons: 116 Cal, 12g Fat, 2g Pro, <1g Sug, 1g Carb, 0g Fib, **NET CARBS: 1**

Dijon Vinaigrette

MAKES 1-3/4 CUPS

Will keep about a week in the refrigerator.

1¼   cups oil
⅓   cup Dijon mustard
⅓   cup garlic red wine vinegar
¼   teaspoon ground black pepper

1. Combine ingredients and mix well.

Per 2 tablespoons: 179 Cal, 20g Fat,<1g Pro, 0g Sug, 1g Carb, 0g Fib, **NET CARBS: 1**

Creamy Caesar Dressing

MAKES 1-1/2 CUPS

My second favorite Caesar salad dressing.

1   medium garlic clove
¼   cup fresh lemon juice
1   tablespoon Dijon mustard
1   teaspoon Worcestershire sauce
½   cup grated Parmesan cheese
1   cup mayonnaise

1. Combine first 4 ingredients in a blender or small food processor, blending until smooth (you can do this by hand if you mince the garlic first).
2. Add cheese and mayonnaise and briefly blend. Chill at least one hour to allow flavors to blend.

Per 2 tablespoons: 151 Cal, 16g Fat, 1g Pro, <1g Sug, 1g Carb, 0g Fib, **NET CARBS: 1**

Raspberry Vinaigrette

MAKES 1/2 CUP

A sweet-tart vinaigrette. Can be made in minutes and chilled until ready to serve.

3   packets Splenda®
¼   teaspoon salt
1   teaspoon Dijon mustard
3   tablespoons raspberry wine vinegar
⅓   cup oil

1. Combine ingredients and mix well.

Per 2 tablespoons: 162Cal, 18g Fat, 0g Pro, 0g Sug, 1g Carb, 0g Fib, **NET CARBS: 1**

Red Wine Garlic Dressing

MAKES 3/4 CUP

My favorite sweet-sour dressing.

6   packets Splenda®
1   garlic clove, thinly sliced
⅓   cup red wine vinegar
⅓   cup oil

1. Combine ingredients and chill at least two hours to blend flavors. Remove garlic before using.

Per 2 tablespoons: 111 Cal, 12g Fat, 0g Pro, 0g Sug, 1g Carb, 0g Fib, *NET CARBS: 1*

Quick Roquefort Dressing

MAKES 1 CUP

This is for those of us who prefer a milder Roquefort dressing.

½   cup purchased Roquefort dressing
½   cup sour cream

1. Combine ingredients and mix well.

Per 2 tablespoons: 107 Cal, 11g Fat, 1g Pro, 1g Sug, 2g Carb, 0g Fib, *NET CARBS: 2*

Roquefort Dressing

MAKES 2 CUPS

Great for a salad.
Great as a dip.

4   ounces Roquefort cheese
6   tablespoons Half & Half
1   small garlic clove, minced
2   cups mayonnaise

1. Combine Roquefort and Half & Half in top of a double boiler. Cook over low heat until cheese is melted, stirring until smooth.
2. Add garlic and mayonnaise. Chill overnight to blend flavors. If mixture is too thick, thin with a little Half & Half.

Per 2 tablespoons: 234 Cal, 25g Fat, 2g Pro, 0g Sug, <1g Carb, 0g Fib, *NET CARBS: <1*

Creamy Italian Dressing

MAKES 1-1/4 CUPS

Serve over salads or as a dip with fresh vegetables.

¾ cup sour cream
⅓ cup mayonnaise
1 tablespoon heavy cream
1 (0.6-oz) package Italian dressing mix
2 packets Splenda®
⅛ teaspoon salt

1. Combine ingredients with 3 tablespoons water and mix thoroughly. Chill to blend flavors.

Per 2 tablespoons: 165 Cal, 17g Fat, 1g Pro, 0g Sug, 3g Carb, 0g Fib, *NET CARBS: 3*

Thousand Island Dressing

MAKES 1-1/3 CUPS

Much better than any purchased dressing I have tried. Serve on Mini Chef Salad on page 188.

½ cup mayonnaise
¼ cup heavy cream, whipped
2 tablespoons finely chopped pimiento
¼ cup finely chopped dill pickles
1 tablespoon finely chopped onion
⅓ cup low-carb ketchup

1. Combine ingredients and mix well. Chill to blend flavors.

Per 2 tablespoons: 100 Cal, 11g Fat, <1g Pro, <1g Sug, 1g Carb, 0g Fib, *NET CARBS: 1*

Spinach Salad Dressing

MAKES 2/3 CUP

Goes well with almost any spinach salad.

2 tablespoons Splenda®
2 tablespoons white vinegar
½ cup mayonnaise

1. Combine ingredients and mix well. Chill to blend flavors.

Per 2 tablespoons: 164 Cal, 17g Fat, 0g Pro, 0g Sug, 1g Carb, 0g Fib, *NET CARBS: 1*

Poppy Seed Dressing

MAKES 2/3 CUP

I tuck a little container of this dressing in my purse when I go out for dinner.

½ teaspoon dry mustard
9 packets Splenda®
3 tablespoons white vinegar
½ cup oil
½ teaspoon poppy seeds

1. Combine ingredients and mix thoroughly. Chill at least one hour. Let stand at room temperature about 30 minutes before serving.

Per 2 tablespoons: 203 Cal, 22g Fat,<1g Pro, 0g Sug, 2g Carb, 0g Fib, *NET CARBS: 2*

Easy Vinaigrette

MAKES 1 CUP

This tasty dressing will keep at least a week in the refrigerator. If too tart, decrease vinegar to ¼ cup or add another Splenda packet.

⅔ **cup olive oil**
⅓ **cup cider vinegar**
1 **teaspoon dry mustard**
½ **teaspoon paprika**
¾ **teaspoon salt**
2 **packets Splenda®**

1. Combine ingredients and whisk until blended. Chill to blend flavors.

Per 2 tablespoons: 164 Cal, 18g Fat, <1g Pro, 1g Sug, 1g Carb, <1g Fib, **NET CARBS: 1**

Raspberry Dressing

MAKES 1/2 CUP

A little different, but very good.

2 **tablespoons raspberry vinegar**
2 **tablespoons low-carb raspberry spread**
⅓ **cup oil**

1. Combine vinegar and raspberry spread in a small bowl.
2. Gradually whisk in oil until blended. Cover. Chill at least 1 hour.

Per 2 tablespoons: 170 Cal, 19g Fat, 0g Pro, 0g Sug, 3g Carb, 0g Fib, **NET CARBS: 3**

Coleslaw Dressing

MAKES 1-1/4 CUPS

Very good in almost any type of coleslaw.

1 **cup mayonnaise**
12 **packets Splenda®**
¼ **cup cider vinegar**

1. Combine ingredients. Cover and chill to blend flavors.

Per 2 tablespoons: 276 Cal, 30g Fat, 0g Pro, 1g Sug, 3g Carb, 0g Fib, **NET CARBS: 3**

Orange Butter

MAKES 1/2 CUP

Serve on low-carb French toast,
pancakes or muffins.

$\frac{1}{2}$ cup butter, softened
1 tablespoon fresh orange zest

1. Beat ingredients until well blended.

Per tablespoon: 101 Cal, 11g Fat, <1g Pro, 0g Sug,
<1g Carb, 0g Fib, **NET CARBS: <1**

Cranberry Sauce

MAKES ABOUT 2 CUPS

Our traditional holiday cranberry sauce.

8 ounces fresh cranberries
1 cup Xylitol
$\frac{1}{4}$ cup low-carb apricot spread
2 tablespoons fresh lemon juice

1. Wash cranberries and discard the bad ones.
2. In medium saucepan, combine Xylitol and 6 tablespoons water. Bring to a boil and cook 3 to 4 minutes. Add cranberries and cook 8 to 10 minutes or until cranberries make a popping sound and become transparent.
3. Remove from heat and stir in apricot spread and lemon juice. Cover and chill before serving.

Per 1/4-cup: 92 Cal, 0g Fat, 0g Pro, 1g Sug,
4g Carb, 1g Fib, **NET CARBS: 3**

Chocolate Sauce

MAKES 1-1/4 CUPS

Use for hot chocolate, chocolate
milk, ice cream toppings, etc.

1 cup heavy cream
4 ounces low-carb dark chocolate

1. In a heavy medium saucepan, bring the cream to a boil. Watch carefully since cream has a tendency to boil up quickly.
2. Remove from heat. Add chocolate, stirring until melted and smooth. Store in refrigerator. Mixture will thicken as it cools.

Per tablespoon: 110 Cal, 10g Fat, 1g Pro, 0g Sug,
2g Carb, 1g Fib, **NET CARBS: 1**

Blueberry Sauce

MAKES 2-1/2 CUPS

This is a wonderful sauce on cheesecake
and ice cream, but must be used sparingly.

1 cup Xylitol
$1\frac{1}{2}$ tablespoons cornstarch
1 teaspoon grated lemon zest
3 cups fresh or frozen blueberries

1. Combine Xylitol, cornstarch and lemon zest in a medium saucepan. Gradually stir in 1 cup water. Cook over medium heat until thickened, stirring frequently.
2. Add blueberries. Bring to a boil then remove from heat. Cover and chill.

Per 2 tablespoons: 39 Cal, 0g Fat, <1g Pro, 2g Sug,
4g Carb, 1g Fib, **NET CARBS: 3**

Clarified Butter

MAKES ABOUT 1-1/2 CUPS

Clarified butter keeps longer, doesn't burn when sautéing and has a pure flavor. Should be used for cooking only.

1   **pound unsalted butter**

1. Melt butter in a small saucepan. Pour into a glass measuring cup and let stand a few minutes, then skim off foam. Carefully pour off butter and discard the sediment that settles on the bottom. Cover and refrigerate and use as needed.

Per entire recipe: 3252 Cal, 368g Fat, 4g Pro, 0g Sug 0g Carb, 0g Fib, **NET CARBS: 0**

Crèam Fraîche

MAKES 2 CUPS

Very good over fresh strawberries or molded salads. Also makes a good substitute for sour cream since it doesn't curdle if brought to a boil.

1   **cup heavy cream**
1   **cup sour cream**

1. Combine cream and sour cream in a small bowl. Cover loosely with plastic wrap and let stand at room temperature overnight or until thickened. Bowl should be placed in a warm spot in the kitchen. Chill until ready to use.

Per tablespoon: 41 Cal, 4g Fat, <1g Pro, 0g Sug, 1g Carb, 0g Fib, **NET CARBS: 1**

Creamy Pesto Sauce

MAKES 2/3 CUP

A nice light sauce. If desired, serve as a side with Pesto Chicken Saltimbocca, page 128.

½   **cup heavy cream**
2   **tablespoons pesto, or to taste**

1. Whip cream until thick. Stir in pesto.

Per 2 tablespoons: 111 Cal, 12g Fat, 1g Pro, <1g Sug, 1g Carb, <1g Fib, **NET CARBS: 1**

Sweet Pepper Sauce

MAKES 1 CUP

Serve over chicken breasts, pork chops or fish.

1   **tablespoon oil**
¼   **cup sliced green onions**
1   **garlic clove, minced**
1   **(7-oz) jar roasted peppers, drained, chopped**
1   **cup whipping cream**
1   **tablespoon chopped fresh basil**

1. Heat oil in small saucepan. Sauté onion and garlic for 1 minute. Add remaining ingredients and simmer 4 to 5 minutes, stirring constantly. Drizzle over choice of meat.

Per 2 tablespoons: 142 Cal, 13g Fat, 1g Pro, <1g Sug, 4g Carb, <1g Fib, **NET CARBS: 4**

Pesto Mayonnaise

MAKES 1 CUP

Keep on hand as a spread for sandwiches and wraps and as a topping for hamburgers.

1   cup mayonnaise
1   tablespoon pesto, or to taste

1. Combine ingredients. Cover and store in the refrigerator.

Per tablespoon: 105 Cal, 11g Fat, <1g Pro, 0g Sug, 0g Carb, 0g Fib, **NET CARBS: 0**

Onion-Mushroom Topping

MAKES 4 SERVINGS

A nice topping for hamburgers and meatloaf.

1   medium onion, sliced, separated into rings
1   cup sliced mushrooms
1   tablespoon butter
½   teaspoon Worcestershire sauce

1. Cook onion and mushrooms in butter in a medium nonstick skillet, until just tender. Add Worcestershire sauce and 1 tablespoon water; stir to blend.

Per serving: 41 Cal, 3g Fat, 1g Pro, 2g Sug, 3g Carb, <1g Fib, **NET CARBS: 3**

Tartar Sauce

MAKES 1 CUP

Make ahead and allow time to chill.

¾   cup mayonnaise
1   teaspoon finely chopped onion
1   tablespoon finely chopped parsley
1   tablespoon finely chopped dill pickle

1. Combine ingredients and mix well. Chill at least one hour to blend flavors.

Per tablespoon: 75 Cal, 8g Fat, 0g Pro, 0g Sug, 0g Carb, 0g Fib, **NET CARBS: 0**

Horseradish Sauce

MAKES 3/4 CUP

For a Prime Rib dinner, fill large mushroom caps with sauce; then, top with chopped chives. Bake 10 to 15 minutes at 325°F until heated through.

¼   cup mayonnaise
½   cup sour cream
1½   teaspoons prepared horseradish
¼   teaspoon onion salt
¼   teaspoon garlic salt

1. Combine ingredients and mix well. Chill at least one hour to blend flavors.

Per tablespoon: 54 Cal, 6g Fat, <1g Pro, 0g Sug, <1g Carb, 0g Fib, **NET CARBS: <1**

Tomato-Basil Sauce

MAKES 2-1/2 CUPS

*Serve over meat, chicken, seafood
or low-carb pasta.*

3   tablespoons oil
3   medium garlic cloves, minced
1   (28-oz) can diced tomatoes
     Salt and pepper
1   tablespoon chopped basil or to taste

1. Heat oil in saucepan over low heat. Add garlic and cook until soft but not brown.
2. Add tomatoes, salt and pepper to taste. Cook over medium heat, 12 to 15 minutes, or until thickened, stirring frequently.
3. Add basil and cook for about 2 minutes.

note: If diced tomatoes are too large, process in a blender or food processor. This takes only a second.

Per 1/4 cup: 50 Cal, 4g Fat, 1g Pro, 2g Sug, 3g Carb, 1g Fib, *NET CARBS: 2*

Bordelaise Sauce

MAKES 2 CUPS

*Especially good with steaks,
beef tenderloin and fondue.*

¼   cup minced shallots
4   tablespoons butter, divided
2   bay leaves, finely crumbled
1   cup Burgundy wine
5   teaspoons cornstarch
1½ cups canned, condensed beef broth,
     undiluted

1. In a small saucepan, cook shallots in 2 tablespoons of the butter. They should be tender but not brown.
2. Add bay leaves and wine; simmer over medium heat until reduced to about 1/3 of original volume.
3. Combine cornstarch and 1/4-cup beef broth, mixing to form a smooth paste. Add to wine mixture along with remaining broth. Cook, stirring frequently, until thickened. Add remaining 2 tablespoons butter.

Per tablespoon: 21 Cal, 1g Fat, 0g Pro, 0g Sug, 1g Carb, 0g Fib, *NET CARBS: 1*

Spicy Barbecue Sauce

MAKES 1-1/2 CUPS

Excellent for basting chicken & ribs.

½ cup olive oil
½ cup fresh lemon juice
2 tablespoons Worcestershire sauce
1½ teaspoons hot sauce
2 tablespoons prepared mustard
¼ cup brown Sugar Twin®

1. Combine ingredients in a small saucepan. Bring to a boil and then remove from heat.

Per tablespoon: 44 Cal, 5g Fat, 0g Pro, 1g Sug, 1g Carb, 0g Fib, **NET CARBS: 1**

Barbecue Sauce

MAKES 1 CUP

You should always have this in your refrigerator. Use for ribs, hamburger patties, grilled chicken, pork chops, as a meatloaf topping, etc.

1 cup low-carb ketchup
½ cup brown Sugar Twin®
1 tablespoon Worcestershire sauce
1 tablespoon prepared mustard
½ teaspoon lemon pepper

1. Combine ingredients and let stand at least an hour to blend flavors.

Per tablespoon: 9 Cal, 0g Fat, 0g Pro, 1g Sug, 2g Carb, 0g Fib, **NET CARBS: 2**

Cook's Tip

If using a barbecue sauce with a high sugar content, brush on chicken or meat during last 15 minutes of cooking time.

Chili Barbecue Sauce

MAKES 2 CUPS

Will keep several days in the refrigerator.

¾ cup low-carb ketchup
½ cup butter
¼ cup white vinegar
¾ cup brown Sugar Twin®
4 teaspoons chili powder
2 teaspoons Worcestershire sauce

1. Combine all ingredients in a medium saucepan. Bring to a boil and then remove from heat.

Per 1/4 cup: 119 Cal, 11g Fat, <1g Pro, 2g Sug, 4g Carb, <1g Fib, **NET CARBS: 4**

Mock Hollandaise Sauce

*Serve warm over broccoli, asparagus
or green beans.*

½ cup sour cream
½ cup mayonnaise
2 teaspoons fresh lemon juice
1 teaspoon prepared mustard

1. Combine all the ingredients in a small
saucepan and cook over very low heat until
heated through.

Per tablespoon: 66 Cal, 7g Fat, 0g Pro, 0g Sug,
<1g Carb, 0g Fib, *NET CARBS: <1*

Pesto Sauce

MAKES 1-1/4 CUPS

Make several batches and freeze.

1½ cups packed fresh basil
⅓ cup pine nuts
2 medium garlic cloves
½ cup grated Parmesan cheese
¾ cup oil

1. Blend ingredients in a blender or food
processor, mixing until smooth. Sauce will
thicken as it stands. Store, tightly covered in
refrigerator.

Per tablespoon: 97 Cal, 10g Fat, 1g Pro, <1g Sug,
<1g Carb, <1g Fib, *NET CARBS: <1*

Cheese Sauce

MAKES ABOUT 1-1/2 CUPS

Serve over broccoli or asparagus.

3 tablespoons butter
3 tablespoons flour
⅓ cup heavy cream
2 tablespoons dry sherry
½ cup (2-oz) Cheddar cheese, shredded
½ cup (2-oz) American cheese, shredded

1. Melt butter in a medium saucepan. Stir in
flour and cook 2 minutes, but do not brown. Add
cream and 2/3 cup water. Cook over low heat,
stirring constantly, until thickened.
2. Add sherry and then gradually add the
cheese. Cook until melted and heated through.
Do not allow to boil.

Per tablespoon: 47 Cal, 4g Fat, 1g Pro, 0g Sug,
1g Carb, 0g Fib, *NET CARBS: 1*

Mustard Sauce

MAKES 1-1/4 CUPS

*A nice sauce to serve with ham.
Can make a day ahead.*

1 cup whipping cream, whipped
½ cup mayonnaise
¼ cup prepared mustard

1. Combine ingredients and mix well. Chill at
least 2 hours before serving.

Per tablespoon: 83 Cal, 9g Fat, <1g Pro, 0g Sug,
<1g Carb, 0g Fib, *NET CARBS: <1*

Sun-Dried Tomato Pesto Sauce

MAKES 1-1/2 CUPS

A very nice distinctive tomato flavor.

- ¾ cup oil-packed sun-dried tomatoes, drained
- ¼ cup pine nuts
- 2 medium garlic cloves
- 1 tablespoon minced fresh basil
- 1½ tablespoons fresh lemon juice
- ½ cup oil

1. Blend ingredients in a blender or food processor, mixing until smooth. Store tightly covered in the refrigerator.

Per tablespoon: 57 Cal, 6g Fat, <1g Pro, 0g Sug, 1g Carb, <1g Fib, **NET CARBS: 1**

Pizza Sauce

MAKES ABOUT 1 CUP

An easy but flavorful pizza sauce.

- ¼ teaspoon garlic powder
- ¼ teaspoon oregano
- ½ teaspoon basil
- ½ cup grated Parmesan cheese
- 1 (8-oz) can tomato sauce

1. Combine all the ingredients and mix well.

Per 2 tablespoons: 31 Cal, 2g Fat, 2g Pro, 1g Sug, 2g Carb, <1g Fib, **NET CARBS: 2**

Cream Gravy

MAKES 2 CUPS

Next time you fry chicken, take the time to make this recipe.

- 4 tablespoons fat from frying chicken
- 4 tablespoons flour
- ½ cup heavy cream
  Salt and pepper

1. Leave 4 tablespoons fat in skillet along with crusty bits that stick to the bottom. Add flour and stir until blended. Cook until just lightly browned, stirring constantly.
2. Gradually stir in cream along with 1-1/2 cups water. Continue cooking, stirring frequently, until thickened, about 5 minutes. Add salt and pepper to taste.
3. If gravy is too thick, stir in a little cream. If too thin, add a little flour mixed with water.

Per 1/4 cup: 123 Cal, 12g Fat, 1g Pro, <1g Sug, 4g Carb, <1g Fib, **NET CARBS: 4**

Company Gravy

MAKES 2-1/2 CUPS

Serve with chicken or pork.

½ **cup finely chopped onion**
2 **tablespoons butter**
2 **tablespoons flour**
1½ **cups chicken broth**
½ **cup heavy cream**
¼ **cup dry white wine**

1. In a small saucepan, cook onion in heated butter until soft. Add flour and cook about 2 minutes, stirring frequently.

2. Remove from heat and gradually stir in broth, cream and wine. Bring to a boil, reduce heat and simmer, stirring frequently until mixture has thickened.

note: For added flavor, if you have a small amount of browned bits from a roast or turkey, stir that into the gravy as it boils.

Per 1/4 cup: 75 Cal, 7g Fat, 1g Pro, <1g Sug, 2g Carb, <1g Fib, ***NET CARBS: 2***

Turkey Gravy

MAKES 4 CUPS

Since this recipe makes a lot, this is the one I use for my daughter's Thanksgiving dinner.

½ **cup fat drippings**
½ **cup flour**
4 **cups turkey broth**
  Salt and pepper

1. After turkey is roasted, pour meat juices into a large measuring cup. Remove 1/2 cup of fat that rises to the top. Discard remaining fat, but reserve the broth.

2. Pour fat into a medium saucepan; heat until hot. Gradually stir in flour and cook over medium heat until lightly browned. Gradually add broth, stirring constantly to blend. Cook, stirring frequently, until thickened. Season with salt and pepper to taste.

tip: If you don't have quite 4 cups broth, add water to make up the difference. If the gravy is too thin, add additional flour mixed with a little water. If too thick, thin with additional broth or water.

Per 1/4 cup: 79 Cal, 7g Fat, 1g Pro, <1g Sug, 3g Carb, <1g Fib, ***NET CARBS: 3***

Pot Roast Gravy

MAKES 2 CUPS

Gravy is a must when making a pot roast.

2 **cups liquid from pot roast**
¼ **cup flour**
  Salt and pepper

1. Remove cooked roast from pot. Make sure there is at least 2 cups of liquid remaining in pot.

2. Combine flour and about 1/4 cup water in a small jar and shake vigorously to mix. Add to pot stirring to blend. Cook over medium-low heat until thickened, stirring frequently. Add salt and pepper to taste.

note: If gravy is too thin, add a little more flour and water. If too thick, add beef broth or water.

Per 1/4 cup: 22 Cal, <1g Fat, 2g Pro, <1g Sug, 4g Carb, <1g Fib, ***NET CARBS: 4***

Brining

Brining is a simple way to enhance flavor and make meats and poultry more tender and juicy. Although salt is the key ingredient, the meat will not taste salty. We have not included the carbs in the brining solution because the amount absorbed into the meat, per serving, is negligible.

Brining Solution

MAKES 4 QUARTS

This very simple brining solution can be used for meats, chicken, turkey, etc.

4   quarts water
⅔   cup kosher salt

1. Combine ingredients, stirring until salt is dissolved.

note: Amount of solution needed may vary with each recipe depending on the size of the poultry or meat. There should be enough to cover completely.

Maple Flavored Brine

MAKES 6-1/2 CUPS

There should be enough brine to cover the meat you are cooking.

6   cups water
¼   cup brown Sugar Twin®
½   cup kosher salt
½   cup no-carb maple syrup

Combine ingredients, stirring until salt is dissolved.

Marinades

We have not included the nutritional analysis in marinade recipes because the amount of marinade absorbed into the meat, per serving, is negligible.

Ginger Marinade

MAKES 1 CUP

A good marinade for beef or chicken.

- ⅓ cup soy sauce
- ⅓ cup brown Sugar Twin®
- 2 tablespoons white vinegar
- 1½ tablespoons Worcestershire sauce
- 1 tablespoon olive oil
- 3 slices fresh ginger

1. Combine ingredients and pour over meat. Cover and chill at least 2 hours or overnight.

Easy Beef Marinade

MAKES 1/2 CUP

Use to marinate sirloin, chuck and flank steak.

- ¼ cup soy sauce
- ¼ cup oil
- 2 tablespoons fresh lemon juice
- 1 tablespoon brown Sugar Twin®
- ¼ teaspoon garlic salt
- ⅛ teaspoon oregano

1. Combine ingredients; pour over meat and marinate in refrigerator several hours or overnight, turning occasionally.

Red Wine Marinade

MAKES 1 CUP

An excellent marinade for beef.

- 1 cup dry red wine
- ¼ cup chopped onion
- 1 medium garlic, minced
- ½ teaspoon dried thyme
- ¼ teaspoon black pepper
- ¼ teaspoon salt

1. Combine ingredients in a small saucepan. Bring to a boil, reduce heat and simmer 2 to 3 minutes. Cover and chill. Will keep about a week in the refrigerator.

Herb Marinade

MAKES 1/2 CUP

A good marinade for fish, chicken and meats.

- ¼ cup oil
- 2 tablespoons lemon juice
- 1½ tablespoons dry red wine
- 1 teaspoon dried thyme
- 1 medium garlic clove, minced
- ¼ teaspoon pepper

1. Combine ingredients until blended.

Soups, Sandwiches, Pizza & Wraps

🍳 Soups
🍳 Sandwiches
🍳 Pizza
🍳 Wraps

Oriental Soup

The next time you prepare a large flank steak, remove a 4-ounce portion to save for this quick and flavorful soup.

4 ounces flank steak
1 teaspoon cornstarch
1 packet Splenda®
2 teaspoons soy sauce
2 cups beef broth
2 cups Bok Choy, sliced thin
   (both green and white parts)

1. Cut beef lengthwise (with the grain) into 1-1/2 to 2-inch strips. Cut each strip across the grain into 1/8-inch slices.

2. Combine cornstarch, Splenda and soy sauce. Add meat; cover and marinate 30 minutes.

3. In medium saucepan, bring broth to a boil. Add Bok Choy; cook 1-1/2 to 2 minutes until just crisp-tender. Add meat and cook about 1 minute.

Per cup: 61 Cal, 2g Fat, 8g Pro, <1g Sug, 2g Carb, 1g Fib, *NET CARBS: 1*

Egg Drop Soup

MAKES 3 CUPS

A nice light prelude to a meal.

3 cups chicken broth
2 large eggs, beaten
⅓ cup snow peas, julienned
   Salt and pepper to taste

1. In medium saucepan, bring broth to a boil. Gradually add eggs, stirring briskly after each addition.

2. Add snow peas and cook 1 to 2 minutes. Season with salt and pepper.

Per cup: 77 Cal, 5g Fat, 6g Pro, 1g Sug, 3g Carb, 1g Fib, *NET CARBS: 2*

Company Egg Soup

MAKES 4 CUPS

As you can see, this is low-carb as well as low-fat and low calories.

3 cups chicken broth
2 large eggs, beaten
⅓ cup chopped green onions
¾ cup sliced mushrooms
¼ cup chopped water chestnuts
1 tablespoon soy sauce

1. In a large saucepan, bring broth to a boil. Gradually add the eggs, stirring briskly after each addition.

2. Add remaining ingredients and cook until mushrooms are tender.

Per cup: 68 Cal, 4g Fat, 5g Pro, 1g Sug, 4g Carb, 1g Fib, *NET CARBS: 3*

Shrimp & Mushroom Soup

MAKES 4 CUPS

*A very small amount of carrots adds just
the color this soup needs.*

4   cups chicken broth
¼   cup shredded carrots
2   cups coarsely chopped Bok Choy (both
    white and green part)
¼   cup finely chopped water chestnuts
2   ounces sliced mushrooms
2   ounces tiny cooked shrimp

1. In large saucepan, bring broth to a boil. Add
carrots, Bok Choy, water chestnuts and mushrooms. Bring to a boil; reduce heat and simmer 3
to 4 minutes or until Bok Choy is just crisp
tender.
2. Add shrimp and heat through.

Per cup: 50 Cal, 2g Fat, 5g Pro, 1g Sug,
5g Carb, 1g Fib, **NET CARBS: 4**

Seasoned Chicken Broth

AMOUNT VARIES

*The nutritional analysis will vary but carbs
are zero as all vegetables are discarded
after simmering.*

4   pounds chicken backs and wings
2   large onions, quartered
3   carrots, sliced
3   celery stalks, cut up
    Salt and pepper to taste

1. Place ingredients in a large pot and add
water to cover. Bring to a boil and skim off foam.

Reduce heat and simmer, 2 to 3 hours.
2. Remove chicken and vegetables and discard.
Strain broth and taste for seasoning. Refrigerate
until cool and lift off fat that congeals on top.
Broth is now ready to use or freeze.

Per serving: nutrients will vary, **NET CARBS: 0**

Chicken-Broccoli Soup

MAKES 6 CUPS

A nice creamy cheese soup.

½   cup chopped onion
1   cup cubed cooked chicken
1   cup broccoli florets
1½ cups heavy cream
¼   teaspoon pepper
1½ cups (6-oz) Cheddar cheese, shredded

1. Place onion and 1/2-cup water in a large
saucepan. Cook until tender.
2. Add chicken, broccoli, cream, pepper and
1-1/4cups water. Bring to a boil, reduce heat and
cook until broccoli is tender. Gradually add
cheese, stirring after each addition, until melted.

Per cup: 352 Cal, 32g Fat, 13g Pro, 1g Sug,
4g Carb, 1g Fib, **NET CARBS: 3**

Grilled Cheese Sandwiches

MAKES 2 SERVINGS

Because of the carbs in the bread, I suggest half a sandwich per serving. I know this isn't much, but add a large green salad and you will have a very satisfying meal.

2   slices low-carb white bread
1   tablespoon low-carb raspberry spread
1   tablespoon finely chopped pecans
1   slice Monterey Jack cheese
2   tablespoons butter, melted

1. Spread 1 slice bread with jam. Sprinkle with pecans and top with cheese. Top with bread.
2. Brush each side with butter and cook in sprayed nonstick skillet until toasted, turning once. Slice diagonally.

Per serving: 244 Cal, 19g Fat, 11g Pro, <1g Sug, 9g Carb, 3g Fib, ***NET CARBS: 6***

Barbecue Beef Filling

MAKES 2-1/2 CUPS

Serve in low-carb tortillas, rolls or hamburger buns.

1   pound lean ground beef
½   cup chopped onion
½   cup Barbecue Sauce, page 209

1. Brown ground beef and onion; drain.
2. Add Barbecue sauce and cook 5 minutes or until liquid is absorbed.

Per 1/2 cup: 180 Cal, 11g Fat, 14g Pro, 2g Sug, 4g Carb, <1g Fib, ***NET CARBS: 4***

Bacon-Cheese Melt

MAKES 4 SERVINGS

Kids love these. Serve with a green salad or Baked Tortilla Chips, page 22.

6   slices bacon, cooked, crumbled
2   tablespoons chopped Plum tomatoes
4   slices low-carb white bread
¾   cup (3-oz) Cheddar cheese, shredded

1. Lightly toast bread on one side.
2. Sprinkle bacon and tomatoes on untoasted side. Top with cheese. Broil until cheese is melted and hot.

Per serving: 196 Cal, 12g Fat, 16g Pro, <1g Sug, 7g Carb, 3g Fib, ***NET CARBS: 4***

French Toasted Sandwich

*To reduce carbs, but still have a fulfilling meal,
serve half a sandwich and add a tossed
salad and fresh raw vegetables.*

2   slices deli ham
2   thin slices cheese
4   slices low-carb white bread
2   large eggs, lightly beaten
½   cup heavy cream
2   tablespoons butter

1. Cut ham and cheese to fit and place between bread slices.
2. Combine eggs, cream and 1/3 cup water. Dip sandwiches in mixture. Brown in heated butter, turning once. Cut in half and serve.

note: Add additional butter, if needed.

Per haf sandwich: 317 Cal, 24g Fat, 16g Pro, <1g Sug, 7g Carb, 3g Fib, *NET CARBS: 4*

Mary's Egg & Cheezies

MAKES 6 SERVINGS

*Darlene made these for us for lunch and
they were delicious. A must try.*

4   large hardboiled eggs, shredded
¼   cup chopped green onion
1   cup (4-oz) Cheddar cheese, shredded
½   cup mayonnaise
6   slices low-carb white bread
6   thin tomato slices

1. Preheat oven to 350°F. Combine first 4 ingredients and mix thoroughly. Spread on bread slices and place bread on the oven rack. Bake 6 to 8 minutes or until heated through and bread is toasted. Top each with a tomato slice.

Per serving: 321 Cal, 25g Fat, 16g Pro, 1g Sug, 8g Carb, 3g Fib, *NET CARBS: 5*

Asparagus-Tuna Melt

MAKES 4 SERVINGS

My kids grew up on tuna melts.

1   (6-oz) can tuna, drained
2   tablespoons chopped onion
⅓   cup mayonnaise
4   slices low-carb white bread
4   cooked asparagus spears, halved
4   slices Swiss cheese

1. Preheat oven to 350°F. Combine tuna and onion with just enough mayonnaise to moisten.
2. Spread bread with tuna mixture. Top each with 2 asparagus halves. Top with a cheese slice. Carefully place on oven rack and bake 6 to 8 minutes or until hot.

Per serving: 341 Cal, 24g Fat, 22g Pro, 1g Sug, 8g Carb, 3g Fib, *NET CARBS: 5*

Sloppy Joes

MAKES 8 SANDWICHES

You can prepare filling ahead, but do not assemble sandwiches until ready to serve.

2   **pounds lean ground beef**
1   **cup chopped onion**
¾   **cup low-carb ketchup**
3   **tablespoons prepared mustard**
2   **teaspoons chili powder**

1. In large skillet, brown ground beef and onion; drain. Add remaining ingredients along with 1/2 cup water. Bring to a boil, reduce heat and simmer 15 to 20 minutes or until liquid is absorbed. Serve as a sandwich using low-carb tortillas or bread.

note: Nutritional analysis is based on filling only.

Per serving: 255 Cal, 15g Fat, 18g Pro, 1g Sug, 4g Carb, <1g Fib, *NET CARBS: 4*

Artichoke-Cheese Melts

MAKES 9 SERVINGS

It's up to you, but I like to sprinkle a little salt on my sandwich before baking.

3   **large hardboiled eggs, shredded**
1½ **cups (6-oz) Cheddar cheese, shredded**
1   **(14-oz) can artichoke hearts, chopped**
¼   **cup mayonnaise**
1   **tablespoon Mild & Creamy Dijon mustard**
    low-carb white bread, toasted.

1. Preheat oven to 350°F. Combine ingredients. Spread 1/3 cup on desired number of bread slices, spreading all the way to the edges. Place on baking pan and bake 6 to 8 minutes or until golden. Makes enough spread for 9 slices of bread.

Per slice: 230 Cal, 14g Fat, 15g Pro, <1g Sug, 9g Carb, 3g Fib, *NET CARBS: 6*

Open-Face Cheese Sandwich

MAKES 4 SERVINGS

A nice cool weather sandwich.

4   **slices bacon, halved**
4   **slices low-carb white bread**
2   **tablespoons mayonnaise**
4   **thin tomato slices**
4   **thin onion slices**
4   **slices Cheddar cheese**

1. Cook bacon until cooked through. Drain.
2. Spread bread with mayonnaise. Top with tomato, onion, bacon and cheese. Broil to melt cheese.

Per serving: 265 Cal, 19g Fat, 17g Pro, 1g Sug, 8g Carb, 3g Fib, *NET CARBS: 5*

Pizza Toppings

Pizza Sauce Creations

- Barbecue sauce, Mozzarella cheese, cooked chicken, chopped red onion

- Pizza sauce, Mozzarella cheese, cooked chicken, chopped tomatoes, green onion

- Pizza sauce, Mozzarella cheese, ham, pineapple tidbits (just a few)

- Pizza sauce, Mozzarella cheese and/or Cheddar cheese & cooked sausage, onion, green pepper, red pepper

- Pizza sauce, Mozzarella cheese, chopped Plum tomatoes, fresh basil, Parmesan cheese

- Stewed tomatoes, drained, basil, olive oil

- Pizza sauce, Mozzarella cheese, pepperoni, cooked sausage, mushrooms

- Pizza sauce or olive oil, Mozzarella cheese, artichoke hearts, coarsely chopped onion, green peppers

- Pizza sauce, Mozzarella cheese, red pepper, basil

- Pizza sauce, Mozzarella and Cheddar cheese, artichoke hearts, pepper strips, sliced ripe olives

Classy Little Pizzas

Some of my favorite pizzas use no sauce at all. Just the cheese. I like to use a combination of 70% Mozzarella and 30% Fontina cheese for the base of the pizzas.

Some favorite toppings are:

- Cheese, arugula, Prosciutto, shaved Parmesan cheese, fresh rosemary, olive oil.

- Cheese, pancetta strips, roasted garlic, rosemary, hot pepper flakes.

- Cheese, artichokes, red pepper strips, asparagus, basil, goat cheese.

- Cheese, sliced pancetta, sliced radicchio, hot pepper flakes, parsley.

Artichoke Cheese Pizza

MAKES 4 SERVINGS

A flavorful, not so traditional, pizza.

1   tablespoon oil
4   (7-inch) low-carb tortillas
¾   small onion, sliced
1½ cups (6-oz) Mozzarella cheese, shredded
1   (9-oz) can artichoke hearts, drained

1. Preheat oven to 400°F. Heat oil in medium skillet. Cook onion until soft, stirring frequently. Drain.
2. Place tortillas on a baking sheet and bake 4 to 5 minutes until lightly toasted. Turn over and sprinkle with cheese. Top with onion and artichokes. Cut artichokes if too large. Bake 8 to 10 minutes or until cheese melts.

Per serving: 237 Cal, 15g Fat, 16g Pro, 2g Sug, 18g Carb, 12g Fib, **NET CARBS: 6**

Barbecue Chicken Pizza

MAKES 2 SERVINGS

A nice after school snack.

2   (7-inch) low-carb tortillas
2   tablespoons Barbecue Sauce, page 209
1   cup cubed cooked chicken
¾   cup (3-oz) Cheddar cheese, shredded
1½ tablespoons chopped green onion

1. Preheat oven to 425°F. Place tortillas on baking sheet and bake 4 minutes. Turn over.

2. Spread with barbecue sauce. Top with remaining ingredients. Bake 8 to 10 minutes or until cheese melts.

Per serving: 303 Cal, 18g Fat, 29g Pro, 1g Sug, 14g Carb, 8g Fib, **NET CARBS: 6**

Chicken-Pesto Pizza

MAKES 4 SERVINGS

One of our favorite pizzas.

4   (7-inch) low-carb tortillas
2   tablespoons pesto
1½ cups (6-oz) Mozzarella cheese, shredded
1½ cups cubed cooked chicken
¼   cup Plum tomatoes, chopped
4   asparagus stems

1. Preheat oven to 400°F. Place tortillas on baking sheet. Layer ingredients in order listed to within 1 inch of edge. Bake 8 to 10 minutes or until golden and heated through.

Per serving: 292 Cal, 16g Fat, 31g Pro, 1g Sug, 14g Carb, 9g Fib, **NET CARBS: 5**

∽ Hint ∾

Because most low-carb tortillas are quite thin, it is best to leave a 1 inch border when sprinkling cheese on top. This will help prevent cheese from flowing over the edge.

Pepperoni Pizza

*Remember to keep the cheese 1 inch
from the edge.*

1   **(10-inch) low-carb tortilla**
⅓   **cup chopped Plum tomatoes**
½   **cup (2-oz) Mozzarella cheese, shredded**
1   **tablespoon grated Parmesan cheese**
    Dash oregano
10   **thin slices pizza pepperoni**

1. Preheat oven to 425°F. Place tortilla on
baking sheet. Layer ingredients in order listed to
within 1 inch of edge. Bake 8 to 10 minutes or
until golden and heated through. Cut in half and
serve.

Per serving: 268 Cal, 19g Fat, 18g Pro, 1g Sug,
13g Carb, 8g Fib, **NET CARBS: 5**

Sausage-Onion Pizza

*Make your own pizza sauce and
keep on hand for last minute pizzas.*

4   **(7-inch) low-carb tortillas**
2   **tablespoons pizza sauce, page 211**
4   **ounces sausage, cooked**
¾   **cup (3-oz) Mozzarella cheese, shredded**
1   **tablespoon chopped green onions**

1. Preheat oven to 400°F. Place tortillas on a
baking sheet and bake 4 to 5 minutes or until
lightly toasted. Turn over and spread with pizza
sauce. Top with remaining ingredients and bake 8
to 10 minutes or until cheese is melted.

Per serving: 188 Cal, 12g Fat, 14g Pro, 1g Sug,
13g Carb, 8g Fib, **NET CARBS: 5**

Almond Egg Salad Wraps

MAKES 6 WRAPS

*Filling can be used as a sandwich, a dip
or a filling for tortillas.*

6   hardboiled eggs, chopped
¼   teaspoon salt
¼   teaspoon dried dill weed
¼   cup chopped slivered almonds
⅓   cup mayonnaise
6   (7-inch) low-carb tortillas

1. Combine first 4 ingredients and add just
enough mayonnaise to moisten. Spread mixture
on tortillas and roll tightly.

Per serving: 243 Cal, 19g Fat, 12g Pro, 0g Sug,
12g Carb, 9g Fib, **NET CARBS: 3**

Turkey Club Wrap

MAKES 1 WRAP

A restaurant favorite.

1   (7-inch) low-carb tortilla
1   tablespoon mayonnaise
2   slices deli turkey
2   slices bacon, cooked, crumbled
1   Plum tomato, chopped
½   cup shredded lettuce

1. Spread tortilla with mayonnaise. Layer
ingredients in order listed. Roll tightly.

Per serving: 345 Cal, 19g Fat, 36g Pro, 1g Sug,
12g Carb, 8g Fib, **NET CARBS: 4**

Beef & Cheese Roll-ups

MAKES 4 SERVINGS

*Try using some of your own favorite
ingredients and you might come up with some
fantastic sandwich ideas.*

4   (7-inch) low-carb tortillas
½   cup soft herb cream cheese spread
8   slices deli roast beef
2   cups (8-oz) Monterey Jack cheese,
    shredded
2   cups shredded lettuce

1. Spread each tortilla with 2 tablespoons
cheese spread. Top with ingredients in order
listed. Roll tightly.

Per serving: 396 Cal, 29g Fat, 29g Pro, <1g Sug,
13g Carb, 8g Fib, **NET CARBS: 5**

Dijonnaise

If you like both Dijon mustard and
mayonnaise on your sandwiches, make
your own Dijonnaise and keep on hand.
All you have to do is mix 1/2 cup
mayonnaise with 2 teaspoons Dijon
mustard (or to taste).

NET CARBS: 0

Veggie Wrap

MAKES 1 SERVING

We seem to think we have to have meat on a sandwich, but this is a nice change and quite delicious.

1   (7-inch) low-carb tortilla
2   tablespoons cream cheese, softened
8   thin slices cucumber
½   cup shredded lettuce
1   tablespoon Plum tomato, chopped

1. Spread tortilla with cream cheese. Top with ingredients in order listed. Roll tightly.

Per serving: 166 Cal, 12g Fat, 8g Pro, 2g Sug, 14g Carb, 8g Fib, *NET CARBS: 5*

Bacon & Tomato Wraps

MAKES 4 SERVINGS

To avoid totally crushing everything, cut the sandwiches with a very sharp or serrated knife.

4   (7-inch) low-carb tortillas
4   tablespoons mayonnaise
4   thin onion slices
4   thin tomato slices
1   cup (4-oz) Cheddar cheese, shredded
4   slices bacon, cooked, crumbled

1. Spread tortillas with mayonnaise. Top with remaining ingredients in order listed. Roll tightly.

Per serving: 304 Cal, 25g Fat, 15g Pro, 1g Sug, 13g Carb, 8g Fib, *NET CARBS: 5*

Turkey-Swiss Wrap

MAKES 1 SERVING

Bacon can be omitted, if desired.

1   (7-inch) low-carb tortilla
1   tablespoon mayonnaise
2   slices deli turkey
2   slices bacon, cooked, crumbled
¼   cup (1-oz) Swiss cheese, shredded
½   cup shredded lettuce

1. Spread tortilla with mayonnaise. Layer remaining ingredients in order listed. Roll tightly.

Per serving: 451 Cal, 27g Fat, 44g Pro, 1g Sug, 14g Carb, 8g Fib, *NET CARBS: 6*

Deli Sub Wrap

MAKES 1 SERVING

A meal in itself, but if really hungry, add dill pickles, raw vegetable sticks and 1/2 cup fresh raspberries.

1   (7-inch) low-carb tortilla
2   slices deli roast beef
1   thin slice Jarlsberg cheese
½   cup alfalfa sprouts
1   teaspoon oil

1. Top tortilla with the next 3 ingredients. Drizzle with oil (you may use less). Roll tightly.

Per serving: 222 Cal, 14g Fat, 20g Pro, 0g Sug, 13g Carb, 8g Fib, *NET CARBS: 5*

Roast Beef Wrap

MAKES 1 SERVING

*Pepper Jack cheese adds a nice
bite to this recipe.*

1   (7-inch) low-carb tortilla
2   teaspoons Mild and Creamy Dijon
    Mustard
2   slices deli roast beef
¼   cup (1-oz) Pepper Jack cheese, shredded

1. Spread tortilla with mustard. Top with roast
beef and cheese. Roll tightly.

Per serving: 220 Cal, 13g Fat, 20g Pro, 0g Sug,
14g Carb, 8g Fib, *NET CARBS: 6*

Tuna Wraps

MAKES 2 SERVINGS

*You can get 2 more wraps by adding 2
hard-boiled eggs, chopped.*

1   (6-oz) can tuna, drained
¼   cup finely chopped celery
¼   cup chopped onion
½   cup (2-oz) Cheddar cheese, shredded
⅓   cup mayonnaise
2   (7-inch) low-carb tortillas

1. Combine first 4 ingredients. Mix with just
enough mayonnaise to moisten. Spread on
tortillas and roll tightly.

Per serving: 505 Cal, 41g Fat, 27g Pro, 1g Sug,
14g Carb, 9g Fib, *NET CARBS: 5*

Tuna & Egg Wraps

MAKES 4 SERVINGS

*We really don't have to give up our tuna
salad after all.*

1   (12-oz) can white tuna, drained
¼   cup finely chopped onion
2   hardboiled eggs, chopped
⅓   cup mayonnaise (or to taste)
4   (7-inch) low-carb tortillas

1. Combine first 4 ingredients. Spread equal
amounts on tortillas and roll tightly.

Per serving: 333 Cal, 22g Fat, 28g Pro, 1g Sug,
12g Carb, 8g Fib, *NET CARBS: 4*

Guacamole Turkey Wrap

MAKES 1 SERVING

Use prepared or purchased guacamole.

1   (7-inch) low-carb tortilla
2   tablespoons guacamole
2   slices deli turkey
2   slices bacon, cooked, crumbled
½   cup shredded lettuce

1. Spread tortilla with guacamole. Top with turkey, bacon, then lettuce. Roll tightly.

Per serving: 273 Cal, 10g Fat, 36g Pro, <1g Sug, 14g Carb, 9g Fib, **NET CARBS: 5**

Guacamole Spread

MAKES 8 SERVINGS

This makes a nice spread for those delicious tortilla wraps we can now enjoy.

1   ripe avocado, mashed
1   tablespoon thick and chunky salsa

Combine ingredients and use as a spread on tortillas or sandwiches.

Per tablespoon: 41 Cal, 4g Fat, 1g Pro, <1g Sug, 2g Carb, 2g Fib, **NET CARBS: 0**

Turkey Wrap

MAKES 1 SERVING

A little bit of sun-dried tomatoes is just what this wrap needs.

1   (7-inch) low-carb tortilla
2   teaspoons mayonnaise
2   teaspoons chopped oil-packed sun-dried tomatoes
2   slices deli turkey
2   thin slices red onion
¼   cup (1-oz) Mozzerella cheese, shredded

1. Layer ingredients in order given and roll up tightly.

Per serving: 340 Cal, 17g Fat, 39g Pro, 1g Sug, 15g Carb, 9g Fib, **NET CARBS: 6**

Veggie Tortilla Wrap

MAKES 1 SERVING

Simple but good.

1   (7-inch) low-carb tortilla
1   tablespoon mayonnaise
¼   cup chopped Plum tomato
    Salt
¼   cup alfalfa sprouts

1. Spread tortilla with mayonnaise. Top with tomato and sprinkle lightly with salt. Top with sprouts and roll tightly.

Per serving: 156 Cal, 13g Fat, 6g Pro, <1g Sug, 12g Carb, 8g Fib, **NET CARBS: 4**

Beef-Provolone Wrap

MAKES 1 SERVING

*Monterey Jack is a good substitute
for the Provolone.*

1   **(7-inch) low-carb tortilla**
1   **tablespoon pesto**
2   **slices deli roast beef**
½ **Plum tomato, chopped**
¼ **cup (1-oz) Provolone, shredded**

1. Spread tortilla with pesto. Layer with remaining ingredients. Roll tightly.

Per serving: 208 Cal, 13g Fat, 19g Pro, 1g Sug, 13g Carb, 9g Fib, **NET CARBS: 4**

Easy Beef Wrap

MAKES 1 SERVING

You can use any flavored cream cheese here.

1   **(7-inch) low-carb tortilla**
2   **tablespoons garlic cream cheese spread**
2   **slices deli roast beef**
1   **thin onion slice, separated**

1. Spread tortilla with cheese spread. Top with roast beef and onion. Roll tightly.

Per serving: 174 Cal, 9g Fat, 17g Pro, 2g Sug, 14g Carb, 8g Fib, **NET CARBS: 6**

Pastrami Wrap

MAKES 1 SERVING

Pastrami is a nice change from roast beef.

1   **(7-inch) low-carb tortilla**
1   **tablespoon mayonnaise**
2   **slices deli pastrami**
1   **tablespoon chopped Plum tomato**
1   **slice (1-oz) Cheddar cheese, julienned**
½ **cup shredded lettuce**

1. Spread tortilla with mayonnaise. Top with pastrami slices, tomato, and cheese. Microwave to heat through and melt cheese.
2. Sprinkle with lettuce and roll tightly.

Per serving: 312 Cal, 23g Fat, 20g Pro, <1g Sug, 12g Carb, 8g Fib, **NET CARBS: 4**

Pastrami & Onion Wrap

MAKES 1 SERVING

Feel free to substitute any meat for the pastrami.

1   **(10-inch) low-carb tortilla**
1   **tablespoon mayonnaise**
3   **slices deli pastrami**
1   **thin slice red onion**
½ **cup shredded lettuce**

1. Spread tortilla with mayonnaise and layer with remaining ingredients. Roll tightly.

Per serving: 257 Cal, 16g Fat, 20g Pro, <1g Sug, 20g Carb, 14g Fib, **NET CARBS: 6**

Egg Salad Wraps

MAKES 6 SERVINGS

A must try. Low in carbs and a good source of protein.

6   large hardboiled eggs, chopped
3   tablespoons dill pickle relish
    Salt and pepper
⅓   cup mayonnaise
6   (7-inch) low-carb tortillas
2   cups shredded lettuce

1. Combine eggs and pickle relish. Add salt and pepper to taste. Add just enough mayonnaise to moisten.
2. Spread egg salad to within one inch of edge of tortillas. Sprinkle with lettuce and roll tightly.

Per serving: 218 Cal, 17g Fat, 12g Pro, 1g Sug, 12g Carb, 8g Fib, **NET CARBS: 4**

Spicy Ham Wraps

MAKES 4 SERVINGS

Just a nice touch of spicy.

½   cup mayonnaise
2   tablespoons chopped ripe olives
1   tablespoon spicy brown mustard
4   (7-inch) low-carb tortillas
8   slices deli ham
1   cup (4-oz) Monterey Jack cheese, shredded

1. Combine first 3 ingredients and spread on tortillas.
2. Layer with ham and cheese. Roll tightly.

Per serving: 401 Cal, 34g Fat, 20g Pro, 1g Sug, 12g Carb, 8g Fib, **NET CARBS: 4**

Beef-Tomato Wrap

MAKES 1 SERVING

Can omit cheese spread and use mayo.

1   (7-inch) low-carb tortilla
2   tablespoons herb cream cheese spread
3   slices deli roast beef
1   small Plum tomato, chopped
½   cup (2-oz) Cheddar cheese, shredded

1. Spread tortilla with cheese spread. Layer with remaining ingredients. Roll tightly.

Per serving: 429 Cal, 30g Fat, 34g Pro, 3g Sug, 15g Carb, 9g Fib, **NET CARBS: 6**

Chicken Caesar Wraps

MAKES 4 SERVINGS

Tastes just like a Caesar salad.

4 cups romaine
2 tablespoons grated Parmesan
¼ cup low-carb Caesar Salad Dressing, see
    page 201
1 cup cubed cooked chicken
4 (7-inch) low-carb tortillas

1. Combine romaine and Parmesan with just enough dressing to lightly coat. Add chicken and spoon mixture on tortillas. Roll tightly.

Per serving: 164 Cal, 10g Fat, 14g Pro, 1g Sug, 14g Carb, 9g Fib, **NET CARBS: 5**

Chicken-Avocado Wraps

MAKES 4 SERVINGS

*The bacon adds a nice
crunch along with the lettuce.*

4 (7-inch) low-carb tortillas
4 tablespoons mayonnaise
1 ripe avocado, mashed
8 slices deli chicken
½ cup bacon, cooked, crumbled
1 cup shredded lettuce

1. Spread tortilla with mayonnaise and avocado.
2. Top with chicken, bacon and lettuce. Roll tightly.

Per serving: 271 Cal, 21g Fat, 13g Pro, <1g Sug, 16g Carb, 12g Fib, **NET CARBS: 4**

Deli Wrap

MAKES 1 SERVING

A nice picnic wrap.

1 (7-inch) low-carb tortilla wrap
1 tablespoon low-carb pizza sauce
2 slices deli ham
2 slices salami
¼ cup (1-oz) Cheddar cheese, shredded
3 thin green pepper slices

1. Spread tortilla with pizza sauce. Layer with remaining ingredients and roll tightly.

Per serving: 304 Cal, 20g Fat, 26g Pro, 1g Sug, 13g Carb, 8g Fib, **NET CARBS: 5**

Chicken-Alfalfa Wrap

MAKES 1 SERVING

Slice on diagonal for more attractive roll-ups.

1 (10-inch) low-carb tortilla
1 tablespoon mayonnaise
3 slices deli chicken
2 tablespoons Plum tomato, chopped
¼ cup alfalfa sprouts

1. Spread tortilla with 1 tablespoon mayonnaise. Layer with remaining ingredients. Roll tightly.

Per serving: 244 Cal, 15g Fat, 21g Pro, 1g Sug, 21g Carb, 15g Fib, **NET CARBS: 6**

Cheeseburger Wraps

MAKES 2 SERVINGS

Tastes just like your favorite cheeseburger.

½ pound lean ground beef
¼ cup chopped onion
½ teaspoon salt
⅛ teaspoon pepper
2 (7-inch) low-carb tortillas
½ cup (2-oz) Cheddar cheese, shredded

1. Brown ground beef and onion; drain. Add salt and pepper. Place mixture in center of tortillas. Sprinkle with cheese. Roll tightly.

Per serving: 371Cal, 25g Fat, 29g Pro, 1g Sug, 13g Carb, 8g Fib, **NET CARBS: 5**

Sausage Wraps

MAKES 4 SERVINGS

1 (12-oz) package sausage
⅓ cup chopped onions
1 (4-oz) can sliced mushrooms, drained, chopped
4 (7-inch) low-carb tortillas
1 cup (4-oz) Monterey Jack cheese, shredded

1. Brown sausage and onion; drain. Add mushrooms and heat through. Place 1/4 of mixture on each tortilla; sprinkle with cheese. Roll tightly.

Per serving: 339 Cal, 26g Fat, 19g Pro, 1g Sug, 15g Carb, 9g Fib, **NET CARBS: 6**

Easy Soft Tacos

MAKES 4 SERVINGS

A hot tortilla wrap is a nice change.

1 pound lean ground beef
4 (7-inch) low-carb tortillas
¾ cup (3-oz) Cheddar cheese, shredded
¼ cup sour cream
¼ cup salsa

1. Brown ground beef; drain. Spread beef in center of tortillas. Top with cheese, sour cream and salsa. Roll to enclose filling.

Per serving: 367 Cal, 26g Fat, 28g Pro, <1g Sug, 12g Carb, 8g Fib, **NET CARBS: 4**

Taco Burger Wraps

MAKES 4 SERVINGS

The degree of heat in the salsa is up to you.

1 pound lean ground beef
⅓ cup thick and chunky salsa
4 (7-inch) low-carb tortillas
¾ cup (3-oz) Cheddar cheese, shredded
3 Plum tomatoes, chopped
1 cup shredded lettuce

1. Brown ground beef; drain. Add salsa and simmer until liquid is absorbed. Microwave tortillas until warm. Fill with meat mixture, layer with cheese, tomatoes and lettuce. Roll tightly.

Per serving: 355 Cal, 23g Fat, 28g Pro, 2g Sug, 15g Carb, 9g Fib, **NET CARBS: 6**

Beef-Salsa Turnovers

MAKES 6 SERVINGS

Use your favorite salsa in this turnover.

1   pound lean ground beef
1   cup thick and chunky salsa
6   (7-inch) low-carb tortillas
2   cups (8-oz) Cheddar cheese shredded

1. Preheat oven to 400°F. In medium skillet, brown ground beef; drain. Add salsa, bring to a simmer and cook 15 minutes or until liquid is absorbed.

2. Place tortillas on baking sheets. Just off center, place a portion of meat mixture. Sprinkle with cheese.

3. Bake just long enough to melt cheese. Remove from oven and fold tortillas in half like a turnover. Press edge to seal.

Per serving: 355 Cal, 24g Fat, 26g Pro, 3g Sug, 14g Carb, 8g Fib, **NET CARBS: 6**

Reuben Wrap

MAKES 1 SERVING

Just like from your favorite deli.

1   (7-inch) low-carb tortilla
1   tablespoon mustard
2   slices deli corned beef
¼   cup (1-oz) Swiss cheese, shredded
½   cup sauerkraut, drained

1. Preheat oven to 350°F. Spread tortilla with mustard. Top with corned beef, then cheese and sauerkraut. Roll-up and secure with a wooden toothpick.

2. Place on a baking sheet and bake 8 to 10 minutes or until tortilla is somewhat toasted and cheese begins to melt.

Per serving: 225 Cal, 12g Fat, 21g Pro, 1g Sug, 16g Carb, 10g Fib, **NET CARBS: 6**

Beef-Sauerkraut Wraps

MAKES 4 SERVINGS

I like this combination of ground beef and sauerkraut.

1   pound lean ground beef
½   cup chopped onion
1   (8-oz) can sauerkraut, drained
1   teaspoon salt
½   teaspoon caraway seeds
4   (7-inch) low-carb tortillas

1. Brown ground beef and onion; drain.

2. Add sauerkraut, salt and caraway seeds and heat through. Place mixture on tortillas and roll to enclose filling.

Per serving: 267 Cal, 16g Fat, 23g Pro, 2g Sug, 15g Carb, 10g Fib, **NET CARBS: 5**

Pizza Wrap

MAKES 1 SERVING

This one you bake in the oven.

1   (10-inch) low-carb tortilla
½   cup (2-oz) Monterey Jack cheese, shredded
1   tablespoon Plum tomato, chopped
1   tablespoon sliced green onions

1. Preheat oven to 350°F. Place tortilla on baking sheet and sprinkle with cheese, then tomato and onions. Roll up rather tightly and bake, seam-side down, 5 to 6 minutes or until cheese is melted.

Per serving: 297 Cal, 20g Fat, 22g Pro, 1g Sug, 20g Carb, 14g Fib, **NET CARBS: 6**

Chicken Turnover

MAKES 1 SERVING

These are quick to make for multiple servings.

1   (7-inch) low-carb tortilla
⅓   cup cubed cooked chicken
2   tablespoons salsa, well-drained
¼   cup (1-oz) Cheddar cheese, shredded

1. Preheat oven to 425°F. Place tortilla on a baking sheet. Arrange chicken over half the tortilla. Top with salsa and sprinkle with cheese.
2. Bake about 1 minute to melt cheese. Fold tortilla over and press to seal.

Per serving: 216 Cal, 12g Fat, 21g Pro, <1g Sug, 13g Carb, 8g Fib, **NET CARBS: 5**

Chicken Stir-Fry Wraps

MAKES 4 SERVINGS

I like to use the larger tortillas for these since they tend to be a little messy.

3   chicken breast halves, skinned, boned
1   tablespoon oil
½   small onion, sliced
1   small green pepper, sliced
    Salt and pepper to taste
4   (10-inch) low-carb tortillas

1. Cut chicken into narrow strips.
2. Heat oil in a large skillet. Add chicken, onion and green pepper and cook over medium-high heat, stirring frequently. Chicken should be cooked through and vegetables crisp-tender. Add salt and pepper to taste.
3. Divide mixture among tortillas and roll tightly.

Per serving: 222 Cal, 9g Fat, 28g Pro, 1g Sug, 20g Carb, 14g Fib, **NET CARBS: 6**

Hot Ham & Cheese Wraps

Makes a nice hot lunch.

4   (7-inch) low-carb tortillas
¼   cup mayonnaise
8   thin slices deli ham
8   thin slices deli chicken
½   cup (2-oz) Swiss cheese, shredded

1. Preheat oven to 325°F. Spread tortillas with mayonnaise. Layer with ham, chicken and cheese. Roll tortillas.
2. Place, seam-side down, on a baking sheet. Bake 4 to 5 minutes or until just heated through.

Per serving: 277 Cal, 18g Fat, 23g Pro, 1g Sug, 13g Carb, 8g Fib, *NET CARBS: 5*

Grilled Hot Dog Wraps

MAKES 4 SERVINGS

Not just for kids.

4   low-carb hot dogs
4   (7-inch) low-carb tortillas
2   tablespoons prepared mustard
½   cup shredded lettuce
4   (1 oz) slices Cheddar cheese

1. Grill or microwave hot dogs to heat through.
2. Microwave tortillas until just warm. Layer with mustard, hot dog, lettuce and cheese. Roll tightly.

Per serving: 342 Cal, 24g Fat, 24g Pro, <1g Sug, 17g Carb, 12g Fib, *NET CARBS: 5*

Hot Dog Wrap

MAKES 1 SERVING

These are really very good.

1   low-carb hot dog.
1   (1-oz) slice Cheddar cheese, halved
2   teaspoons prepared mustard
1   tablespoon dill pickle relish
1   (7-inch) low-carb tortilla

1. Split hot dog lengthwise. Place, cut-side down, in small skillet and brown turning once. Top with cheese and let melt.
2. Spread tortilla with mustard. Place hot dog in center and top with relish. Roll tightly.

Per serving: 348 Cal, 24g Fat, 24g Pro, <1g Sug, 18g Carb, 12g Fib, *NET CARBS: 6*

Hot Dogs

For variety, top hot dogs with the following ingredients:

- Chili, Cheddar cheese, diced onions
- Sautéed onions
- Sauerkraut and caraway seeds
- Mustard, relish, chopped onion, peppers, and pickle spears (Chicago style)
- Sauerkraut and Swiss cheese

Canadian Bacon Wrap

MAKES 1 SERVING

Low-carb tortillas have come to the rescue for low-carb dieters desperate to be able to make sandwiches.

1   (7-inch) low-carb tortilla
1   tablespoon mayonnaise
2   thin slices Canadian bacon, julienned
1   tablespoon chopped Plum tomato
1   (1-oz) slice Swiss cheese, julienned

1. Spread tortilla with mayonnaise. Top with Canadian bacon, tomato and cheese. Microwave to heat through and melt cheese. Roll tightly.

Per serving: 300 Cal, 23g Fat, 18g Pro, 1g Sug, 13g Carb, 8g Fib, *NET CARBS: 5*

Swiss-Ham Wrap

MAKES 1 SERVING

For larger appetites, use a 10-inch tortilla for only 2 extra net carbs.

1   (7-inch) low-carb tortilla
1   tablespoon Dijonnaise, see page 225
2   slices deli ham
¼   cup (1-oz) Swiss cheese, shredded
½   cup shredded lettuce

1. Spread tortilla with mayonnaise. Layer with remaining ingredients. Roll tightly.

Per serving: 267 Cal, 17g Fat, 23g Pro, 0g Sug, 15g Carb, 9g Fib, *NET CARBS: 6*

Italian Sausage Wraps

MAKES 2 SERVINGS

A hot lunch is always welcome.

1   tablespoon oil
¼   cup coarsely chopped onion
¼   cup chopped green pepper
⅓   cup sauerkraut, drained
2   Italian sausages, cooked
2   (7-inch) low-carb tortillas

1. Heat oil in a small skillet. Cook onion and pepper until crisp tender. Add sauerkraut and sausages and heat through. Place mixture on tortillas and roll tightly.

Per serving: 188 Cal, 14g Fat, 11g Pro, 1g Sug, 15g Carb, 10g Fib, *NET CARBS: 5*

Vegetables

- ♨ Asparagus
- ♨ Beans
- ♨ Broccoli
- ♨ Brussels Sprouts
- ♨ Cabbage
- ♨ Cauliflower
- ♨ Kale
- ♨ Mixed Vegetables
- ♨ Mushrooms
- ♨ Spinach
- ♨ Squash
- ♨ Zucchini

Asparagus & Almonds

Can serve with almost any meal.

1¼ pounds asparagus, trimmed
1 tablespoon butter
1 tablespoon slivered almonds

1. Slice asparagus diagonally into 1-1/2 inch pieces.
2. Cook in a large skillet in 1/2 cup water, until crisp-tender, about 5 to 7 minutes. Drain. Remove and keep warm.
2. Toast almonds in butter until golden. Return asparagus to skillet and heat through.

Per serving: 50 Cal, 4g Fat, 2g Pro, 1g Sug, 3g Carb, 2g Fib, *NET CARBS: 1*

Asparagus with Parmesan Cheese Sauce

MAKES 4 SERVINGS

This makes 4 servings, but if you have four people who love asparagus, you need to double the recipe.

1 pound asparagus, trimmed
1 tablespoon butter
1 tablespoon flour
2 tablespoons heavy cream
¼ cup (1-oz) Cheddar cheese, shredded
3 tablespoons grated Parmesan cheese

1. Steam asparagus until just crisp-tender.

2. Meanwhile, melt butter in a small saucepan. Stir in the flour and cook about 1 minute. Combine cream with 6 tablespoons water. Gradually add to flour mixture. Cook until thickened, stirring frequently.
3. Gradually add the Cheddar and stir until melted. Add Parmesan and stir to melt.
4. Place asparagus on a serving plate and top with the sauce.

Per serving: 115 Cal, 9g Fat, 5g Pro, 1g Sug, 4g Carb, 1g Fib, *NET CARBS: 3*

Scalloped Asparagus

MAKES 4 SERVINGS

Very rich and very good. Choose asparagus with thin stalks, if possible.

1 pound asparagus, trimmed
1 cup heavy cream
1 large hardboiled egg, chopped
½ teaspoon salt
¼ cup (1-oz) Swiss cheese, shredded

1. Preheat oven to 400°F. Heat cream in a small saucepan. Reduce to a simmer and cook until thickened.
2. Place asparagus in a sprayed 11x7-inch baking dish. Sprinkle with the egg and salt. Pour cream over top. Sprinkle with cheese. Cover with foil. Bake 10 minutes. Uncover and bake 5 to 10 minutes or until asparagus is tender and cheese is lightly browned.

Per serving: 264 Cal, 25g Fat, 6g Pro, 1g Sug, 4g Carb, 1g Fib, *NET CARBS: 3*

Asparagus and Red Peppers

MAKES 4 SERVINGS

*A colorful vegetable dish to serve
with almost any menu.*

1¼ **pounds asparagus, trimmed**
½   **small red pepper, cut into narrow strips**
1   **tablespoon butter**
    Dash black pepper
1   **tablespoon grated Parmesan cheese**

1. Place asparagus and pepper strips in a
medium skillet and add 1/4 cup water. Cover and
cook 5 to 7 minutes or until crisp-tender; drain.

2. Add butter and pepper and toss to coat.
Sprinkle with Parmesan.

Per serving: 64 Cal, 3g Fat, 4g Pro, 2g Sug,
6g Carb, 3g Fib, *NET CARBS: 3*

Family Favorite Asparagus

MAKES 4 SERVINGS

*Serve with Quiche Lorraine
and a small Caesar salad.*

1   **pound asparagus, trimmed**
1   **tablespoon butter**
2   **tablespoons chopped hazelnuts**
¼   **teaspoon dried basil**
⅛   **teaspoon ground pepper**
2   **tablespoons grated Parmesan cheese**

1. Heat 1/4 cup water in a medium skillet. Add
asparagus and cook on medium-high heat 4 to 6
minutes or until just crisp-tender. Drain. Remove
and set aside.

2. Add butter to skillet and sauté hazelnuts
until lightly toasted. Return asparagus to skillet;
season with basil and pepper and heat through.
Place on serving plate and sprinkle with
Parmesan.

Per serving: 71 Cal, 6g Fat, 3g Pro, 1g Sug,
3g Carb, 2g Fib, *NET CARBS: 1*

Asparagus & Bacon

Serve with ham or roast beef.

1   **pound asparagus, trimmed**
2   **tablespoons no-carb vinaigrette dressing**
4   **slices bacon, cooked, crumbled**

1. Trim asparagus and place in a medium skillet. Add enough hot water to cover. Cook, over medium heat, until just crisp-tender. Remove and drain thoroughly.
2. Toss with just enough dressing to lightly coat. Cover and chill no longer than 1 hour.
3. Place on serving dish and sprinkle with bacon.

Per serving: 84 Cal, 7g Fat, 4g Pro, 1g Sug, 2g Carb, 1g Fib, **NET CARBS: 1**

Green Beans Dijon

MAKES 6 SERVINGS

Just as good without the almonds.

1   **tablespoon butter**
1   **tablespoon slivered almonds**
2   **teaspoons lemon juice**
1   **teaspoon Dijon mustard**
1   **pound green beans, cooked**

1. Heat butter in a small skillet. Add almonds and lightly toast. Stir in the lemon juice and mustard. Pour over hot beans and toss gently to coat.

Per serving: 45 Cal, 3g Fat, 2g Pro, 1g Sug, 5g Carb, 2g Fib, **NET CARBS: 3**

Green Beans & Bacon

MAKES 6 SERVINGS

My mother used to cook her green beans for hours; something unheard of today. Although the flavor was quite different, it was delicious.

1   **pound green beans, trimmed**
1½   **tablespoons butter**
8   **slices bacon, cooked, crumbled**
    Salt and pepper

1. Cook beans in a large pot of boiling salted water until just crisp-tender, about 4 minutes or so. They will turn a bright green. Drain.
2. Heat butter in a large skillet; add beans and toss. Add bacon and heat through. Season with salt and pepper.

Per serving: 91 Cal, 6g Fat, 4g Pro, 1g Sug, 5g Carb, 2g Fib, **NET CARBS: 3**

Deviled Green Beans

MAKES 4 SERVINGS

The horseradish adds a little zip to the recipe.

⅓   **cup finely chopped onion**
3   **tablespoons butter**
1   **tablespoon prepared horseradish**
1   **tablespoon prepared mustard**
1   **(14.5-oz) can green beans, drained**

1. In a medium skillet, cook onion in butter until soft. Add horseradish and mustard. Add green beans and heat through.

Per serving: 101 Cal, 9g Fat, 1g Pro, 1g Sug, 5g Carb, 2g Fib, **NET CARBS: 3**

Steamed Green Beans

PER 1/2 CUP

A simple and fresh way to enjoy beans in season.

Desired amount of fresh green beans

1. Rinse beans and snap off ends. Cook in steamer rack over boiling water 10 to 15 minutes until just crisp tender.
2. Or drop into a large pot of boiling water and cook 4 to 8 minutes or until just crisp-tender.

note: Unless you grow your own green beans, really fresh green beans are hard to find. Don't purchase them unless they feel firm and crisp to the touch.

Per 1/2 cup: 17 Cal, 0g Fat, 1g Pro, 1g Sug, 4g Carb, 2g Fib, *NET CARBS: 2*

Fried Green Beans

MAKES 4 SERVINGS

Great substitute for fries.

1   **pound fresh green beans, trimmed**
    oil

1. Rinse beans and pat dry.
2. Heat 1/4 inch oil in a large skillet over medium-high heat (375°F). Add 1 layer of green beans and cook until bright green, about 30 seconds. Drain on paper towels and keep warm. Repeat.

note: If desired, toss with a little salt and pepper. These are quite a conversation piece because the beans have an interesting wrinkled look. Your guests will wonder how you did it.

Per serving: 65 Cal, 4g Fat, 2g Pro, 2g Sug, 8g Carb, 4g Fib, *NET CARBS: 4*

German Style Green Beans

MAKES 4 SERVINGS

A nice sweet-sour flavor.

1   **pound green beans, cooked**
4   **slices bacon, cooked, crumbled**
1   **tablespoon finely chopped onion**
2   **packages Splenda®**
1   **tablespoon red wine vinegar**

1. Cook onion in 1 tablespoon bacon drippings.
2. Add Splenda and vinegar, then the beans and bacon. Cook until heated through.

Per serving: 68 Cal, 3g Fat, 4g Pro, 2g Sug, 8g Carb, 3g Fib, *NET CARBS: 5*

Broccoli with Cheese Sauce

MAKES 6 SERVINGS

A nice vegetable casserole dish.

1¼ pounds broccoli, trimmed
3 tablespoons butter
¼ cup flour
¼ cup heavy cream
½ cup (2-oz) sharp Cheddar cheese, shredded
   Salt and pepper to taste

1. Steam broccoli until crisp-tender.
2. Meanwhile, melt butter in a medium saucepan. Quickly stir in the flour and cook 1 minute. Remove from heat. Gradually stir in the cream and 1-1/4 cups water until smooth. Cook, stirring frequently, until thickened.
3. Reduce heat and gradually stir in the cheese until melted. Add salt and pepper to taste. Place broccoli in a serving dish and top with some of the sauce. Pass remaining sauce at the table.

Per serving: 166 Cal, 13g Fat, 6g Pro, <1g Sug, 9g Carb, 3g Fib, **NET CARBS: 6**

Broccoli Stir-Fry

MAKES 4 SERVINGS

During the Christmas holidays, add 1/4 cup chopped pimiento.

4 cups broccoli florets
1 tablespoon oil
6 thin slices fresh ginger
1 garlic clove, minced
1 packet Splenda®
½ teaspoon salt

1. Steam broccoli until just crisp-tender.
2. Heat oil in a medium skillet. Add ginger and garlic. Cook 1 minute.
3. Add broccoli, Splenda, salt and 1 tablespoon water. Cook, stirring frequently, until heated through. Remove ginger before serving.

Per serving: 52 Cal, 4g Fat, 2g Pro, 0g Sug, 4g Carb, 2g Fib, **NET CARBS: 2**

Broccoli-Tomato Dish

MAKES 4 SERVINGS

This recipe has both eye and taste appeal.

4 cups broccoli florets
1 tablespoon butter, melted
¼ teaspoon oregano
   Salt and pepper to taste
2 medium tomatoes
⅓ cup (1½-oz) Mozzarella cheese, shredded

1. Preheat oven to 350°F. Cook broccoli until just crisp-tender. Toss with butter, oregano, salt and pepper. Place in center of a 10-inch oven-proof dish.
2. Cut tomatoes into 16 wedges and arrange around the edge. Sprinkle with cheese. Bake 5 minutes or until tomatoes are heated through and cheese is melted.

Per serving: 95 Cal, 5g Fat, 5g Pro, 2g Sug, 8g Carb, 3g Fib, **NET CARBS: 5**

Onion & Broccoli Stir-Fry

MAKES 6 SERVINGS

Can substitute asparagus or zucchini for the broccoli.

4　cups broccoli florets
1　tablespoon oil
1　medium onion, thin wedges
½　cup sliced celery
1½　teaspoons cornstarch
1½　teaspoons soy sauce

1. Cook broccoli until just partially cooked.
2. Heat oil in a medium skillet or a wok. Add broccoli, onion and celery and cook, over medium-high heat, until crisp-tender.
3. Combine remaining ingredients until smooth. Add to vegetables and cook about 2 minutes, stirring frequently.

Per serving: 46 Cal, 3g Fat, 2g Pro, 1g Sug, 5g Carb, 2g Fib, **NET CARBS: 3**

Broccoli Meringue

MAKES 8 SERVINGS

This is one recipe where the broccoli needs to be cooked beyond crisp tender. It should be a little on the soft side.

5　cups broccoli florets
2　large egg whites, room temperature
¼　teaspoon salt
½　cup (2-oz) Edam, Cheddar or Swiss cheese, shredded
½　cup mayonnaise

1. Microwave or steam broccoli; drain thoroughly. Place in a sprayed 8x8-inch baking dish.
2. Beat egg whites and salt until stiff peaks form. Fold in the cheese and mayonnaise. Spread evenly over broccoli. Broil 5 to 6 inches from heat for 2 to 3 minutes, or until golden brown.

Per serving: 145 Cal, 13g Fat, 4g Pro, 0g Sug, 2g Carb, 1g Fib, **NET CARBS: 1**

Broccoli with Bacon

MAKES 4 SERVINGS

A nice company dish.

4　slices bacon, cooked, crumbled
4　cups broccoli florets
3　tablespoons butter
¼　cup whole pecans
　　Salt and pepper

1. Cook broccoli in a large saucepan of simmering water until just crisp-tender, about 3 to 4 minutes. Drain.
2. Meanwhile, heat butter in large skillet over medium heat. Add pecans and cook 1 minute. Add broccoli and bacon. Sprinkle with pepper.

Per serving: 176 Cal, 16g Fat, 5g Pro, <1g Sug, 5g Carb, 3g Fib, **NET CARBS: 2**

Lemon Broccoli

MAKES 4 SERVINGS

*Just a touch of lemon adds that extra flavor
to please most appetites.*

1   **pound broccoli spears**
1½ **tablespoons butter**
1   **tablespoon fresh lemon juice**
    Dash ground black pepper

1. Place broccoli in a sprayed 11x7-inch
baking dish. Add about 1/4 cup water. Cover
lightly and microwave 4 to 6 minutes or until
bright green and just crisp-tender; drain.
2. Combine remaining ingredients and microwave to melt butter. Pour over broccoli.

Per serving: 78 Cal, 5g Fat, 3g Pro, 2g Sug,
8g Carb, 4g Fib, *NET CARBS: 4*

Broccoli Mustard Cream

MAKES 3 SERVINGS

Keep extra packages of broccoli in the freezer.

1   **(10-oz) package frozen broccoli**
⅓   **cup mayonnaise**
⅓   **cup sour cream**
1   **teaspoon prepared mustard**
½   **teaspoon lemon juice**

1. Cook broccoli according to package
directions; drain. Place in serving dish.
2. Meanwhile, combine remaining ingredients
in small saucepan. Cook over low heat until
heated through. Pour over broccoli.

Per serving: 258 Cal, 25g Fat, 4g Pro, 1g Sug,
6g Carb, 3g Fib, *NET CARBS: 3*

Cauliflower Cheese Deluxe

MAKES 6 SERVINGS

1   **(20-oz) package frozen cauliflower,
    thawed**
¼   **cup finely chopped onion**
    Salt and pepper
1   **cup heavy cream**
1   **cup (4-oz) Cheddar cheese, shredded**

1. Preheat oven to 350°F. Place cauliflower in
a sprayed 8x8-inch baking dish. Sprinkle with
onion, salt and pepper. Pour cream over top and
sprinkle with cheese. Bake 25 to 30 minutes or
until cauliflower is tender.

Per serving: 234 Cal, 21g Fat, 7g Pro, 1g Sug,
6g Carb, 3g Fib, *NET CARBS: 3*

Judy's Cauliflower Dish

MAKES 6 SERVINGS

Some of our best recipes come from our friends.

1 **(20-oz) package frozen cauliflower**
  Salt and pepper
1 **cup mayonnaise**
1 **tablespoon prepared mustard**
1 **cup (4-oz) Cheddar cheese, shredded**

1. Preheat oven to 350°F. Place thawed cauliflower in a sprayed 8x8-inch baking dish. Bake 8 minutes. Sprinkle with salt and pepper.
2. Combine mayonnaise and mustard. Spread over cauliflower. Bake 8 minutes.
3. Sprinkle with cheese and bake 8 to 10 minutes or until cauliflower is tender.

Per serving: 365 Cal, 36g Fat, 6g Pro, 1g Sug, 4g Carb, 3g Fib, *NET CARBS: 1*

Cabbage Stir-Fry

MAKES 4 SERVINGS

For color, add a small shredded carrot.

2 **tablespoons oil**
6 **cups cabbage, 1 to 1½-inch slices**
  Salt and pepper

1. In large skillet, heat oil over medium heat.
2. Add cabbage and 1/4 cup water. Cook until just crisp-tender, about 8 to 10 minutes, stirring occasionally. Season with salt and pepper.

Per serving: 85 Cal, 7g Fat, 1g Pro, 0g Sug, 6g Carb, 2g Fib, *NET CARBS: 4*

Mock Mashed Potatoes

MAKES 6 SERVINGS

It would be a stretch to call these mashed potatoes, but I do think this is a very good substitute.

1 **(20-oz) package frozen cauliflower**
3 **tablespoons butter**
3 **tablespoons whipping cream**
  Salt and pepper

1. Cover cauliflower with water and cook until tender; drain. Place in mixer bowl.
2. Heat butter and cream in microwave. Gradually add to cauliflower, mixing to a mashed potato consistency. Add salt and pepper to taste.

Per serving: 94 Cal, 8g Fat, 2g Pro, 1g Sug, 4g Carb, 3g Fib, *NET CARBS: 1*

Cauliflower-Broccoli Dish

MAKES 6 SERVINGS

Simple but tasty.

1 **small head cauliflower, cut into florets**
1 **cup frozen broccoli florets**
2 **tablespoons butter**
  Salt and pepper

1. In medium saucepan, add cauliflower and 1/2 cup water. Bring to a boil, cover and cook until almost tender, about 8 minutes.
2. Add broccoli and cook until vegetables are tender. Drain. Add butter and season with salt and pepper.

Per serving: 51 Cal, 4g Fat, 2g Pro, 1g Sug, 4g Carb, 2g Fib, *NET CARBS: 2*

Sweet-Sour Brussels Sprouts

MAKES 4 SERVINGS

Even if you aren't too fond of Brussels sprouts, you just might enjoy this recipe.

¾ pound Brussels sprouts
¼ cup finely chopped onion
1 tablespoon olive oil
3 tablespoons cider vinegar
2 tablespoons Xylitol
¼ teaspoon dry mustard

1. Wash and trim Brussels sprouts. Cook onion in heated oil in a medium skillet.
2. Stir in vinegar, Xylitol, mustard and then the Brussels sprouts. Bring to a boil, reduce heat. Cover and simmer 10 to 12 minutes or until crisp tender.

variation: For a special dinner, sprinkle the cooked Brussels sprouts with cooked crumbled bacon.

Per serving: 84 Cal, 4g Fat, 2g Pro, 3g Sug, 8g Carb, 3g Fib, **NET CARBS: 5**

Brussels Sprouts Sauté

MAKES 4 SERVINGS

A taste tester favorite.

1 pound Brussels sprouts
¼ cup butter
½ teaspoon basil
   Salt and pepper to taste

1. Trim Brussels sprouts and remove outer leaves. Cut each into 3 or 4 slices.

2. Heat butter in medium skillet. Add remaining ingredients and toss to coat. Cook 8 to 10 minutes or until just crisp-tender.

Per serving: 145Cal, 12g Fat, 3g Pro, 2g Sug, 9g Carb, 3g Fib, **NET CARBS: 6**

Eggplant Parmesan

MAKES 12 SLICES

For added color, top with a little marinara or spaghetti sauce.

1 eggplant, about ¾ pound
½ cup low-carb dry white bread crumbs
3 tablespoons grated Parmesan cheese
1 large egg, lightly beaten
½ cup (2-oz) Mozzarella cheese, shredded

1. Preheat oven to 375°F. Cut eggplant into 1/4 inch slices (do not peel).
2. Combine bread crumbs and Parmesan. Dip eggplant in egg, then in crumb mixture. Place on sprayed or Silpat®-lined baking sheet. Bake 20 to 25 minutes or until lightly browned and cooked through.
3. Sprinkle cheese on slices and bake just until cheese is melted.

Per serving: 38 Cal, 2g Fat, 3g Pro, 1g Sug, 2g Carb, 1g Fib, **NET CARBS: 1**

Sautéed Kale

There are many reasons to include kale in our diet. It has several disease fighting components and is high in vitamin A as well as calcium and potassium.

1   large bunch kale, about 10 ounces
1½ tablespoons oil
    Salt and pepper
2   teaspoons fresh lemon juice

1. Strip kale leaves from stems. Rinse and drain well.
2. Heat oil in large nonstick skillet. Add kale and cook, covered, for 1 minute. Uncover. Cook, stirring, for 1 minute or until just wilted. Sprinkle with salt, pepper and lemon juice.

Per serving: 66 Cal, 5g Fat, 1g Pro, 1g Sug, 4g Carb, 2g Fib, **NET CARBS: 2**

Grilled Portabello Mushrooms

Portobello mushrooms are made for summer grilling.

4   large portabello mushrooms
1   tablespoon finely chopped garlic
½   cup olive oil
1   tablespoon balsamic vinegar
    Salt and pepper

1. Preheat grill. Remove mushroom stems. Combine garlic, oil and vinegar. Brush liberally on top sides of mushrooms. Lightly brush the bottom sides. Place top-side down on grill. Cook about 4 minutes on each side or until tender.
2. Salt and pepper each side. Place on cutting board and slice on the bias.

Per serving: 222 Cal, 14g Fat, 3g Pro, <1g Sug, 6g Carb, 2g Fib, **NET CARBS: 4**

Sautéed Mushrooms

This goes nicely with grilled or broiled steaks.

2   tablespoons butter
1   tablespoon oil
8   ounces mushrooms, whole or sliced
½   cup coarsely chopped onion
1   garlic clove, minced

1. Heat butter and oil in a medium skillet. Add remaining ingredients and cook, stirring frequently, 4 to 5 minutes or until cooked through.

Per serving: 102 Cal, 9g Fat, 2g Pro, 2g Sug, 4g Carb, 1g Fib, **NET CARBS: 3**

Grilled Onions

Serve with hamburgers, steaks, pork or chicken.

2   **medium onions, sliced 1-inch thick**
2   **tablespoons butter**
    Salt and pepper

1. Brush onion slices with butter and place on heated grill. Cook until just crisp-tender and lightly browned, turning once. Sprinkle with salt and pepper.

Per serving: 73 Cal, 6g Fat, 1g Pro, 2g Sug, 6g Carb, 1g Fib, **NET CARBS: 5**

Squash & Red Peppers

MAKES 6 SERVINGS

Colorful as well as good for you.

2   **tablespoons oil**
½   **cup red onion, sliced**
1   **small red pepper, ¼-inch strips**
3   **yellow squash, sliced**
1   **teaspoon dried basil**
    Salt and pepper

1. Heat oil in medium skillet. Cook onion until just tender.
2. Add red pepper and cook until just crisp-tender.
3. Add squash and basil. Cook until crisp-tender, 8 to 10 minutes, stirring frequently.
4. Add salt and pepper to taste.

Per serving: 51 Cal, 5g Fat, <1g Pro, 1g Sug, 2g Carb, <1g Fib, **NET CARBS: 2**

Spaghetti Squash

PER 1/2 CUP SERVING

Serve as a substitute for pasta.

1   **spaghetti squash**
2   **tablespoons butter**

1. Preheat oven to 350°F. Cut squash in half lengthwise. Remove seeds and place, cut-side down, in a shallow pan. Add a small amount of water, about 1/2 cup, and bake 40 to 50 minutes or until cooked through. With a fork, pull into strands and toss with just enough butter to lightly coat. Servings depend on the size of the squash.

Per 1/2 cup: 54 Cal, 4g Fat, <1g Pro, 2g Sug, 5g Carb, 1g Fib, **NET CARBS: 4**

Sautéed Spinach

The garlic adds a lot of flavor.

1   **pound spinach, rinsed, stemmed**
1   **tablespoon oil**
1   **medium garlic, finely chopped**
1   **tablespoon pine nuts**
    Shaved Parmesan cheese

1. Heat oil in a large skillet. Add garlic and cook until soft, but not brown. Add spinach and cook over medium-high heat 2 to 3 minutes. Stir frequently until slightly wilted.

2. Add pine nuts and toss to coat. Place on serving plate and garnish with Parmesan.

Per serving: 69 Cal, 6g Fat, 3g Pro, <1g Sug, 4g Carb, 2g Fib, *NET CARBS: 2*

Spinach Stir-Fry

MAKES 6 SERVINGS

Don't skimp on the spinach. I am always amazed at how much it cooks down.

3   **bunches fresh spinach**
4½ **tablespoons olive oil**
⅓   **cup slivered almonds**
2   **tablespoons soy sauce**
1   **teaspoon sesame seeds (optional)**

1. Remove stems from spinach, rinse and spin dry.

2. Heat oil in a large wok or Dutch oven. Add spinach and cook, stirring frequently, until leaves just start to wilt, this doesn't take long so don't walk away from it.

3. Add almonds and soy sauce. Spoon into serving bowl and sprinkle with sesame seeds.

Per serving: 167 Cal, 14g Fat, 7g Pro, 1g Sug, 7g Carb, 4g Fib, *NET CARBS: 3*

Baked Tomato Halves

MAKES 6 SERVINGS

If desired, top with a dab of sour cream just before serving.

3   **medium tomatoes**
1   **cup low-carb soft white bread crumbs**
2   **tablespoons butter**
¼   **teaspoon dried basil**

1. Preheat oven to 350°F. Cut tomatoes in half cross-wise. Place in a shallow baking dish.

2. Combine remaining ingredients and sprinkle on tomatoes. Bake 15 to 20 minutes or until tomatoes are heated through, but still firm.

Per serving: 68 Cal, 4g Fat, 3g Pro, 2g Sug, 6g Carb, 2g Fib, *NET CARBS: 4*

Zucchini-Tomato Casserole

MAKES 6 SERVINGS

For crisp vegetables, watch the cooking time carefully. If you prefer the vegetables soft and juicy, cook a few minutes longer.

2   medium zucchini, sliced
    Salt and pepper
1   medium onion, thinly sliced
1   green pepper, thinly sliced
2   medium tomatoes, sliced
1½   cups (6-oz) Cheddar cheese, shredded

1. Preheat oven to 350°F. Place zucchini in a sprayed 2-quart deep casserole dish; sprinkle with salt and pepper.

2. Top with onions and then the green pepper and tomatoes. Sprinkle with cheese. Bake 50 to 60 minutes.

Per serving: 136 Cal, 10g Fat, 8g Pro, 3g Sug, 5g Carb, 1g Fib, **NET CARBS: 4**

Zucchini Patties

MAKES 21 PATTIES

This is a great way to use up all that zucchini from the garden that keeps on growing and growing.

1½   pounds zucchini
½   teaspoon salt
½   medium garlic clove, finely chopped
2   large eggs, lightly beaten
⅓   cup grated Parmesan cheese
2   tablespoons oil

1. Wash zucchini and coarsely shred. Combine with salt and let stand 15 minutes. Squeeze with hands to release most of the liquid. Drain on paper towels.

2. Add garlic, eggs and cheese. Heat oil in large nonstick skillet over medium-high heat. Mound heaping tablespoons of zucchini in skillet; flatten slightly if necessary. Fill the skillet, but don't crowd. Cook 6 to 8 minutes, turning once, until golden. Repeat.

Per patty: 28 Cal, 1g Fat, 2g Pro, 0g Sug, 1g Carb, <1g Fib, **NET CARBS: 1**

Sautéed Zucchini

MAKES 4 SERVINGS

An easy simple recipe.

3   zucchini, 8 ounces each
2   tablespoons oil
½   teaspoon grated lemon zest
    Salt and pepper

1. Cut zucchini into matchstick size pieces.

2. Heat oil in medium skillet over medium heat. Add zucchini and sauté, stirring frequently, until just tender. Add lemon zest and season with salt and pepper.

Per serving: 81 Cal, 7g Fat, 2g Pro, 2g Sug, 4g Carb, 2g Fib, **NET CARBS: 2**

Zucchini-Parmesan Dish

MAKES 4 SERVINGS

The Parmesan adds a nice touch.

1   **pound small zucchini, sliced**
2   **teaspoons oil**
½   **teaspoon lemon zest**
¼   **teaspoon ground black pepper**
1   **tablespoon grated Parmesan cheese**

1. Cook zucchini in heated oil about 4 minutes or until just crisp-tender. Drain off any excess oil. Toss lightly with remaining ingredients.

Per serving: 40 Cal, 3g Fat, 2g Pro, 2g Sug, 3g Carb, 1g Fib, **NET CARBS: 2**

Three Pepper Stir-Fry

MAKES 4 SERVINGS

This colorful stir-fry compliments almost any main course. Also makes a nice pizza topping.

2   **tablespoons oil**
1   **medium red, yellow and green pepper, sliced into ¼-inch rings**
1   **medium onion, sliced, separated into rings**
    Salt and pepper to taste

1. Heat oil in a large nonstick skillet. Add vegetables and cook, over medium heat, until crisp-tender, stirring occasionally. Season with salt and pepper.

tip: The peppers should remain a bright color; if they've lost their color, you know they have cooked too long.

Per serving: 88 Cal, 7g Fat, 1g Pro, 2g Sug, 7g Carb, 1g Fib, **NET CARBS: 6**

Steamed Vegetable Mix

MAKES 6 SERVINGS

You get a little taste of carrots without going over your carb budget for the day.

1   **medium onion, thin wedges, separated**
1   **small carrot, thinly sliced**
1   **medium red pepper, narrow strips**
1   **medium-small zucchini, sliced**
1   **tablespoon butter**
    Salt and pepper to taste

1. Place first 3 ingredients in a large steamer

basket. Place over boiling water; cover and cook 6 minutes.

2. Add zucchini; continue cooking 3 to 4 minutes or until vegetables are crisp-tender. Place in a large serving bowl and toss with butter, salt and pepper.

Per serving: 37 Cal, 2g Fat, <1g Pro, 2g Sug, 5g Carb, 1g Fib, **NET CARBS: 4**

Roasted Vegetables

MAKES 8 SERVINGS

Vegetables can be roasted in the oven or on a grill.

½ **pound Brussels sprouts, halved**
1 **pound fresh green beans, trimmed**
¾ **cup chopped green onions**
1 **teaspoon dried basil or rosemary**
2 **tablespoons oil**
Salt and pepper to taste

1. Preheat oven to 425°F. In a small stock pot, cook Brussels sprouts in 2 inches of water for 3 minutes.

2. Add green beans and cook 4 to 5 minutes or until they turn a bright green--no longer, please. Drain thoroughly.

3. In a sprayed shallow roasting pan, combine vegetables with remaining ingredients. Bake 10 to 12 minutes or until lightly roasted.

Per serving: 62 Cal, 4g Fat, 2g Pro, 2g Sug, 7g Carb, 3g Fib, **NET CARBS: 4**

Sautéed Onions and Peppers

MAKES ENOUGH FOR 8 (7-INCH)TORTILLAS

Serve with chicken or beef fajitas.

1 **tablespoon of olive oil**
¼ **teaspoon paprika**
½ **red and green peppers, julienned**
2 **medium onions, thin wedges**
Salt and pepper to taste

1. Heat oil in a large skillet. Stir in paprika. Add peppers and onions. Cook until just crisp tender.

Per serving: 23 Cal, 2g Fat, 0g Pro, 1g Sug, 2g Carb, <1g Fib, **NET CARBS: 2**

Sesame Vegetable Stir-Fry

MAKES 4 SERVINGS

Quick and easy! If you want a little more color, add 1/4 cup chopped red peppers.

1 **tablespoon oil**
2 **cups cauliflower florets**
2 **cups broccoli florets**
1 **tablespoon soy sauce**
1 **teaspoon toasted sesame seeds**

1. Heat oil in a medium skillet over medium-high heat. Add cauliflower and broccoli and cook, stirring frequently, until just crisp-tender. Stir in soy sauce. Sprinkle with sesame seeds.

Per serving: 58 Cal, 4g Fat, 3g Pro, 1g Sug, 4g Carb, 2g Fib, **NET CARBS: 2**

Sautéed Mixed Vegetables

MAKES 8 SERVINGS

A great accompaniment to steak.

2   tablespoons oil
2   medium onions, thin wedges
½   pound mushrooms, sliced
1   medium green pepper, narrow strips
3   tablespoons dry sherry
½   teaspoon salt (optional)

1. Heat oil in a large skillet. Add vegetables and sherry and cook over medium heat until vegetables are crisp-tender. Sprinkle with salt, if using.

Per serving: 54 Cal, 4g Fat, 1g Pro, 2g Sug, 4g Carb, 1g Fib, *NET CARBS: 3*

Tomatoes & Sour Cream

MAKES 6 SERVINGS

Adds color to your meal.

¼   cup mayonnaise
½   cup sour cream
2   tablespoons finely chopped onion
¼   teaspoon dried dill weed
3   medium firm ripe tomatoes
    Salt and pepper

1. Combine mayonnaise, sour cream, onion and dill weed. Cover and chill.
2. Preheat broiler. Cut tomatoes in half crosswise and place, cut-side up, in a shallow baking pan. Sprinkle with salt and pepper. Place pan on a rack positioned about 3 inches from heat. Broil tomatoes about 5 minutes or until heated through but still firm. Place on a serving plate or individual plates and spoon sour cream sauce over top.

Per serving: 127 Cal, 12g Fat, 1g Pro, 2g Sug, 5g Carb, 1g Fib, *NET CARBS: 4*

Onion Blossoms

MAKES 4 SERVINGS

These little gems team well with grilled chicken, steaks or fish.

4   small sweet onions
2   tablespoons butter, melted
    Salt and pepper
1   tablespoon chopped parsley

1. Preheat oven to 350°F. Peel onions, but don't cut off the root end, as this is the only thing that will hold the onion together.
2. Cut onions almost to the root, cutting into 8 wedges. Place in a sprayed 8x8-inch baking dish.
3. Pour butter over onions and sprinkle with salt and pepper. Cover dish with foil and bake 30 minutes. Remove foil and baste onions with liquid. Bake 10 to 15 minutes or until tender. Remove from oven and sprinkle with parsley. Carefully lift blossoms and place on each serving plate.

Per serving: 80 Cal, 6g Fat, 1g Pro, 3g Sug, 7g Carb, 1g Fib, *NET CARBS: 6*

Desserts

Patrick's Almond Cookies

MAKES 18 COOKIES

Xylitol saves you 12 grams of carbohydrates per 1/2 cup over Splenda®.

2 large egg whites, room temperature
¼ teaspoon almond extract
½ cup Xylitol
1 cup almond flour

1. Preheat oven to 350°F. Beat egg whites until stiff. Add extract; fold in Xylitol and almond flour.

2. Drop by heaping teaspoons, placing 2 inches apart, on sprayed or Silpat®-lined baking sheet. Bake 10 to 12 minutes or until lightly browned and center is almost firm. Cool on rack.

Per cookie: 51 Cal, 3g Fat, 2g Pro, 0g Sug, 1g Carb, <1g Fib, **NET CARBS: 1**

Macaroons

MAKES 18 MACAROONS

These are best eaten within a few hours of being made.

2 large egg whites
½ teaspoon vanilla extract
9 packets Splenda®
1 cup unsweetened shredded coconut

1. Preheat oven to 300°F. Beat egg whites until foamy. Add vanilla. Gradually add the Splenda and beat until soft peaks form.

2. Fold in coconut. Drop by tablespoons, 2 inches apart on sprayed baking sheet. Bake 20 to 25 minutes or until lightly browned. Cool on rack.

Per macaroon: 40 Cal, 3g Fat, 1g Pro, <1g Sug, 2g Carb, 1g Fib, **NET CARBS: 1**

Pecan Macaroons

MAKES 30 MACAROONS

These are best served same day made or frozen.

2 cups chopped pecans
2 large eggs, lightly beaten
1 cup Splenda®

1. Preheat oven to 350°F. Finely grind pecans in a small food processor or blender. Place in bowl and add eggs and Splenda, mixing well.

2. Place mounded teaspoons on sprayed or Silpat®-lined baking sheet. Bake 8 to 10 minutes or until somewhat firm. Cool on rack.

Per macaroon: 63 Cal, 6g Fat, 1g Pro, <1g Sug, 2g Carb, 1g Fib, **NET CARBS: 1**

Vanilla-Almond Cookies

MAKES 26 COOKIES

These taste a lot like shortbread cookies.

2   cups almond flour
½   cup Splenda®
½   cup butter, softened
1   teaspoon vanilla extract.

1. Preheat oven to 325°F. Combine all the ingredients until blended. Drop heaping teaspoons onto a sprayed or Silpat®-lined baking sheet. Try to stay as round as possible. Flatten slightly with a fork. Bake 15 to 20 minutes or until somewhat firm.

Per cookie: 82 Cal, 8g Fat, 2g Pro, 0g Sug, 2g Carb, 1g Fib, **NET CARBS: 1**

Chocolate Coconut Drops

MAKES 25 CANDIES

Delicious! Do try this recipe.

7   ounces low-carb chocolate, broken
4   ounces low-carb white chocolate, broken
1   cup chopped pecans
¾   cup unsweetened shredded coconut

1. Melt chocolates in heavy medium saucepan over very low heat. Stir until smooth.
2. Add nuts and coconut. Drop by mounded teaspoons onto waxed paper or Silpat®-lined baking sheet. Allow to set at room temperature or chill until firm.

Per candy: 107 Cal, 8g Fat, 1g Pro, <1g Sug, 3g Carb, 2g Fib, **NET CARBS: 1**

Sugar Cookies

MAKES 22 COOKIES

Nice with a cup of coffee.

¼   cup butter, softened
1   large egg, lightly beaten
1   teaspoon vanilla extract
1   cup Splenda® plus 1 tablespoon
1¼ cups almond flour

1. Preheat oven to 375°F. Beat butter until smooth. Add egg and vanilla and blend as best you can. Add the 1 cup Splenda and almond flour.
2. Spoon heaping teaspoons on baking sheet. Press to 1/4-inch thickness. Sprinkle with remaining Splenda. Bake 9 to 11 minutes or until lightly browned.

Per cookie: 63 Cal, 5g Fat, 2g Pro, 0g Sug, 3g Carb, 1g Fib, **NET CARBS: 2**

Chocolate-Coconut Candies

MAKES 24 CANDIES

These get quite hard if refrigerated.

2   (3.5-oz) bars low-carb dark chocolate
1¼ cups unsweetened shredded coconut.
½   teaspoon almond extract

1. Melt chocolate in heavy small saucepan over low heat.
2. Add coconut and extract. Drop by mounded teaspoons onto baking pan. Let stand until set.

Per candy: 69 Cal, 6g Fat, 1g Pro, <1g Sug, 2g Carb, 1g Fib, **NET CARBS: 1**

Cran-Pecan Chocolate Bark

MAKES 24 CANDIES

Just a tiny bit of dried cranberries adds a nice touch.

12   ounces low-carb milk chocolate
1   tablespoon shortening
¼   cup dried cranberries
¾   cup finely chopped pecans

1. In small heavy saucepan, melt chocolate and shortening over very low heat. Remove from heat and stir in cranberries and 1/4 cup pecans.

2. Pour into a buttered, then wax paper lined 11x7-inch baking dish; spread evenly. Sprinkle with remaining pecans; press lightly. Chill about 45 minutes to set. Remove and break into small pieces.

Per piece: 97 Cal, 8g Fat, 1g Pro, 1g Sug, 3g Carb, 2g Fib, **NET CARBS: 1**

What is Coulis?

Coulis is a fruit that has been sweet-ened, processed in a blender or food processor and then pressed through a sieve to remove the seeds. What you then have is a nice sauce to serve over or under a dessert or to decorate a plate.

Fruit Kabobs with Chocolate Sauce

MAKES 4 SERVINGS

Serve as a dessert or as a garnish with grilled chicken.

4   small strawberries
4   cantaloupe cubes
4   pineapple chunks
4   large raspberries

   Chocolate Sauce:
½   cup heavy cream
7   ounces low-carb milk chocolate

1. Heat cream in small saucepan over low heat.

2. Break up chocolate and add to cream, stirring until smooth.

3. Alternate fruit on small skewers, using 1 piece of each fruit.

4. Spoon 2 tablespoons chocolate sauce on dessert plates, tilting to coat somewhat. Place a fruit kabob in center of each plate. Drizzle each with 1 tablespoon chocolate sauce.

Per kabob: 331 Cal, 27g Fat, 3g Pro, 1g Sug, 9g Carb, 6g Fib, **NET CARBS: 3**

Ice Cream Towers

MAKES 1 SERVING

*Low-carb ice cream is quite high in carbs
considering that a serving size is only 1/2 cup.
The paper cups are the 5-ounce size.*

½   cup low-carb vanilla ice cream
1   (1-oz) low-carb Toffee bar

1. Press 1/4 cup ice cream in bottom of paper
cup. Sprinkle with half the toffee. Repeat layers.
Cover with plastic wrap and freeze. Remove
paper just before serving.
note: If you can afford the carbs, drizzle a
small plate with fruit Coulis, page 259 and top
with "Towers." This makes a stunning company
dessert.

Per serving: 249 Cal, 18g Fat, 5g Pro, 2g Sug,
8g Carb, 4g Fib, *NET CARBS: 4*

Variations

- Chocolate and vanilla ice cream with
  toffee bars
- Chopped chocolate bars (with or without
  nuts)
- Chopped strawberries
- Raspberries or blueberries
- Toasted unsweeted shredded coconut
- Chopped nuts
- Fruit spread
- Chocolate sauce
- Chopped peanut cups

Berries & Cream

MAKES 8 SERVINGS

Serve in small wine glasses.

½   cup heavy cream
1   cup low-carb vanilla ice cream, softened
3   cups strawberries, sliced
7   packets Splenda®
¼   teaspoon almond extract

1. Whip cream until stiff. Combine with ice
cream. Freeze.
2. Combine strawberries and Splenda. Chill.
3. Before serving, remove cream mixture from
freezer and let stand 15 minutes.
4. Combine berries with almond extract. Fold
into cream mixture.

Per serving: 110 Cal, 8g Fat, 2g Pro, 3g Sug,
8g Carb, 2g Fib, *NET CARBS: 6*

Ice Cream & Amaretto

MAKES 1 SERVING

An elegant but quick and easy dessert.

1   (½-cup) scoop low-carb vanilla ice cream
1   teaspoon Amaretto liqueur
1   tablespoon whipped cream sweetened
    with Xylitol
1   teaspoon sliced almonds

1. Spoon ice cream into a wine glass or small
dessert dish. Spoon Amaretto over top. Top with
whipped cream and sprinkle with almonds.

Per serving: 194 Cal, 14g Fat, 5g Pro, 4g Sug,
9g Carb, 4g Fib, *NET CARBS: 5*

Ice Cream Balls

MAKES 1 SERVING

With more and more delicious low-carb ice creams on the market, we can now enjoy these once forbidden desserts.

½ **cup low-carb vanilla ice cream**
    nuts or coconut, to coat

1. Form ice cream into a ball. This is easier to do if the ice cream is frozen quite firm. Choose a variation below. Place in muffin tin; cover and freeze. When ready to serve, place in a wine glass or dessert dish.

note: You will need to total the carbs based on the ingredients you use. A carbohydrate gram counter will give you these counts. Coconut should be unsweetened. Add toppings as your carb count allows.

Ice Cream only: 140 Cal, 10g Fat, 4g Pro, 2g Sug, 7g Carb, 4g Fib, **NET CARBS: 3**

Variations

- Ice cream, unsweetened shredded coconut, chocolate sauce
- Ice cream, almonds, strawberries
- Ice cream, pecans, chocolate sauce
- Ice cream, unsweetened shredded coconut, raspberries
- Ice cream, unsweetened shredded coconut, blueberry sauce

Cook's Tip
Small servings of low-carb berries are now allowed on low-carb diets--even Atkins. Those lowest are raspberries, strawberries, blueberries, and blackberries.

Chocolate Fondue

MAKES 1-1/2 CUPS

Serve with fresh strawberries, low-carb marsh-mallows and toasted buttered low-carb bread sticks.

3 **(3.5-oz) bars low-carb dark chocolate**
½ **cup heavy cream**
3 **tablespoons sugar-free raspberry syrup**

1. Break chocolate into small pieces. Add to small fondue pot or saucepan. Add cream and syrup. Cook over low heat, stirring until chocolate is melted and smooth.

Per 2-tablespoons: 143 Cal, 12g Fat, 1g Pro, 0g Sug, 3g Carb, 3g Fib, **NET CARBS: 0**

Cream De Menthe Dessert

MAKES 1 SERVING

An easy dessert for St. Patrick's Day.

½   cup low-carb vanilla ice cream
1   teaspoon Cream De Menthe

1. Spoon ice cream into a small dessert dish. Drizzle Cream De Menthe over top.

Per serving: 161 Cal, 10g Fat, 4g Pro, 4g Sug, 9g Carb, 4g Fib, *NET CARBS: 5*

Sandy's Raspberry Delight

MAKES 5 SERVINGS

If desired, garnish with whipped cream.

1   (0.6-oz) package sugar-free raspberry
     gelatin
1   cup low-carb vanilla ice cream
1   cup raspberries
¼   cup chopped pecans

1. Combine jello with 1 cup boiling water, stirring until completely dissolved. Add ice cream and whisk until blended. Refrigerate until the thickness of uncooked egg whites, about 20 minutes.

2. Stir in raspberries and pecans. Spoon into small serving dishes and refrigerate until firm.

Per serving: 124 Cal, 8g Fat, 4g Pro, 2g Sug, 7g Carb, 4g Fib, *NET CARBS: 3*

Ice Cream Parfait

MAKES 1 SERVING

Fill your most attractive small parfait or wine glasses with ice cream and freeze for a nice frosty look.

1   low-carb toffee bar
⅓   cup low-carb chocolate ice cream
⅓   cup low-carb vanilla ice cream

1. Finely crush toffee bar. Fill glass with the chocolate ice cream. Sprinkle with half the toffee. Add vanilla ice cream, then rest of toffee.

Per serving: 295 Cal, 21g Fat, 6g Pro, 3g Sug, 10g Carb, 5g Fib, *NET CARBS: 5*

Low Carb Variations

- Vanilla ice cream, sliced strawberries
- Vanilla ice cream, raspberries
- Vanilla Ice cream, blueberries
- Vanilla ice cream, grated low-carb chocolate
- Strawberry ice cream, sliced strawberries
- Chocolate ice cream, grated low-carb chocolate & nuts

Ben's Strawberries

MAKES 24

My Grandson, Ben, ate about a dozen of these before I could get them on the serving tray.

8 ounces Mascarpone cheese, softened
⅓ cup Splenda®
1 tablespoon Grand Marnier
24 medium-small strawberries

1. Combine cheese, Splenda and Grand Marnier until smooth.
2. Spoon into a pastry bag fitted with a small star tip. Cut strawberries in half lengthwise and pipe a small mound of cheese mixture onto center. Serve as soon as possible. Sprinkle very lightly with a little Splenda, if desired.

Per two halves: 25 Cal, 2g Fat, <1g Pro, <1g Sug, 1g Carb, <1g Fib, **NET CARBS: 1**

Choco-Raspberry Dessert

MAKES 1 SERVING

Have a barbecue and serve this for dessert.

⅓ cup fresh raspberries
½ cup low-carb chocolate ice cream
1 tablespoon Chocolate Sauce, see page 205

1. Place 1/4 cup raspberries in blender and blend just until pureed.
2. Place ice cream in small serving dish. Pour puree over top. Drizzle with chocolate sauce. Garnish with remaining raspberries.

Per serving: 227Cal, 16g Fat, 5g Pro, 4g Sug, 13g Carb, 7g Fib, **NET CARBS: 6**

Strawberry-Raspberry Dessert

MAKES 4 SERVINGS

A colorful dessert and so few carbs.

2 cups fresh raspberries
¼ cup Xylitol
4 ½-cup scoops low-carb strawberry ice cream
   A few thin strips of lemon peel (optional)

1. Puree raspberries and Xylitol just briefly in a blender.
2. Place ice cream in small serving dishes and spoon sauce over top. If desired, garnish with lemon strips. If you just happen to have 4 mint leaves hanging around, add those to add a bit more color.

Per serving: 202 Cal, 10g Fat, 5g Pro, 5g Sug, 14g Carb, 8g Fib, **NET CARBS: 6**

Chocolate Pots De Créme

This very rich chocolate dessert is traditionally served in tiny pot-shaped pots de créme cups.

9	**ounces low-carb dark chocolate, broken up**
3	**tablespoons Splenda®**
1	**tablespoon, plus 1½ teaspoons oil**
1½	**teaspoons vanilla extract**
¼	**cup heavy cream**

1. Place first 4 ingredients in a blender or food processor.

2. Combine cream with 1/2 cup water. Microwave until boiling. Pour over chocolate mixture and process until smooth. Pour into 4 small cups or custard dishes. Cover. Chill 2 to 3 hours before serving. Garnish with whipped cream and grated chocolate, if desired.

Per serving: 356 Cal, 28g Fat, 3g Pro, <1g Sug, 9g Carb, 8g Fib, **NET CARBS: 1**

Coconut-Mint Dessert

Since we can have only 1/2 cup ice cream for a serving, this is pretty good.

½	**cup butter**
1¾	**cups unsweetened shredded coconut**
6	**cups low-carb mint chocolate chip ice cream, softened**

1. Melt butter in small skillet. Add coconut and cook, stirring frequently, until golden.

2. Press onto bottom of sprayed 8x8-inch dish. Add ice cream. Cover. Freeze until ready to serve. Remove about 10 minutes before serving for easier slicing.

Per serving: 296 Cal, 27g Fat, 5g Pro, 3g Sug, 10g Carb, 6g Fib, **NET CARBS: 4**

Mocha Mousse

MAKES 4 SERVINGS

If you use the same brand dark chocolate I used, you shouldn't have to add a sweetener.

⅓ cup hot strong coffee
6 ounces low-carb dark chocolate, broken up
1 teaspoon vanilla extract
1 cup heavy cream, whipped

1. Place coffee and chocolate in a 4 cup glass measuring cup. Microwave about 1 minute or until chocolate is soft. Add vanilla and let cool to room temperature.

2. Fold whipped cream into chocolate until mixed. Spoon into 4 small dessert dishes.

Per serving: 396 Cal, 36g Fat, 3g Pro, <1g Sug, 7g Carb, 5g Fib, *NET CARBS: 2*

White Chocolate Mousse

MAKES 4 SERVINGS

A recipe for white chocolate fans.

4 ounces low-carb white chocolate
1½ cups heavy cream
½ teaspoon vanilla extract
¼ cup sliced strawberries

1. Melt chocolate in a heavy small saucepan over very low heat.

2. Meanwhile, whip cream and vanilla until firm, but not stiff. Add the white chocolate and beat until blended. Watch carefully, the mixture should be a little thicker, but not curdled.

3. Layer with strawberries in small parfait or wine glasses.

variation: Place mousse in a small serving bowl and surround bowl with fresh berries and serve as a dip.

Per serving: 441 Cal, 33g Fat, 3g Pro, 1g Sug, 5g Carb, <1g Fib, *NET CARBS: 5*

Pistachio Dessert

MAKES 8 SERVINGS

This is so good, it is sometimes hard to limit your servings.

1 quart low-carb vanilla ice cream, softened
⅓ cup heavy cream plus ½ cup
1 (1-oz) package sugar-free instant pistachio pudding
1 packet Splenda®
¼ cup chopped pecans

1. In mixer bowl, blend ice cream, the 1/3 cup heavy cream, 2/3 cup water and pudding mix. Spoon into 8 dessert dishes. Chill until set.

2. When ready to serve, whip the 1/2 cup cream with Splenda. Spoon over pudding and sprinkle with nuts.

Per serving: 263 Cal, 22g Fat, 5g Pro, 2g Sug, 8g Carb, 4g Fib, *NET CARBS: 4*

Fried Gouda & Strawberries

You may have a hard time convincing your guests this is low carb. May also be served as an appetizer or first course.

4 (½-inch thick) slices Gouda cheese, 3½ x 2-inches, remove rind
2 tablespoons flour
1 egg, lightly beaten
¼ cup low-carb dry white bread crumbs
1¼ cups oil
½ cup sliced sweetened strawberries

1. Dip cheese slices in flour and lightly coat all sides.
2. Dip in egg, then in bread crumbs to cover. Place on a rack and let stand 15 minutes.
3. Heat oil in medium skillet over medium-high heat. Brown until golden on both sides, turning once. The cheese will be soft. If it starts to ooze, remove immediately. Place briefly on paper towels. Place on small serving plates and top with strawberries.

note: This would be equally as good with raspberries.

Per serving: 177 Cal, 13g Fat, 10g Pro, 2g Sug, 6g Carb, 1g Fib, **NET CARBS: 5**

Chocolate Covered Strawberries

MAKES 20 SERVINGS

We have to have discipline when eating these, they are so good.

1 (3.5-oz) bar low-carb dark chocolate
1 teaspoon shortening
20 medium-size strawberries

1. Break chocolate into 1-inch pieces. Place in heavy small saucepan along with the shortening. Heat, over low heat, until melted and smooth.
2. Dip strawberries into chocolate and place, point-side up on a dish. Place in refrigerator to set. Serve same day made.

Per strawberry: 28 Cal, 2g Fat, <1g Pro, 1g Sug, 2g Carb, 1g Fib, **NET CARBS: 1**

Strawberries Grand Marnier

MAKES 4 SERVINGS

If desired, top with whipped cream or serve with French toast or crepes.

2 cups sliced strawberries
¼ cup Xylitol
1 tablespoon Grand Marnier
1 teaspoon fresh orange zest

1. Combine all ingredients. Cover and chill until ready to serve.

Per serving: 66 Cal, <1g Fat, 1g Pro, 5g Sug, 8g Carb, 2g Fib, **NET CARBS: 6**

Coconut Custard

A nice creamy custard.

4   large eggs, lightly beaten
⅓   cup Splenda®
½   teaspoon vanilla extract
1   cup heavy cream
¼   cup unsweetened shredded coconut
    Nutmeg

1. Preheat oven to 325°F. Combine eggs, Splenda, and vanilla. Combine cream with 2 cups water and gradually add to egg mixture. Stir in coconut.

2. Place 6 ungreased 10-ounce ramekins in a 13x9-inch baking dish. Fill ramekins. Sprinkle lightly with nutmeg.

3. Fill baking dish with 1-inch of boiling water. Carefully place dish in oven. Bake 30 to 40 minutes or until center is just set (still some jiggle left). Let cool on rack. Cover with plastic wrap and chill in refrigerator.

Per serving: 218 Cal, 20g Fat, 5g Pro, 1g Sug, 4g Carb, 1g Fib, **NET CARBS: 3**

Lemon Cheesecake

MAKES 12 SERVINGS

This is good. Creamy with a light touch of lemon. If desired serve on individual plates drizzled with raspberry Coulis, page 259. Garnish with whipped cream and thin strands of lemon peel.

1   (3-oz) package sugar-free lemon gelatin
2   (8-oz) packages cream cheese, softened
½   cup Xylitol
½   cup sour cream
¼   cup heavy cream

1. Thoroughly mix the lemon gelatin with 1/4 cup boiling water, stirring until dissolved.

2. In mixer bowl, combine remaining ingredients and beat until smooth and light. Add gelatin and beat until smooth. Spoon into a lightly sprayed 9-inch pie dish. Chill 3 to 4 hours or until set.

variation: If a crust is desired, Press-in-Pan Pie Crust (page 271) will add only 1 gram of net carbs per slice.

Per serving: 213 Cal, 17g Fat, 7g Pro, 0g Sug, 2g Carb, 0g Fib, **NET CARBS: 2**

Fantastic Cheesecake

MAKES 16 SERVINGS

*One of our most popular recipes
adapted to low-carb cooking.*

3   tablespoons graham cracker crumbs
3   (8-oz) packages cream cheese, softened
4   large eggs
¾   cup plus 1 cup sour cream
1   cup Splenda® plus ¼ cup
4   tablespoons fresh lemon juice, divided

1. Preheat oven to 350°F. Lightly spray a 9-inch springform pan. Add graham cracker crumbs and rotate to cover bottom and sides. Discard loose crumbs.

2. In mixer bowl, beat cream cheese until smooth.

3. Add eggs, one at a time, and mix well.

4. Add the 3/4 cup sour cream, 1 cup Splenda and 2 tablespoons lemon juice. Mix until blended and smooth. Pour into pan and bake 35 to 40 minutes or until just firm. Do not over-bake; the center should still jiggle just a little.

5. Meanwhile, combine the 1 cup sour cream, 1/4 cup Splenda and 2 tablespoons lemon juice. Carefully pour over baked cheesecake and spread over top. Bake 5 minutes. Place pan on rack and cool. Cover and chill.

note: For a smoother cheesecake, it is very important to have all ingredients at room temperature. Also, the carbs can be reduced by 2 carbs per serving by using the sugar substitute Xylitol. The consistency will be a little different, but is still very good.

Per serving: 233 Cal, 21g Fat, 6g Pro, 1g Sug, 5g Carb, 0g Fib, ***NET CARBS: 5***

White Chocolate Cheesecake

MAKES 16 SERVINGS

*As with any cheesecake, watch
carefully so as not to overcook.*

3   (8-oz) packages cream cheese, softened
1   cup Splenda®
5   large eggs
1   teaspoon vanilla extract
½   cup heavy cream
8   ounces low-carb white chocolate, chopped

1. Preheat oven to 325°F. Beat cream cheese and Splenda until smooth, but do not overmix. Add eggs, one at a time, mixing well. Add extract.

2. In medium saucepan, bring cream to a boil, then remove from heat. Add white chocolate and stir until melted. Slowly add to cream cheese, beating until mixed. Pour into a sprayed 9-inch springform pan.

3. Bake 40 to 50 minutes or until set on the sides, but still soft in the center. Let cool on rack. Cover and chill overnight.

Per serving: 269 Cal, 19g Fat, 6g Pro, <1g Sug, 4g Carb, 0g Fib, ***NET CARBS: 4***

Chocolate Pie

MAKES 10 SERVINGS

Crust can be made a day or two ahead.

1   baked Press-in-Pan pie crust, page 271
1   (3.5-oz) bar low-carb dark chocolate
1¾   cups heavy cream, divided
1   (3-oz) package cream cheese, softened
⅓   cup Splenda®

1. Melt chocolate and 2 tablespoons cream in a small heavy saucepan. Mix until smooth.

2. In the mixer bowl, beat cream cheese until smooth. Beat in the Splenda. Add 2 tablespoons of the cream and the chocolate mixture.

3. Whip remaining cream and fold into the chocolate mixture. Spoon into the pie crust and chill until set.

Per serving: 301 Cal, 29g Fat, 5g Pro, <1g Sug, 6g Carb, 2g Fib, **NET CARBS: 4**

Chocolate-Peppermint Pie

MAKES 10 SERVINGS

For chocolate-peppermint fans.

1   baked Press-in-Pan pie crust, page 271
1   quart low-carb chocolate ice cream, softened
1   teaspoon peppermint extract
1   (1 oz) no-carb toffee bar, crushed

1. Combine ice cream and peppermint extract. Spoon into pie crust. Sprinkle with toffee.

Per serving: 205 Cal, 16g Fat, 6g Pro, 2g Sug, 8g Carb, 4g Fib, **NET CARBS: 4**

Fruit Pie

MAKES 10 SERVINGS

Wonderful summer pie.

1   baked Press-in-Pan pie crust, page 271
1   (0.3-oz) package sugar-free raspberry gelatin
2   cups low-carb vanilla ice cream, softened
1½   cups sliced strawberries
½   cup whipping cream, whipped

1. Dissolve gelatin in 1-1/4 cups boiling water. Stir in the ice cream until dissolved. Chill until slightly thickened.

2. Fold in strawberries and pour into pie crust. Chill until set. Top each serving with whipped cream.

Per serving: 191 Cal, 16g Fat, 5g Pro, 2g Sug, 8g Carb, 3g Fib, **NET CARBS: 5**

Peanut Butter Pie

If desired, garnish with whipped cream and a chocolate covered almond or coffee bean.

1   baked Press-in-Pan pie crust, page 271
1   (8-oz) package cream cheese, softened
1   cup low-carb creamy peanut butter spread
1   cup Splenda®
1   cup whipping cream

1. In mixer bowl, beat cream cheese until smooth.
2. Add remaining ingredients and beat until blended and smooth. Pour into pie shell. Chill until firm.

Per serving: 336 Cal, 31g Fat, 9g Pro, 3g Sug, 8g Carb, 2g Fib, **NET CARBS: 6**

Peanut Butter Ice Cream Pie

This is an ice cream dessert, so the servings are small, but also very rich.

1   baked Press-in-Pan pie crust, page 271
1   quart low-carb vanilla ice cream, softened
¼   cup low-carb peanut butter spread

1. Place very soft ice cream in a bowl. Lightly swirl in the peanut butter. Spoon into pie shell. Cover and freeze.

Per serving: 194 Cal, 16g Fat, 6g Pro, 2g Sug, 8g Carb, 4g Fib, **NET CARBS: 4**

Mile High Toffee Pie

If desired, top with low-carb chocolate sauce and whipped cream.

1   baked Press-in-Pan pie crust, page 271
1   quart low-carb chocolate ice cream, softened
¾   quart low-carb vanilla ice cream, softened
½   cup crushed no-carb toffee bars

1. Spoon chocolate ice cream into pie crust. Sprinkle with toffee. Spoon vanilla ice cream over top. Freeze. Cover until ready to serve.

variations: Add toffee and 1/2 cup pecans to vanilla ice cream.

Per serving: 320 Cal, 24g Fat, 9g Pro, 3g Sug, 13g Carb, 7g Fib, **NET CARBS: 6**

Graham Cracker Crust

MAKES ONE 9-INCH CRUST

There isn't a lot of crust here, but it does work.

8   (2½-inch) graham cracker squares,
    crushed
2   tablespoons butter, melted

1. Preheat oven to 350°F. Combine ingredients
and press onto bottom and sides of a 9-inch
baking dish (do not go over rim). Bake 6 to 8
minutes or until just starting to brown. Cool
before filling.

Per 1/8 crust: 55 Cal, 3g Fat, <1g Pro, 2g Sug,
5g Carb, <1g Fib, *NET CARBS: 5*

Press-in-Pan Pie Crust

MAKES ONE 9-INCH PIE CRUST

A truly versatile pie crust.

1   cup almond flour
3   packets Splenda®
1   tablespoon butter, chilled
1   large egg yolk

1. Preheat oven to 350°F. Place flour and
Splenda in a bowl. Cut in the butter.
2. Add egg yolk and mix until smooth. Press
into bottom and up sides of a 9-inch pie dish.
Bake 8 to 10 minutes or until just lightly
browned.

Per 1/8 crust: 104 Cal, 9g Fat, 4g Pro, 1g Sug,
3g Carb, 1g Fib, *NET CARBS: 2*

Almond Pie Crust

MAKES ONE 9-INCH CRUST

Almond is a nice flavor for pie crust.

1¼   cups almond flour
3   packets Splenda®
4   tablespoons butter, softened

1. Preheat oven to 350°F. Combine almond
flour and Splenda. Add butter and mix until a
soft dough forms.
2. Press into bottom and sides (not rim) of a
lightly sprayed 9-inch pie dish. Bake 9 to 10
minutes or until very lightly browned. Cool.

Per 1/8 crust: 151 Cal, 14g Fat, 4g Pro, 0g Sug,
4g Carb, 2g Fib, *NET CARBS: 2*

Pecan Crust

MAKES ONE 9-INCH PIE CRUST

Easy to make.

2   cups finely ground pecans
⅓   cup brown Sugar Twin®
¼   cup butter, melted

1. Preheat oven to 350°F. Combine all ingredients until well mixed. Press into bottom and sides
(but not rim) of sprayed 9-inch pie dish. Bake 10
to 12 minutes or until toasted. Cool.

Per 1/8 crust: 258 Cal, 27g Fat, 3g Pro, 2g Sug,
5g Carb, 3g Fib, *NET CARBS: 2*

Coconut-Pecan Crust

MAKES ONE 10-INCH CRUST

*This crust best fits a 10-inch pie dish
(with low sides--not a deep dish).*

1¾ cups unsweetened shredded coconut
½   cup finely chopped pecans
2   tablespoons almond flour
½   cup butter, melted

  1. Preheat oven to 375°F. Combine first 3 ingredients. Stir in butter until well mixed. Press into bottom and up sides of a 10-inch pie dish. Bake 8 to10 minutes or until lightly browned. Let cool.

Per 1/12 crust: 201 Cal, 20g Fat, 1g Pro, 1g Sug, 4g Carb, 2g Fib, *NET CARBS: 2*

Coconut Crust

MAKES ONE 9-INCH CRUST

*This crust works really well with pies
that do not have to be baked.*

½   cup butter
1¾ cups unsweetened shredded coconut

  1. Melt butter in medium skillet over low heat. Stir in coconut. Remove from heat and let stand about 5 minutes to soften the coconut.
  2. Over medium-low heat, lightly toast the coconut, stirring frequently.
  3. Press evenly over bottom and sides, but not the rim, of a 9-inch pie dish.

Per 1/12 crust: 156 Cal, 16g Fat, 1g Pro, 1g Sug, 3g Carb, 2g Fib, *NET CARBS: 1*

๑ Hints ๑

Instant Soft Butter
Forget to soften the butter? Place the un-wrapped butter in a resealable plastic bag and flatten with a rolling pin.

Grating Chocolate
This can be easily done by using the large holes on your grater.

Egg Whites
Egg whites will have a higher volume if beaten at room temperature. However, they are more easily separated from the yolk if done when the eggs are cold.

Index

A

B

Cookies

D

Poultry - see Chicken, Cornish Hens or Turkey

Q

Quiche

R

S

Salads

Salad Dressings

Salsa

Sandwiches

Sauces

Seafood

Seasoning

Shellfish - See Seafood

W

Wraps

Z

Great Meals Begin With Six Ingredients Or Less

Six Ingredients or Less Diabetic Cookbook -288 pages and over 400 delicious low-fat and low-carb recipes. Includes nutritional analysis and diabetic exchanges.

Six Ingredients or Less Low-Carb - 288 pages and over 600 delicious quick and easy recipes to help you creatively cook with only 0 to 6 Net carbs per recipe. Includes all food categories including desserts, pasta dishes and slow cooker recipes in a plastic comb-bound binding.

Six Ingredients or Less Cookbook - New revised and expanded edition of our all-purpose cookbook. Over 600 recipes and 352 pages of delicious foods from everyday cooking to company entertaining.

Six Ingredients or Less Light & Healthy - 224 pages devoted to great cooking you and your family will enjoy. Recipes also include the nutritional analysis.

Six Ingredients or Less Pasta and Casseroles - 224 pages of recipes for today's busy life-styles. The original and low-fat version is given for each recipe.

Six Ingredients or Less Slow Cooker - 224 pages of easy stress-free recipes, letting the slow cooker do the work for you.

Six Ingredients or Less Families on the Go - Our quickest and easiest recipes yet. Designed to get you in and out of the kitchen fast. 288 pages.

Diabetic Cookbooks	(____) # of copies	$19.95 each	$_____
Low-Carb Cooking	(____) # of copies	$19.95 each	$_____
Six Ingredients or Less	(____) # of copies	$18.95 each	$_____
Light & Healthy	(____) # of copies	$12.95 each	$_____
Pasta & Casseroles	(____) # of copies	$14.95 each	$_____
Slow Cooker	(____) # of copies	$16.95 each	$_____
Families on the Go	(____) # of copies	$16.95 each	$_____

Plus Postage & Handling (First book $3.75, each add'l book, add $1.50) $_____
Washington residents add 8.8% sales tax or current tax rate $_____
                                                    Total $_____

Please Print or Type

Name _____ Phone (___) _____

Address _____

City _____ State _____ Zip _____

MC or Visa _____ Exp _____

Signature _____

sixingredientsorless.com or info@sixingredientsorless.com.
1-800-423-7184